FIFTH EDITION

Focus on
Grammar 2A

Irene E. Schoenberg

Focus on Grammar 2: An Integrated Skills Approach, Fifth Edition, Volume A

Copyright © 2017, 2012, 2006, 2000 by Pearson Education, Inc.
All rights reserved.

No part of this publication may be reproduced, stored in a retrieval system, or transmitted in any form or by any means, electronic, mechanical, photocopying, recording, or otherwise, without the prior permission of the publisher.

Pearson Education, 221 River Street, Hoboken, NJ 07030

Staff credits: The people who made up the *Focus on Grammar 2, Fifth Edition, Volume A* team, representing content creation, design, manufacturing, marketing, multimedia, project management, publishing, rights management, and testing, are Pietro Alongi, Rhea Banker, Elizabeth Barker, Stephanie Bullard, Jennifer Castro, Tracey Cataldo, Aerin Csigay, Mindy DePalma, Dave Dickey, Warren Fischbach, Pam Fishman, Nancy Flaggman, Lester Holmes, Gosia Jaros-White, Leslie Johnson, Barry Katzen, Amy McCormick, Julie Molnar, Brian Panker, Stuart Radcliffe, Jennifer Raspiller, Lindsay Richman, Robert Ruvo, Alexandra Suarez, Paula Van Ells, and Joseph Vella.

Text design and layout: Don Williams
Composition: Page Designs International
Project supervision: Bernard Seal
Contributing editors: Julie Schmidt and Bernard Seal

Cover image: Andy Roberts / Getty Images

Printed in the United States of America

ISBN 10: 0-13-413267-X
ISBN 13: 978-0-13-413267-9

6 2022

Contents

WELCOME TO
FOCUS ON GRAMMAR
FIFTH EDITION

BUILDING ON THE SUCCESS of previous editions, *Focus on Grammar* continues to provide an integrated-skills approach to engage students and help them understand, practice, and use English grammar. Centered on thematic instruction, *Focus on Grammar* combines comprehensive grammar coverage with abundant practice, critical thinking skills, and ongoing assessment, helping students accomplish their goals of communicating confidently, accurately, and fluently in everyday situations.

New in the Fifth Edition

New and Updated Content
Focus on Grammar continues to offer engaging and motivating content that appeals to learners from various cultural backgrounds. Many readings and activities have been replaced or updated to include topics that are of high interest to today's learners.

Updated Charts and Redesigned Notes
Clear, corpus-informed grammar presentations reflect real and natural language usage and allow students to grasp the most important aspects of the grammar. Clear signposting draws attention to common usage, the difference between written and spoken registers, and common errors.

Additional Communicative Activities
The new edition of *Focus on Grammar* has been expanded with additional communicative activities that encourage collaboration and the application of the target grammar in a variety of settings.

Expanded Writing Practice
Each unit in *Focus on Grammar* now ends with a structured "From Grammar to Writing" section. Supported by pre-writing and editing tasks, students engage in activities that allow them to apply the target grammar in writing.

New Assessment Program
The new edition of *Focus on Grammar* features a variety of new assessment tools, including course diagnostic tests, formative and summative assessments, and a flexible gradebook. The assessments are closely aligned with unit learning outcomes to inform instruction and measure student progress.

Revised MyEnglishLab
The updated MyEnglishLab offers students engaging practice and video grammar presentations anywhere, anytime. Immediate feedback and remediation tasks offer additional opportunities for successful mastery of content and help promote accuracy. Instructors receive instant access to digital content and diagnostic tools that allow them to customize the learning environment to meet the needs of their students.

The *Focus on Grammar* Approach

At the heart of the *Focus on Grammar* series is its unique and successful four-step approach that lets learners move from comprehension to communication within a clear and consistent structure. The books provide an abundance of scaffolded exercises to bridge the gap between identifying grammatical structures and using them with confidence and accuracy. The integration of the four skills allows students to learn grammar holistically, which in turn prepares them to understand and use English more effectively.

STEP 1: Grammar in Context integrates grammar and vocabulary in natural contexts such as articles, stories, dialogues, and blog posts. Students engage with the unit reading and theme and get exposure to grammar as it is used in real life.

STEP 2: Grammar Presentation presents the structures in clear and accessible grammar charts and notes with multiple examples of form and meaning. Corpus-informed explanations and examples reflect natural usage of the target forms, differentiate between written and conversational registers whenever appropriate, and highlight common errors to help students avoid typical pitfalls in both speaking and writing.

STEP 3: Focused Practice provides numerous and varied contextualized exercises for both the form and meaning of the new structures. Controlled practice ensures students' understanding of the target grammar and leads to mastery of form, meaning, and use.

STEP 4: Communication Practice provides practice with the structures in listening exercises as well as in communicative, open-ended speaking activities. These engaging activities provide ample opportunities for personalization and build students' confidence in using English. Students also develop their critical thinking skills through problem-solving activities and discussions.

Each unit now culminates with the **From Grammar to Writing** section. Engaging and motivating writing activities encourage students to apply grammar in writing through structured tasks from pre-writing that contain writing models to editing.

Recycling

Underpinning the scope and sequence of the *Focus on Grammar* series is practice that allows students to use target structures and vocabulary many times, in different contexts. New grammar and vocabulary are recycled throughout the book. Students have maximum exposure, leading them to become confident in using the language in speech and in writing.

Assessment

Extensive testing informs instruction and allows teachers and students to measure progress.

- **Unit Reviews** at the end of every unit assess students' understanding of the grammar and allow students to monitor their own progress.

- **Diagnostic Tests** provide teachers with a valid and reliable means to determine how well students know the material they are going to study and to target instruction based on students' needs.

- **Unit Review Tests, Mid- and End-of-Term Review Tests, and Final Exams** measure students' ability to demonstrate mastery of skills taught in the course.

- The **Placement Test** is designed to help teachers place students into one of the five levels of the *Focus on Grammar* course.

The Importance of Context

A key element of *Focus on Grammar* is presenting important grammatical structures in context. The contexts selected are most relevant to the grammatical forms being introduced. Contextualized grammar practice also plays a key role in improving fluent use of grammar in communicative contexts. It helps learners to develop consistent and correct usage of target structures during all productive practice.

The Role of Corpus

The most important goal of *Focus on Grammar* has always been to present grammar structures using natural language. To that end, *Focus on Grammar* has incorporated the findings of corpus linguistics,* while never losing sight of what is pedagogically sound and useful. By taking this approach, *Focus on Grammar* ensures that:

- the language presented reflects real, natural usage

- themes and topics provide a good fit with the grammar point and elicit the target grammar naturally

- findings of the corpus research are reflected in the syllabus, readings, charts, grammar notes, and practice activities

- examples illustrate differences between spoken and written registers, and formal and informal language

- students are exposed to common errors in usage and learn how to recognize and avoid errors in their own speech and writing

Focus on Grammar Efficacy

The fifth edition of *Focus on Grammar* reflects an important efficacy initiative for Pearson courses—to be able to demonstrate that all teaching materials have a positive impact on student learning. To support this, *Focus on Grammar* has been updated and aligned to the **Global Scale of English** and the **Common European Framework** (CEFR) to provide granular insight into the objectives of the course, the progression of learning, and the expected outcomes a learner will be able to demonstrate upon successful completion.

To learn more about the Global Scale of English, visit www.English.com.

Components

Student Books with Essential Online Resources include access codes to the course audio, video, and self-assessment.

Student Books with MyEnglishLab offer a blended approach with integration of print and online content.

Workbooks contain additional contextualized practice in print format.

Digital Teacher's Resources include printable teaching notes, GSE mapping documents, answer keys, audio scripts, and downloadable tests. Access to the digital copy of the student books allows teachers to project the pages for whole-class instruction.

FOG Go app allows users to access the student book audio on their mobile devices.

---

* A principal resource has been Douglas Biber et al, *Longman Grammar of Spoken and Written English*, Harlow: Pearson Education Ltd., 1999.

The *Focus on Grammar* Unit

Focus on Grammar introduces grammar structures in the context of unified themes. All units follow a four-step approach, taking learners from grammar in context to communicative practice. Thematic units add a layer to learning so that by the end of the unit students will be able to discuss the content using the grammar points they have just studied.

STEP 1 — GRAMMAR IN CONTEXT

Before You Read activities create interest and elicit students' knowledge about the topic.

Vocabulary exercises help students improve their command of English.

Engaging, high-interest **readings** in a variety of genres present the target structures in natural and realistic contexts. As students read, they encounter the form, meaning, and use of the grammar.

Comprehension and **Discussion** activities focus on the meaning of the text and draw students' attention to the target structures.   **NEW!**

Grammar Charts present the structures in a clear, easy-to-read format.

STEP 2 GRAMMAR PRESENTATION

SIMPLE PRESENT: AFFIRMATIVE AND NEGATIVE STATEMENTS

Affirmative Statements

Subject	Verb	
I You* We They	eat like	noodles.
He She It	has	

Negative Statements

Subject	Do not / Does not	Base Form of Verb	
I You We They	do not don't	eat like have	noodles.
He She It	does not doesn't		

* *You* can be singular or plural.

ADVERBS AND EXPRESSIONS OF FREQUENCY

Adverbs of Frequency

Subject	Adverb	Verb	
I You We They	usually almost never	cook	on holidays.
He She		cooks	
It		rains	

Adverbs of Frequency with *Be*

Subject	Be	Adverb	
I	am		
You We They	are	usually almost never	busy.
He She It	is		

Adverbs of Frequency

always	100%
almost always	↑
frequently	
usually	
often	
sometimes	50%
rarely / seldom	
almost never	↓
never	0%

Expressions of Frequency

Emiko cooks	every day. twice a week. three times a month. several times a year. once in a while.

88 Unit 8

NEW!

The newly designed **Grammar Notes** highlight the main point of each note, making navigation and review easier. Simple corpus-informed **explanations** and **examples** ensure students' understanding.

GRAMMAR NOTES

1 Count and Non-Count Nouns

There are **count nouns** and **non-count nouns**.

Nouns such as *apple*, *table*, and *menu* are **count nouns**. We call them count nouns because we **can count** them.	I ate one pear and two apples.
Nouns such as *milk*, *juice*, and *sugar* are **non-count nouns**. We call them non-count nouns because we **cannot count** them.	We need milk, juice, and sugar.
Some nouns can be both **count** and **non-count** nouns.	He bought three **cakes** for the party. *(count noun)* He ate some **cake**. *(non-count noun)*

USAGE NOTE In informal speaking, some non-count nouns are used as count nouns.

I'd like **two coffees** and **two sodas**.
(= I'd like two cups of coffee and two cans of soda.)

BE CAREFUL! Do not add *-s* or *-es* to a non-count noun.

I need milk.
NOT I need milks.

2 Indefinite Articles *A, An*

Use *a* or *an* to talk about a person or thing for the first time, or when it is not clear which person or thing you mean.

Use *a* or *an* before a **singular count noun**.	I bought a **pear** and an **apple**.
Remember to use *a* before a **consonant sound**.	A: Do you want a **steak**? B: No. I want a **small** pasta dish.
Remember to use *an* before a **vowel sound**.	A: Did you eat an **appetizer**? B: Yes. I had an **avocado** salad.

BE CAREFUL! Do not put *a, an*, or a number before a non-count noun.

I want **rice**.
NOT I want a rice.

3 Definite Article *The*

Use *the* when it is clear which person or thing you mean.

You can use *the* before singular count nouns, plural nouns, and non-count nouns:

• singular count nouns	**The restaurant** is open. *(Both the speaker and listener know which restaurant.)*
• plural nouns	A: Do you have any napkins? B: Yes. The **napkins** are over there. *(the napkins that A asked about)*
• non-count nouns	**The soup** is delicious.

Articles with Count and Non-Count Nouns; *Some / Any*   **311**

NEW!

Clear signposting provides corpus-informed notes about common usage, differences between spoken and written registers, and common errors.

PRONUNCIATION NOTE

Regular Past Tense Endings

Regular simple past verbs end in three sounds: **/d/**, **/t/**, or **/ɪd/**.

• /d/	He **arrived** late.
• /t/	They **worked** at a hotel.
• /ɪd/	She **waited** for him at the airport.

Pronunciation Notes are now included with the grammar presentation to highlight relevant pronunciation aspects of the target structures and to help students understand authentic spoken English.

NEW!

Discover the Grammar activities develop students' recognition and understanding of the target structures before they are asked to produce them.

Controlled practice activities lead students to master form, meaning, and use of the target grammar.

STEP 3 FOCUSED PRACTICE

EXERCISE 1
DISCOVER THE GRAMMAR

A GRAMMAR NOTES 1, 3
A student is people watching in her psychology class. Underline all the uses of the present progressive.

I'm in my psychology class. This semester we're studying child psychology. Today's class is almost over. Julia and Maria are closing their books. Our teacher is returning a test. Bob has a smile on his face. He always gets a good grade. Ryan isn't smiling. Maybe his grade is low. Shoko is texting under the table. Jon isn't listening to the teacher. He's thinking about lunch. I can hear his stomach. It's making noises.

B Write the base form of the underlined words in A.

1. _____study_____   4. _____   7. _____
2. _____   5. _____   8. _____
3. _____   6. _____

EXERCISE 2 AFFIRMATIVE AND NEGATIVE STATEMENTS

GRAMMAR NOTES 1–3 Complete the sentences with the present progressive forms of the verbs in parentheses.

1. I'm tired of studying. I'm taking _____ a break and _____ around.
    (take)   (look)
2. Julie and Maria _____ games, and Bob _____ someone.
                     (play)   (text)
3. Shoko and Ryan _____ homework, and Jon _____ the paper.
                   (do)   (read)
4. It _____ outside now. People _____ umbrellas.
    (rain)   (use)
5. Some people _____ at the door. They _____ for the rain to stop.
                (stand)   (wait)
6. I _____ homework. I'm looking at the people in the library.
    (not / do)
7. It _____ now. It _____ .
    (not / snow)   (rain)
8. They _____ at this moment. They _____ .
         (not / study)   (relax)
9. This semester, Hugo _____ five courses. He _____ hard.
                        (take)   (work)
10. This week in psychology class, we _____ about the behavior of
                                       (learn)
    three-year-old children.

176 Unit 16

EXERCISE 2 ADVERBS OF MANNER

GRAMMAR NOTES 1–2 Complete each sentence. Change the adjectives in parentheses to adverbs.

1. The audience listened ____carefully____
                              (careful)
2. He spoke _____
              (quick)
3. Sally writes _____ .
                 (good)
4. They speak Spanish _____ .
                       (fluent)
5. He spoke _____ .
             (clear)
6. He drove _____ .
             (fast)
7. Did he drive _____ ?
                (dangerous)
8. Did they sing _____ ?
                  (bad)
9. The movie began _____ .
                    (slow)
10. It rained _____ last night.
               (hard)
11. She woke up _____ .
                 (early)
12. He stayed up _____ .
                  (late)

EXERCISE 3 LINKING VERBS

GRAMMAR NOTE 3 Match the beginnings of the sentences with the endings.

__c__ 1. She looks   a. awful. I hate heavy metal music.
____ 2. He looks   b. happy. I guess he gave a good talk.
____ 3. The soup tastes   c. sick. Does she have a fever?
____ 4. Her speech was   d. good. Are they baking cookies?
____ 5. This CD sounds   e. great. People clapped for a long time.
____ 6. Their home smells   f. terrible. Don't eat it.

EXERCISE 4 ADVERBS OF MANNER AND ADJECTIVES

GRAMMAR NOTES 1–3 Complete the conversations. Circle the correct answers.

1. A: How was the debate?
   B: Good. Both sides spoke good / (well)
2. A: How was the food at the reception after the debate?
   B: It tasted bad / badly.

Adverbs of Manner **395**

A **variety of exercise types** engage students and guide them from recognition and understanding to accurate production of the grammar structures.

Editing exercises allow students to identify and correct typical mistakes.

EXERCISE 6
EDITING

GRAMMAR NOTES 1–7
Correct the paragraph. There are eight mistakes. The first mistake is already corrected. Find and correct seven more.

                                    usually start
In the United States, people start usually the New Year holiday on New Year's Eve. Many people plans celebrations weeks in advance. My cousin always invite friends to a party. My parents usually goes to a restaurant with friends. Many people watch an event on TV just before midnight. On New Year's Day, people usually am relax from the night before. My brother watches football games on TV, and my sister is go to her friend's home. I sleeps all day long and not do anything.

Happy New Year

Go to MyEnglishLab for more focused practice.

X The *Focus on Grammar* Unit

Listenings in a variety of genres allow students to hear the grammar in natural contexts.

STEP 4   COMMUNICATION PRACTICE

EXERCISE 7   LISTENING

🔊 34:02 **A** Listen to a quiz show about animals. Read the questions. Choose the correct answers.

1. The first question asks, "Which land animal has the longest gestation period?"
   A gestation period is _____.
   a. the time the baby is inside its mother   **b.** the time the baby learns to walk

2. The second question asks, "Which animal is _____?"
   a. the fattest   **b.** the fastest

3. The third question asks, "Which animal is _____?"
   a. the loudest   **b.** the proudest

4. The last question asks, "Which animal is _____?"
   a. the smallest   **b.** the deadliest

🔊 34:02 **B** Listen again. What were the answers to the four questions in the quiz show? Choose from the words in the box.

ant	cheetah	cow	horse	monkey	peacock
bear	cockroach	elephant	lion	mosquito	tiger

Question 1: the Asian _____

Question 2: the _____

Question 3: the howler _____

Question 4: the _____

C Work with a partner. Say two statements about animals using the superlative. Your partner decides if they are true or false. Take turns.

EXAMPLE: A: The Asian elephant is the loudest land animal.
              B: That's not true. The howler monkey
                  is the loudest land animal.

The Superlative   423

In the **listening activities**, students practice a range of listening skills. A **new step** has been added in which partners complete an activity that relates to the listening and uses the target grammar.

NEW!

Engaging **communicative activities** (conversations, discussions, presentations, surveys, and games) help students synthesize the grammar, develop fluency, and build their problem-solving skills.

EXERCISE 7   WHAT DO I REALLY MEAN?

ROLE PLAY How we speak gives a different meaning to a sentence. Work with a partner. Say the following sentences in the ways in the box or choose your own ways. Your partner guesses how you're talking.

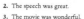

| angrily | decisively | questioningly | sadly | sarcastically |

1. I love English grammar.
   EXAMPLE: A: I love English grammar.
                 B: You're speaking sarcastically.
                 A: You're right.

2. The speech was great.

3. The movie was wonderful.

4. I love to exercise.

5. It's mine, all mine.

EXERCISE 8   WHAT AM I DOING?

GAME Work in groups. Choose a verb and an adverb from the list. Act it out in front of your group. They say what you're doing.

Verbs		Adverbs	
dance	sing	badly	quietly
drive	speak	carefully	quickly
eat	walk	nervously	slowly
listen		noisily	

398   Unit 32

Go to MyEnglishLab for more communication practice.

FROM GRAMMAR TO WRITING

A **From Grammar to Writing** section, now in every unit, helps students to confidently apply the unit's grammar to their own writing. **NEW!**

FROM GRAMMAR TO WRITING

A BEFORE YOU WRITE Read about a student's pet. Then complete the chart with information about your pet or a pet you know about. Work with a partner. Use the chart to tell your partner about the animal.

I have a beautiful parakeet. His feathers are bright green. His name is Chichi. He is two years old. He lives in a cage in my living room. Sometimes he flies around the room. Chichi can sing very beautifully. Chichi couldn't do anything when he was younger. But now he can sit on my finger and eat from my hand. He can't speak, but I'm happy about that. I tell him all my secrets, and he doesn't tell anyone. That's a wonderful quality. I love my Chichi.

	Student's Pet	My Pet
Kind of animal	bird / parakeet	
Description	green feathers	
Name	Chichi	
Age	two years old	
Home	cage	
Abilities	sit on finger / eat from hand	

B WRITE Write a paragraph about a pet. Use the paragraph in A and your chart. Use *can, can't, could,* or *couldn't.*

C CHECK YOUR WORK Read your paragraph in B. Underline *can, can't, could,* or *couldn't* and the verb that follows. Use the Editing Checklist to check your work.

Editing Checklist

Did you...?
- [ ] follow *can, can't, could,* and *couldn't* with the base form of the verb
- [ ] use *can* for the present and *could* for the past
- [ ] check your spelling

D REVISE YOUR WORK Read your paragraph again. Can you improve your writing? Make changes if necessary.

158   Unit 13

Go to MyEnglishLab for more writing practice.

The **Before You Write** task helps students generate ideas for their writing assignment. They typically contain writing models for students to analyze and emulate.

In the **Write** task, students are given a writing assignment and guided to use the target grammar.

Check Your Work includes an Editing Checklist that allows students to proofread and edit their compositions.

In **Revise Your Work**, students are given a final opportunity to improve their writing.

UNIT **REVIEW**

Unit Reviews give students the opportunity to check their understanding of the target structures. Students can check their answers against the Answer Key at the end of the book. They can also complete the Review on MyEnglishLab.

UNIT 25 **REVIEW**

Test yourself on the grammar of the unit.

A Complete the sentences. Circle the correct answers.

1. Do you want to start / starting a business?
2. I hope to sell / selling my business next year.
3. She decided to return / returning to school.
4. She hopes to become / becoming a pilot.
5. She enjoys to fly / flying and to see / seeing the world.

B Complete the sentences with the correct forms of the verbs in parentheses.

1. She doesn't want _____ evenings.
   (work)
2. Her boss refuses _____ her hours.
   (change)
3. She's thinking about _____ her job and _____ back to school.
   (quit)   (go)
4. Her English keeps _____ .
   (improve)

C Write sentences. Put the words in parentheses in the correct order.

1. _____
   (helping / people / she / enjoys)
2. _____
   (to / graduate / in June / expect / we)
3. _____
   (to / trying / study / are / they)
4. _____
   (avoids / and / he / eating / candy / ice cream)

D Correct the paragraph. There are six mistakes.

MyEnglishLab delivers rich online content to engage and motivate **students**.

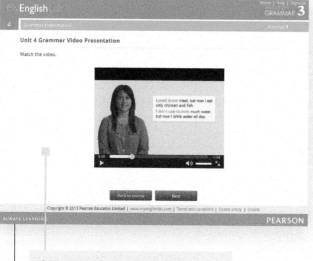

Grammar Coach videos give additional grammar presentations.

NEW!

MyEnglishLab delivers innovative teaching tools and useful resources to **teachers**.

MyEnglishLab provides students with:

- rich interactive practice in grammar, reading, listening, speaking, and writing
- immediate and meaningful feedback on wrong answers **NEW!**
- remediation activities
- grade reports that display performance and time on task

With **MyEnglishLab**, teachers can:

- view student scores by unit and activity
- monitor student progress on any activity or test
- analyze class data to determine steps for remediation and support

MyEnglishLab also provides teachers with:

- a digital copy of the student book for whole-class instruction
- downloadable assessments, including the placement test, that can be administered on MyEnglishLab or in print format
- printable resources including teaching notes, suggestions for teaching grammar, GSE mapping documents, answer keys, and audio scripts

Scope and Sequence

LISTENING	SPEAKING	WRITING	VOCABULARY
A conversation about athletes ■ Can identify key details about people in conversations that are conducted clearly and slowly	■ Can discuss likes and dislikes ■ Can describe something in a simple list of points	■ Can write personal information about a friend or colleague, using notes for guidance	athlete fan (n) in the middle only popular the rest of
A conversation about classmates ■ Can recognize and describe basic information about people in conversations that are conducted clearly and slowly	■ Can ask simple questions to find out more about someone ■ Can use brief, everyday expressions to ask for and give personal details	■ Can write a detailed list of questions about a familiar place	excuse me office on time right (adj) room (n)
A series of phone messages ■ Can extract key factual information from a recorded phone message	■ Can communicate in routine tasks that require simple, direct exchanges of information, such as descriptions of the weather and everyday activities	■ Can write a paragraph about a personal experience (first day of school)	afraid (of) difficult nervous principal (n) AWL surprise (n)
A lecture about art ■ Can identify important details in a brief lecture about a famous artist	■ Can give a brief presentation about people, places, or things	■ Can write short, basic descriptions of people, places, or things	all over occasion public (n) striking (adj) to be born
A telephone conversation ■ Can recognize details in a conversation about a vacation if delivered slowly and clearly	■ Can share information about known places ■ Can offer opinions and comment on statements provided by one's peers	■ Can write a detailed paragraph about a location that has personal significance	climate comfortable dry safe (adj) unusual
A recorded description ■ Can infer information about a location by recognizing important details in a recorded description	■ Can give directions to help one's peers find information on a map or brochure	■ Can write a short invitation to a party or event, including important details like time and location	app dinosaur huge interested locate AWL tour (n)

AWL = Academic Word List item

LISTENING	SPEAKING	WRITING	VOCABULARY
A product advertisement ■ Can follow the main points in a recorded advertisement	■ Can discuss what to do and where to go, and make arrangements to meet ■ Can give basic advice about everyday topics, using simple language	■ Can write an advertisement for a hotel, using a model for guidance	advice dead island nap (n) pray secret
A conversation about holidays ■ Can take detailed notes on a short conversation, listing both main ideas and supporting details	■ Can work with one's peers to prepare a short presentation about a holiday or custom ■ Can describe habits and routines	■ Can write a paragraph about a favorite holiday or tradition, using notes for support	at the stroke of culture AWL eve get together look ahead tradition AWL
A conversation about roommates ■ Can identify a speaker's likes and dislikes in a simple conversation	■ Can answer simple questions in a face-to-face survey ■ Can use a limited range of fixed expressions to describe objects, possessions, or products	■ Can write a simple email that provides personal information and asks routine questions	bother (v) easygoing messy outgoing private (adj) stay up
A conversation about dreams ■ Can identify key details in a conversation about dreams	■ Can give and elicit personal information about sleep habits, taking turns with a partner	■ Can ask for personal details in written form and use the material to write an interview	author (n) AWL guest nightmare remember unfortunately
A conversation about a place ■ Can provide directions to someone, based on information heard in a prior conversation	■ Can gather information about a place from a partner or group, summarize it, and present it to others	■ Can write a short description of a favorite place to shop	aquarium including (prep) indoor join luxury parking space
A conversation about possessions ■ Can identify ownership of possessions in a conversation that's delivered slowly and clearly	■ Can describe an everyday object in detail, also indicating who owns it ■ Can ask and answer questions about possessions	■ Can write a detailed paragraph that describes people in one's family	back (prep) composition excellent grade (n) AWL recognize

AWL = Academic Word List item

LISTENING	SPEAKING	WRITING	VOCABULARY
A conversation about dolphins ■ Can identify abilities of animals in a short conversation	■ Can offer one's opinions or beliefs about a common topic to a partner or group ■ Can exchange information on animals and their behavior	■ Can write a paragraph about a pet, using notes for guidance	genius intelligent AWL invent professor surprised (adj)
A conversation between a doctor and a patient ■ Can identify foods that a patient can or cannot have due to allergies or adverse reactions	■ Can tell a peer or medical professional what one can or cannot eat ■ Can communicate simple rules and regulations	■ Can write a note that describes the dietary restrictions of oneself or of others	dairy in common nutritious recipe substitute AWL
A telephone conversation between friends ■ Can use the information from a phone call to describe the location of people or objects	■ Can describe basic activities or events that are happening at the time of speaking	■ Can write a short narrative about what is currently happening in one's life or immediate environment	bored departure detective AWL psychologist AWL suit
A telephone conversation about family ■ Can identify a speaker's current location and describe what he or she is doing	■ Can rehearse a structured conversation with a partner, using prompts for guidance ■ Can discuss basic activities or events that are happening at the time of speaking	■ Can write a telephone conversation between friends about seeing a famous person	catch a cold cough fever scene still (adv)
A series of phone messages ■ Can identify a speaker's main purpose in a phone call or recorded message	■ Can express a variety of likes and dislikes to one's peers ■ Can collaborate with peers to prepare for and participate in a debate	■ Can write a short fictional story about everyday events, using an illustration as a prompt	connect constantly AWL feature (n) AWL improve waterproof
A conversation about a trip to Japan ■ Can confirm the length of time that someone did something in a conversation about travel	■ Can give a description of everyday topics, such as past habits, plans, and experiences ■ Can ask and answer simple questions about the past	■ Can write a detailed email about a vacation	cancel freeze land (v) miss (v) pick up

AWL = Academic Word List item

LISTENING	SPEAKING	WRITING	VOCABULARY
A story about the past ■ Can confirm important details from an oral story about past events	■ Can use time markers to tell a story that has a sequence of events	■ Can write a short descriptive story	appear border (v) fight (v) ride (v) run away unlucky
A conversation about a movie ■ Can take detailed notes during a conversation, using them to answer detailed *wh-* questions based on that information	■ Can take turns with a partner, asking questions about their favorite book, play, or movie ■ Can ask and answer questions about the life of a famous writer	■ Can write a series of questions and answers about the life of a famous person	exact jealousy mystery (n) play (n) pride (n)
A conversation about a quiz show ■ Can answer *wh-* questions based on information in a short conversation	■ Can take turns with a partner or group, asking questions about famous people and past events ■ Can discuss one's childhood in detail and prompt similar responses from others	■ Can write a short autobiographical passage, using a series of *wh-* questions for guidance	admire base on notice routine statue
A conversation about a building ■ Can follow a slow-paced conversation about a location or place and provide key details about it	■ Can describe future plans and intentions using a variety of time markers ■ Can discuss a life-changing event with a partner or small group	■ Can write a letter or email that expresses and defends an opinion on a controversial topic	against announce gain increase in my opinion tuition
A conversation between a TV news reporter and two people ■ Can identify who the main speaker is referring to in a conversation with multiple participants	■ Can make predictions about future events, providing an opinion or rationale for each prediction ■ Can offer suggestions or solutions to help others with everyday problems and complaints	■ Can write a paragraph that offers detailed predictions about future events	disappear majority memory robot spend time

AWL = Academic Word List item

UNIT	GRAMMAR	READING

▼ PART **8** CONTINUED

24 *May* or *Might* for **Possibility** Page 285 THEME The Weather	■ Can use *might* and *may* to express likelihood in the present and the immediate future ■ Can use *will* and *won't* to express what is certain and what is impossible ■ Can use *be going to* to ask questions about future possibility	News Report: *The Weather Forecast* ■ Can identify detailed information in a weather report
25 **Gerunds and Infinitives** Page 295 THEME Careers	■ Can use gerunds and infinitives after certain verbs	Magazine Article: *The Right Career for You* ■ Can match people with their characteristics based on information in a magazine article

PART 9

Count / Non-Count Nouns; *Much/Many*; Quantifiers

26 **Articles with Count and Non-Count Nouns;** *Some/Any* Page 308 THEME Restaurants and Food	■ Can use indefinite articles to refer to general subjects and definite articles to refer to specific subjects ■ Can use *some* and *any* as quantifiers with count and non-count nouns PRONUNCIATION Indefinite Articles	Restaurant Review: *Kassandra's Food Reviews* ■ Can understand recommendations in restaurant reviews
27 *How much* and *How many*; **Quantifiers** Page 322 THEME Desserts	■ Can ask for information about quantity with *how much/many* ■ Can use *a lot, a few*, and *a little* to refer to quantities with nouns ■ Can describe quantities using *(not) any, a lot, much*, or *many*	Conversation Transcript: *International Desserts* ■ Can identify the quantities of things that were listed in a short conversation about food
28 *Too many* and *Too much*; *Enough* + **Noun** Page 335 THEME The Right Place to Live	■ Can express sufficiency and insufficiency with *enough* and *too* ■ Can use *too many* and *too few* with plural count nouns and *too much* and *too little* with non-count nouns	Blog Post: *Dream Locations* ■ Can identify important details about specific locations or cities

LISTENING	SPEAKING	WRITING	VOCABULARY
A conversation about a trip ■ Can distinguish what actions a speaker takes when he or she is debating among several possibilities	■ Can explain why certain objects or actions might be necessary in certain situations ■ Can explain reasons and possibilities for different situations and events ■ Can discuss possible or tentative plans with a partner or small group	■ Can write a weather report that makes predictions about the present and future	commute (n) flood (v) highway mild predict (v) storm (n)
A lecture about design ■ Can identify how a speaker feels about his or her job after listening to a short lecture	■ Can discuss career interests with a partner or in small groups ■ Can use a short questionnaire to elicit information from others and then communicate that information to one's peers	■ Can write a paragraph about future career goals and aspirations, detailing how these goals will be achieved	career chef compete deadline lawyer salary
A conversation about party preparations ■ Can recognize a great number of details in a conversation about everyday topics	■ Can use simple phrases to order a meal ■ Can offer recommendations to others about food and restaurants	■ Can write a review of a restaurant that includes information about its prices, food quality, atmosphere, and service	atmosphere delicious main course menu reservation service (n)
A conversation about a recipe ■ Can list the ingredients in a recipe that was discussed in a conversation about food	■ Can work with others to answer items on a quiz about desserts ■ Can research and discuss how much of an item is needed to make a specific kind of food	■ Can write a simple conversation between a shopper and a clerk, referring back to a list of items	ingredient in season neighborhood prepare pretty good taste
A conversation about real estate ■ Can recognize and recall specific details about apartments described in a conversation	■ Can describe the pros and cons of living in the city versus the suburbs ■ Can provide a list of criticisms about one's hometown or city	■ Can write a letter to a newspaper or blog that describes a major problem in one's hometown or city	cosmopolitan crime pollution traffic transportation AWL unemployment

AWL = Academic Word List item

LISTENING	SPEAKING	WRITING	VOCABULARY
A conversation about a business trip ■ Can recognize and recall specific details about someone else's travel or work plans	■ Can describe cultural and business customs in one's home country and around the world ■ Can explain the meaning of different body language in one's home country	■ Can write one or two paragraphs that provide someone with advice on how to do business in one's home country	confusion head for insult (v) reception timing (n)
A conversation about academics ■ Can identify what things a speaker must do in order to achieve his or her academic or career goals	■ Can describe rules and requirements at different schools ■ Can discuss and determine ways to solve common problems that occur in schools	■ Can write a paragraph about the different types of rules at a school	average (n) due (adj) fail midterm outline (n) pass (v)
A conversation about a city ■ Can identify what changes are happening in a speaker's hometown or current environment	■ Can describe the similarities and differences between popular locations ■ Can compare and contrast the transportation systems of two major cities	■ Can write a paragraph that compares and contrasts the different ways one can get around a major city	coast (n) diverse AWL personality population wonder (v)
A presentation about public speaking ■ Can identify and recall specific instructions in a talk or a lecture given at a slow, clear pace	■ Can use tone to communicate different levels of emotion, such as excitement or anger ■ Can describe the way someone is performing an action	■ Can write a paragraph about a talent, providing specific examples of the actions one does well	applause appreciate AWL audience fact joke (n) serious
A conversation about two employees ■ Can infer information about the characteristics of people who are being discussed in a conversation	■ Can offer criticisms of plans about things to do during one's free time ■ Can explain why something isn't sufficient or appropriate for a given situation	■ Can write a paragraph that contains complaints about a store	according to in her eyes point of view point out sincerely solution
A quiz show about animals ■ Can, after listening to a speaker, recall detailed information and distinguishing characteristics about animals	■ Can conduct a survey, reporting the results to one's peers ■ Can discuss the characteristics of different animals in detail	■ Can write a paragraph that provides a thorough description of animals encountered at a zoo or in one's local area	centimeter extinct inch kilogram pound (n) species

AWL = Academic Word List item

About the Author

Irene E. Schoenberg has taught ESL for more than two decades at Hunter College's International English Language Institute and at Columbia University's American Language Program. She holds a master's degree in TESOL from Columbia University. She has trained ESL and EFL teachers at Columbia University's Teachers College, the New School University, and Hunter College's English Language Institute. She has given workshops and academic presentations at conferences, English language schools, and universities in Brazil, Canada, Chile, Dubai, El Salvador, Guatemala, Japan, Mexico, Nicaragua, Peru, Taiwan, Thailand, Vietnam, and throughout the United States. She is the author of *Talk about Trivia*; *Talk about Values*; *Speaking of Values 1: Conversation and Listening*; *Topics from A to Z*, Books 1 and 2; and *Focus on Grammar 2* (editions 1–5). She is the co-author with Jay Maurer of the *True Colors* series and *Focus on Grammar 1* (editions 1–4) and is one of the authors of *Future 1: English for Results* and *Future 3: English for Results*.

Acknowledgments

I'd like to thank **Bernard Seal** for expertly overseeing the fifth edition of the *Focus on Grammar* series. He not only found very talented people for me to work with, but he tirelessly worked to ensure that the series is consistent, complete, and appealing to look at.

I want to thank **Julie Schmidt**, my development editor, for her insight, thoughtful comments, and devotion to the project. It amazed me at how quickly she was able to return material with perceptive suggestions and comments. My thanks to **Diane Piniaris** for her fine work on the initial units.

Many thanks are extended to **Don Williams** for his talent at designing the pages and choosing photographs so that the readings and the exercises are visually engaging. The book is beautiful!

Thanks to **Gosia Jaros-White**, Publisher at Pearson Education, for her role in managing the entire series.

I thank **Marjorie Fuchs** and **Jay Maurer** for offering helpful and honest suggestions whenever I asked.

As always, I thank **my students** at Hunter College's *International English Language Institute* whose desire to learn English teaches me so much about the challenge of language learning; and my colleagues, **Ruth French** and **Victor Wheeler**, for giving me great feedback on any questions I had about grammar or methodology.

I thank **Joanne Dresner** for her original vision and guidance of the *Focus on Grammar* series.

Finally, I'd like to thank my family for their love and support: **Harris**, **Dan**, **Dahlia**, **Jonathan**, **Laura**, **Olivia**, **Ella**, and **Drew**.

Reviewers

We are grateful to the following reviewers for their many helpful comments.

Susanna Aramyan, Glendale Community College, Glendale, CA; **Homeretta Ayala**, Baltimore Co. Schools, Baltimore, MD; **Barbara Barrett**, University of Miami, Miami, FL; **Rebecca Beck**, Irvine Valley College, Irvine, CA; **Crystal Bock Thiessen**, University of Nebraska-PIESL, Lincoln, NE; **Janna Brink**, Mt. San Antonio College, Walnut, CA; **Erin Butler**, University of California, Riverside, CA; **Joice Cain**, Fullerton College, Fullerton, CA; **Shannonine M. Caruana**, Hudson County Community College, Jersey City, NJ; **Tonya Cobb**, Cypress College, Cypress, CA; **David Cooke**, Mt. San Antonio College, Walnut, CA; **Lindsay Donigan**, Fullerton College, Fullerton, CA; **Mila Dragushanskya**, ASA College, New York, NY; **Jill Fox**, University of Nebraska, Lincoln, NE; **Katalin Gyurindak**, Mt. San Antonio College, Walnut, CA; **Karen Hamilton**, Glendale Community College, Glendale, CA; **Electra Jablons**, International English Language Institute, Hunter College, New York, NY; **Eva Kozlenko**, Hudson County Community College, Jersey City, NJ; **Esther Lee**, American Language Program, California State University, Fullerton, CA; **Yenlan Li**, American Language Program, California State University, Fullerton, CA; **Shirley Lundblade**, Mt. San Antonio College, Walnut, CA; **Thi Thi Ma**, Los Angeles City College, Los Angeles, CA; **Marilyn Martin**, Mt. San Antonio College, Walnut, CA; **Eve Mazereeuw**, University of Guelph English Language Programs, Guelph, Ontario, Canada; **Robert Mott**, Glendale Community College, Glendale, CA; **Wanda Murtha**, Glendale Community College, Glendale, CA; **Susan Niemeyer**, Los Angeles City College, Los Angeles, CA; **Wayne Pate**, Tarrant County College, Fort Worth, TX; **Genevieve Patthey-Chavez**, Los Angeles City College, Los Angeles, CA; **Robin Persiani**, Sierra College, Rocklin, CA; **Denise Phillips**, Hudson County Community College, Jersey City, NJ; **Anna Powell**, American Language Program, California State University, Fullerton, CA; **JoAnna Prado**, Sacramento City Community College, Sacramento, CA; **Mark Rau**, American River College, Sacramento, CA; **Madeleine Schamehorn**, University of California, Riverside, CA; **Richard Skinner**, Hudson County Community College, Jersey City, NJ; **Heather Snavely**, American Language Program, California State University, Fullerton, CA; **Gordana Sokic**, Douglas College, Westminster, British Columbia, Canada; **Lee Spencer**, International English Language Institute, Hunter College, New York, NY; **Heather Stern**, Irvine Valley College, Irvine, CA; **Susan Stern**, Irvine Valley College, Irvine, CA; **Andrea Sunnaa**, Mt. San Antonio College, Walnut, CA; **Margaret Teske**, Mt. San Antonio College, Walnut, CA; **Johanna Van Gendt**, Hudson County Community College, Jersey City, NJ; **Daniela C. Wagner-Loera**, University of Maryland, College Park, MD; **Tamara Williams**, University of Guelph, English Language Programs, Guelph, Ontario, Canada; **Saliha Yagoubi**, Hudson County Community College, Jersey City, NJ; **Pat Zayas**, Glendale Community College, Glendale, CA

Credits

PHOTO CREDITS

2–3: One/Fotolia; 4: (center left) Benis Arapovic/Shutterstock, (center top) Ahmad Faizal Yahya/Fotolia, (center bottom) Andrey Yurlov/Shutterstock, (right top) Isantilli/Shutterstock, (right bottom) Galina Barskaya/Fotolia; 5: Mangostock/Shutterstock; 8: (top) Klublu/Fotolia, (bottom left) Massimhokuto/Fotolia, (bottom right) Melis/Shutterstock; 9: Everett Collection; 11: (row 1, left to right) Czeasar B. Dancel/Newscom, Maxisport/Shutterstock, AGIF/Shutterstock, AFLO Sports/Newscom, (row 2, left to right) Chatchai Somwat/Shutterstock, Scott W. Grau/Icon Sportswire/Newscom, Walter Bieri/EPA/Newscom, Gabriel Mitrache/Shutterstock; 12: (left to right) Oneinchpunch/Shutterstock, Oliveromg/Shutterstock, MBI/Fotolia, SGr/Fotolia, ArenaCreative/Fotolia, Albe84/Fotolia; 15: Anton Gvozdikov/Shutterstock; 22: (top center) Leungchopan/Fotolia, (center left) Phartisan/123RF; 23: Shipfactory/Shutterstock; 25: Racorn/123RF; 28: Racorn/Shutterstock; 33: (background) Oly5/Fotolia, (left to right) S Bukley/Shutterstock, S_bukley/Shutterstock, Dave Bedrosian/Geisler-Fotopress/picture alliance/Newscom, Denis Makarenko/Shutterstock, Featureflash Photo Agency/Shutterstock; 40–41: Toniflap/Shutterstock; 42: (left) Charles Platiau/Reuters, (right) Simone Capozzi/Fotolia, (right inset) Henri Cartier-Bresson/Magnum Photos; 46: (top right) Photka/Fotolia, (inset) Tyler Olson/Fotolia; 47: Henri Cartier-Bresson/Magnum Photos; 49: (top right) Vvoe/Fotolia, (top right inset) Kokhanchikov/Fotolia, (center right) Jeremy Richards/Shutterstock; 50: Cartier-Bresson/Magnum; 51: (center) Sergii Figurnyi/Fotolia, (inset) Jonathan Tichon/Shutterstock; 52: (top) jayzynism/Fotolia, (inset) ImagesBazaar/Alamy Stock Photo; 54: (center) Pakhnyushchyy/Fotolia; 54–55: kilinson/Fotolia; 57: EvanTravels/Fotolia; 58: queen21/Fotolia; 61: Roman Samokhin/Fotolia; 63: (bottom) Luciano Corbella/Dorling Kindersley, (center left) Butterfly Hunter/Shutterstock, (center right) herraez/Fotolia; 67: (center left) Sailorr/Fotolia, (center right) gdvcom/Fotolia, (bottom left) Felix Lipov/Shutterstock, (bottom right) Toniflap/Shutterstock; 69: alice_photo/Fotolia; 70: (row 1, left to right) Joerg Hackemann/123RF, karakotsya/Shutterstock, Sean Nel/Shutterstock, (row 2, left to right) Anatoly Tiplyashin/Shutterstock, Elnur/Fotolia, Archer/Fotolia; 74–75: Ollyy/Shutterstock; 76: (bottom left) Vasilis_Liappis/Shutterstock, (inset) Julia Sudnitskaya/Shutterstock; 76–77: jessicahyde/Fotolia; 84: (top left) mefanti/Fotolia, (inset) chones/Fotolia; 86: (center left) Topntp/Fotolia, (bottom right) JackF/Fotolia; 87: Angel Simon/Fotolia; 91: Wckiw/Fotolia; 92: Robert Wallace/Newscom; 94: (background) Dwph/Fotolia, (center) Jenifoto/Fotolia; 98: (background) Scisetti Alfio/Fotolia; 103: Voyagerix/Fotolia; 105: (background) Scisetti Alfio/Fotolia; 115: Ljupco Smokovski/Fotolia; 116: Wrangler/Fotolia; 117: Rudall30/Fotolia; 120–121: ImageZoo/Alamy Stock Photo; 122: (center) Kiev Victor/Shutterstock, (bottom right) Philip Lange/Shutterstock; 122–123: (background) Anelina/Fotolia; 123: S-F/Shutterstock; 126: (row 1, left to right) Angorius/Fotolia, Andrey Starostin/Fotolia, Tarasov vl/Fotolia, Rh2010/Fotolia, Beerphotographer/Fotolia, Arcady/Fotolia, (row 2, left to right) Yuriy Shevtsov/Fotolia, Vladimir Solovev/Fotolia, Alex Ishchenko/Fotolia, Nuwatphoto/Fotolia, Lanych/Fotolia, GoodMood Photo/Fotolia, (row 3, left to right) Rgvc/Fotolia, Ki33/Fotolia, kovaleva_ka/Fotolia, AVD/Fotolia, Antonioguillem/Fotolia; 129: (left to right) Fotolia, Nito/Fotolia, Pictorial Press Ltd/Alamy Stock Photo, Stokkete/Shutterstock; 132: (row 1, left to right) Elnur/Fotolia, Monticello/Shutterstock, Pixelrobot/Fotolia, (row 2, left to right) Nuwatphoto/Fotolia, Ivan kmit/Fotolia, Pixelrobot/Fotolia, Africa Studio/Fotolia, (row 3, left to right) Yeko Photo Studio/Shutterstock, Claudio Divizia/Fotolia, Pixs4u/Fotolia; 133: (background) Fotopak/Fotolia; 135: (top right) Picsfive/123RF, (center) WavebreakMediaMicro/Fotolia; 140: (bottom) Mtkang/123RF, (inset) Jane September/Shutterstock; 143: SnowWhiteimages/Shutterstock; 146: Naiauss/Fotolia; 148–149: avirid/Fotolia; 150–151: Farinoza/Fotolia; 151: Four Oaks/Shutterstock; 154: iurii/Shutterstock; 156: virsuziglis/Fotolia; 157: (top left) flib/123RF, (top center) Hintau Aliaksei/Shutterstock, (top right) Eric Isselee/Shutterstock, (center left) Valentyna Chukhlyebova/Shutterstock, (center) Potapov Alexander/Shutterstock, (center right) AuntSpray/Shutterstock, (bottom left) Eric Isselee/123RF, (bottom right) Eric Isselee/123RF; 158: full image/Fotolia; 160: Igor Mojzes/Fotolia; 167: nadia1992/Fotolia; 170–171: Odua Images/Fotolia; 172: (center left) Frederic Cirou/PhotoAlto/Alamy Stock Photo, (bottom

left) Milton Brown/Westend61 GmbH/Alamy Stock Photo; 173: alt.PIX Pte Ltd/Alamy Stock Photo; 176: (background) Picsfive/Shutterstock; 181: goir/Fotolia; 183: (bottom right) katusha161107/Fotolia, (inset) AF archive/Alamy Stock Photo; 187: Spectral-Design/Fotolia; 188: Everett Collection; 191: BillionPhotos.com/Fotolia; 194–195: (background) wassanamuk/123RF, (inset) rondabroc.com/Fotolia; 198: canbedone/Fotolia; 199: Iryna Tiumentseva/Fotolia; 200: Alex/Fotolia, (inset) J.J.Brown/Fotolia; 201: Africa Studio/Fotolia, (inset) am/Fotolia; 206–207: lesslemon/Fotolia; 208: (center) Sergii Figurnyi/Fotolia, (center right) Hung Chung Chih/Shutterstock, (top right) Amy Nichole Harri/Shutterstock, (bottom left) swisshippo/Fotolia; 213: Andrew Zarivny/Shutterstock; 214: (top left) Kaesler Media/Fotolia, (center, top to bottom) Oxlock/Fotolia, Mediterranean/Fotolia, carmenbobo/Fotolia; 216: (background) Scisetti Alfio/Fotolia, (inset) Steinar/Fotolia, (bottom right) cozyta/Shutterstock; 217: Dan Schreiber/Shutterstock; 220–221: (background) alexzaitsev/Fotolia; 223: (background) picsfive/Fotolia; 224: (top right) Romuald Meigneux/SIPA/Newscom, (bottom left) Robin Platzer/Twin Images/LFI/Photoshot/Newscom; 226: (top) Staff/Mirrorpix/Newscom, (bottom) aopsan/Fotolia; 227: (inset) Xalanx/123RF, (top) Darkbird/Fotolia; 228: Jolopes/Fotolia; 229: (background) Paladin1212/Fotolia, (inset) Lynea/Fotolia; 231–232: (background) Weedezign/Fotolia, (center right) Sailorr/Fotolia, (bottom right) Tony Baggett/Fotolia; 235: Nickolae/Fotolia; 237: Pictorial Press Ltd/Alamy Stock Photo; 239: Peter Jordan/Alamy Stock Photo; 240: Classic Image/Alamy Stock Photo; 242–243: Anahtiris/Fotolia; 246: Everett Historical/Shutterstock; 247: Kristin Callahan/Ace Pictures/Newscom; 248: Thinkstock/Stockbyte/Getty Images; 250: Max dallocco/Fotolia, (inset) Pictorial Press Ltd/Alamy Stock Photo; 254: Juliapankk/Fotolia; 256–257: Andresr/Shutterstock; 259: 3103/Shutterstock; 264: Nancy10/Fotolia; 265: (background) Torsakarin/Fotolia; 267: Alex/Fotolia; 268: (background) Romantsubin/Fotolia, (inset) P666/Fotolia, (bottom right) LaCozza/Fotolia; 269: Leungchopan/Fotolia; 270: (background) Tolgatezcan/Fotolia; 272–273: (background) graystone/Fotolia, (inset) Steve Young/Fotolia; 277: Sergey Nivens/Fotolia; 278: (inset) Alex White/Fotolia; 279: Diana Hlevnjak/Fotolia; 280: (left) luismolinero/Fotolia, (right) Zdenka Darula/Fotolia; 282: rcfotostock/Fotolia; 285: (background) oconner/Fotolia, (inset) Lisa Young /123RF; 289: Colorlife/Fotolia; 291: Elnur/Fotolia; 292: WavebreakMediaMicro/Fotolia; 293: naum/Fotolia; 295–296: (background) zephyr_p/Fotolia, (center left) Boyarkina Marina/Fotolia, (bottom left) BillionPhotos.com/Fotolia, (center right) Cathy Yeulet/123RF; 301: (background) gold36/Fotolia; 302: (bottom left) alice_photo/Fotolia, (top left) puckillustrations/Fotolia, (top center) barani83/Fotolia, (top right) kutukupret/Fotolia, (bottom center) NH7/Fotolia, (bottom right) adynue/Fotolia; 304: illustrart/Fotolia; 306–307: Sam Spiro/Fotolia; 308: Fanfo/Fotolia; 309: BillionPhotos.com/Fotolia; 314: Shutterstock; 315: agongallud/Fotolia; 316: mates/Fotolia; 317: Agongallud/Fotolia; 318: (background) Torsakarin/Fotolia, (bottom left) Mizina/Fotolia, (bottom center) Bitt24/Shutterstock, (bottom right) MSPhotographic/Fotolia; 322: ThitareeS/Fotolia; 327: (bottom left) SolisImages/Fotolia, (bottom center) eZeePics Studio/Fotolia, (bottom right) Jenifoto/Fotolia; 329: (left to right) Arvind Balaraman/Shutterstock, Stuart Atton/123RF, Eyewave/Fotolia, CWCreative/Fotolia, Gradt/Fotolia, A v.d. Wolde/Shutterstock; 330: (top) dream79/Fotolia, (center) Diana Taliun/Fotolia; 330–331: (background) scottchan/Fotolia; 332: (background) B.Melo/Fotolia, (center left) LeNi/Shutterstock, (bottom left) Denise Kappa/Shutterstock; 333: B.Melo/Fotolia; 335: Spiritofamerica/Fotolia; 336: Pecold/Fotolia; 338: Elbud/Shutterstock; 343: (bottom left) f11photo/Fotolia, (bottom right) Konstantin L/Fotolia; 344: Picsfive/Fotolia; 346–347: Drivepix/Fotolia; 348: Michaeljung/Fotolia; 352: Arekmalang/Fotolia; 353: IAKODCI IUK VIACHESLAV/Shutterstock; 355: Paylessimages/Fotolia; 357: Nutcd32/Shutterstock; 358: (top left) Slaweek/Fotolia, (bottom right) Edyta Pawlowska/Shutterstock; 359: (background) Tolgatezcan/Fotolia; 361: Zurijeta/Shutterstock; 365: AdMedia/Splash News/Newscom; 366: Forgiss/Fotolia; 367: Stelios Filippo/Fotolia; 368: (center left) karen roach/Shutterstock, (center right) Gomolach/Fotolia, (bottom left) Worldofvector/Fotolia, (bottom left inset) Martialred/Fotolia,

Continued on page 463

Be: Present and Past

2

PART 1

OUTCOMES

- Use the verb *be* in simple present statements
- Recognize details in a short description
- Recognize important information in a conversation about people
- Talk about sports and famous athletes
- Write sentences about a classmate

OUTCOMES

- Ask and answer *yes/no* and *wh-* questions in the simple present
- Answer questions about details in a conversation
- Recognize main ideas and details in a conversation about two people
- Ask questions about a person and a place
- Write a list of questions about a place

OUTCOMES

- Use the verb *be* in the simple past
- Ask and answer questions about the past with *was/were*
- Correct false statements from an article
- Recognize detailed information in phone messages
- Talk about the weather
- Talk about the first day of school
- Write a paragraph about your first day of school

Present of *Be*: Statements

SPORTS

OUTCOMES
- Use the verb *be* in simple present statements
- Recognize details in a short description
- Recognize important information in a conversation about people
- Talk about sports and famous athletes
- Write sentences about a classmate

STEP 1 GRAMMAR IN CONTEXT

BEFORE YOU READ

Look at the photos. Work with a partner. Answer the questions.

1. What are three popular sports in your country?

2. What's your favorite sport?

MOST POPULAR SPORTS IN THE WORLD

Basketball

Cricket

Soccer

Ice hockey

Tennis

READ

01|01 Read this article about Ana and soccer.

Ana and Soccer

Hi, I'm Ana Silva. I'm from São Paulo, Brazil. I'm a soccer fan. Soccer is the number-one sport in my country. It's the number-one sport in the world. It is popular in Africa, Asia, Europe, South America, and North America. But the name "soccer" is not popular all over the world. Only people in the

United States and Canada call the sport "soccer." People in the rest of the world call it "football."

This is a photo of me with my cousins Julia and Marco. They are with me at a soccer game. Julia is in the middle. She's a student at the University of São Paulo. Marco is in high school. He's in his last year. We are all soccer fans. We're athletes, too. I'm a soccer player, but Julia and Marco are not. They're tennis players. But we all love soccer. Of course we love soccer—we are Brazilians!

AFTER YOU READ

A VOCABULARY **Complete the sentences. Circle the correct answers.**

1. Ronaldo is her favorite soccer player. His photo is on her wall. She's a <u>fan / student</u> of Ronaldo.

2. That hockey team is new. It's <u>only / over</u> two years old.

3. All the students in our school like hockey. It is a <u>popular / bad</u> sport here in Canada.

4. Ahmed is good at all sports. He's a very good <u>athlete / friend</u>.

5. This is a photo of my friends and me. Jon is on the left. Natalie is on the right. I'm <u>in the world / in the middle</u>.

6. Ten of my classmates love sports. <u>The rest of / The name of</u> my classmates are not interested in sports.

B COMPREHENSION **Read the statements. Check (✓) *True* or *False*.**

	True	False
1. In the photo, Ana is with her brother and sister.	☐	☐
2. Ana is from Brazil.	☐	☐
3. Brazil is in São Paulo.	☐	☐
4. Football is the number-one sport in Brazil.	☐	☐
5. Julia and Marco aren't soccer players.	☐	☐
6. Ana and her cousins aren't soccer fans.	☐	☐

C DISCUSSION **Work with a partner. Compare your answers in B. Then say two things about Ana and her cousins and two things about soccer.**

PRESENT OF *BE*: STATEMENTS

Affirmative Statements

Singular		
Subject	*Be*	
I	**am**	
You	**are**	
Mike He	**is**	a student.
Carrie She		
Hockey It		a sport.

Plural		
Subject	*Be*	
Marco and I We	**are**	cousins.
You and Julie You		
Ivona and Boris They		
Seoul and Tripoli They		cities.

Negative Statements

Singular		
Subject	*Be + not*	
I	**am not**	from Istanbul.
You	**are not**	
He	**is not**	
She	**is not**	
It	**is not**	new.

Plural		
Subject	*Be + not*	
We	**are not**	in Seoul.
You	**are not**	
They	**are not**	

Contractions

Affirmative Contractions			
I am	→ **I'm**	we are	→ **we're**
you are	→ **you're**	you are	→ **you're**
he is	→ **he's**	they are	→ **they're**
she is	→ **she's**		
it is	→ **it's**		

Negative Contractions					
I am not	→ **I'm not**		we are not	→ **we're not**	**we aren't**
you are not	→ **you're not**	**you aren't**	you are not	→ **you're not**	**you aren't**
he is not	→ **he's not**	**he isn't**	they are not	→ **they're not**	**they aren't**
she is not	→ **she's not**	**she isn't**			
it is not	→ **it's not**	**it isn't**			

GRAMMAR NOTES

1 Present Forms of *Be*

The **present of** *be* has three forms: *am*, *is*, and *are*.	
• *am*	I **am** a student.
• *is*	He **is** from São Paulo.
• *are*	They **are** athletes.

2 Negative Statements

Use *not* after a form of *be* to make a negative statement.	
• *am not*	I **am not** from Turkey.
• *is not*	Seattle **is not** in Canada.
• *are not*	We **are not** hockey players.

3 Contractions

Use **contractions** (short forms) in speaking and informal writing.	I**'m** from Mexico. I**'m not** from Ecuador. She**'s** from Morocco. She **isn't** from Egypt. They**'re** from Brazil. They **aren't** from Argentina.
There are two negative contractions for *is not*.	It**'s not** difficult. It **isn't** difficult.
There are two negative contractions for *are not*.	We**'re not** single. We **aren't** single.
BE CAREFUL! There is only one negative contraction for *am not*.	I**'m not** from Ecuador. NOT I ~~amn't~~ from Ecuador.

4 Subjects and Verbs

All sentences have a **subject** and a **verb**.	**SUBJECT**	**VERB**	
	I	*am*	from São Paulo.
	Julia	*is*	a soccer fan.
	My cousin and I	*are*	soccer fans.
BE CAREFUL! You cannot make a sentence without a subject. You cannot make a sentence without a verb.	**Julia is** a soccer fan. NOT ~~Is a soccer fan.~~ *(No subject)* NOT ~~Julia a soccer fan.~~ *(No verb)*		

5 Subjects, Nouns, and Subject Pronouns

The **subject** is a **noun** or a **pronoun**. Subject pronouns replace subject nouns.	SUBJECT NOUN **Marco Silva** is a student. SUBJECT PRONOUN **He** is from São Paulo.
BE CAREFUL! You cannot put a subject pronoun right after a subject noun.	**Marco is** from São Paulo. NOT Marco ~~he~~ is from São Paulo.

EXERCISE 1 DISCOVER THE GRAMMAR

GRAMMAR NOTES 1–3 Read the paragraph. Underline the forms of *be*.

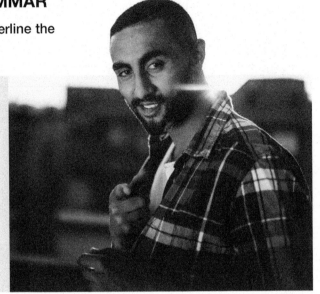

Mourad <u>is</u> from Casablanca. It's the largest city in Morocco. Mourad is a big soccer fan. He isn't a soccer player, but he loves the game. His sister and two brothers are soccer players. They're all excited about the World Cup.

EXERCISE 2 AFFIRMATIVE STATEMENTS

GRAMMAR NOTE 1 Complete the sentences with *am*, *is*, or *are*.

1. Soccer _____*is*_____ popular all over the world.

2. Football _____ popular in the United States and Canada.

3. Football and soccer _____ different sports.

4. Aaron Rodgers and Lionel Messi _____ great athletes.

5. Aaron Rodgers _____ a great football player.

6. Lionel Messi _____ a great soccer player.

7. I _____ a football fan. I love football.

8. My cousins and I _____ soccer fans. We love soccer.

EXERCISE 3 AFFIRMATIVE AND NEGATIVE STATEMENTS

GRAMMAR NOTES 1–3 Complete the paragraphs with affirmative or negative forms of *am*, *is*, or *are*. More than one answer is sometimes possible.

Parminder Nagra _____*is*_____ a talented actor.
1.

She and Keira Knightley _____ the stars of
2.

the 2002 movie *Bend It Like Beckham*. It _____
3.

a comedy. In the movie, Parminder _____ a
4.

young Indian girl in England. She _____ a
5.

good soccer player, and she loves soccer. But her

parents _____ traditional. They
6.

_____ happy. They do not want her to play
7. (not)

soccer. They say, "Soccer _____ for girls.
8. (not)

Marriage _____ for girls. Look at your sister.
9.

Your sister _____ a soccer player, and she
10. (not)

_____ about to marry." Parminder says, "I
11.

_____ my sister."
12. (not)

EXERCISE 4 SUBJECT PRONOUNS AND AFFIRMATIVE CONTRACTIONS

GRAMMAR NOTES 3, 5 Change the underlined words to pronouns and contractions of *be*.

1. Cricket is popular in India. ~~Cricket is~~ *It's* the number-one sport there.

2. Mr. Patel is a cricket fan. <u>Mr. Patel is</u> a soccer fan, too.

3. Soccer is a great sport. <u>Soccer is</u> popular all over the world.

4. <u>My partner and I are</u> on a soccer team.

5. Ms. Cameron is an English teacher. <u>Ms. Cameron is</u> a basketball coach, too.

6. Basketball and baseball are great sports. <u>Basketball and baseball are</u> exciting games.

7. My favorite sport is basketball. <u>Basketball is</u> fun to watch.

8. <u>My cousin and I are</u> at a basketball game in this photo. <u>My cousin and I are</u> in the middle of the row.

EXERCISE 5 AFFIRMATIVE OR NEGATIVE STATEMENTS

GRAMMAR NOTES 1–4 **Write true sentences with the correct simple present forms of *be*.**

1. I _'m or 'm not_ a tennis player.

2. My mother _____ a baseball fan.

3. My father _____ a soccer fan.

4. Soccer _____ popular in my country.

5. Soccer _____ popular all over the world.

6. My friends and I _____ cricket fans.

7. Tennis and ping-pong _____ my favorite sports.

8. I _____ a good tennis player.

9. I _____ a good cricket player.

10. My parents _____ good athletes.

EXERCISE 6 EDITING

GRAMMAR NOTES 1–5 **Read the sentences about a soccer movie. There are seven mistakes. The first mistake is already corrected. Find and correct six more.**

1. "The Beautiful Game" _is_ a movie about soccer.

2. It a documentary.

3. Soccer players from all over Africa in the movie.

4. One boy he is good at soccer.

5. The boy goes to the United States. His parents is happy and unhappy.

6. His mother says, "I'm happy. His future good."

7. She says, "I unhappy. He isn't near us."

EXERCISE 7   LISTENING

01|02   **A**   Study the chart. Then listen to a conversation about athletes. Write the sport and country of origin for each of these famous athletes. Use the words in the boxes.

Sport:	baseball	basketball	golf	soccer	tennis

Country:	Argentina	Brazil	Japan	Portugal	Romania	United States

Name	LeBron James	Lionel Messi	Cristiano Ronaldo	Masahiro Tanaka
Sport	*Basketball*			
Country	*United States*			

Name	Michelle Wie	Alex Morgan	Marta Vieira da Silva	Simona Halep
Sport				
Country				

01|02   **B**   Listen again and check your answers in A.

C   Work in pairs. Use the information in the chart in A to talk about the athletes.

EXAMPLE: A: LeBron James is a basketball player from the United States.
            B: Lionel Messi is . . .

EXERCISE 8 TRUE OR FALSE?

Ⓐ GAME Prepare for the game in B. Complete the sentences. Write three true sentences and one false sentence.

1. **a.** My favorite athlete is _____ .

   b. He / She is _____ .

2. **a.** My cousin and I are _____ .

   b. We are _____ .

Ⓑ Work in a group. Read your sentences to the group. The group guesses the false sentence. Take turns.

EXAMPLE: **A:** My favorite athlete is Serena Williams. She's from South Africa. My cousin and I are tennis players. We are tennis fans, too.

B: Serena Williams isn't from South Africa.

A: That's right. She's from the United States.

EXERCISE 9 PING-PONG IS BORING!

Ⓐ DISCUSSION Prepare for the discussion in B. Complete the chart with one or more words about each sport. Use the words in the box or your own ideas.

| boring | dangerous | exciting | fun | interesting | popular in my country | relaxing |

ping-pong	volleyball	running	swimming	skateboarding	snowboarding
Fun					

Ⓑ Work in a group. Talk about each sport in A.

EXAMPLE: **A:** Ping-pong is fun.

B: I agree. It's exciting, too.

C: I'm not a big ping-pong fan. I think it's boring.

A: OK. Volleyball is next. So, what do you think?

Ⓒ Tell the class three things you agree on.

EXAMPLE: We agree on three things. First, . . . Second, we think that . . . Third, . . .

FROM GRAMMAR TO WRITING

A BEFORE YOU WRITE Look at the chart. Complete the "You" column. Then work with a partner. Talk about yourself. Then listen and take notes about your partner.

	Example	You	Your Partner
Name	Tom Cummins Nickname: Tommy		
City, Country	Toronto, Canada		
A sport in your country	Hockey: very popular in Canada		
Your family and this sport	My two brothers: hockey players and hockey fans		
You and sports	Not a hockey player, not a big hockey fan My favorite sport: snowboarding		

B WRITE Write eight sentences about your partner. Use your notes in A. Use the verb *be* in every sentence.

EXAMPLE: My partner's name is Tom Cummins.
         His nickname is Tommy. . . .

C CHECK YOUR WORK Read your sentences in B. Underline all examples of the verb *be*. Use the Editing Checklist to check your work.

Editing Checklist
Did you . . . ?
☐ use *am* with *I*, *is* with *he/she/it*, and *are* with *you/we/they*
☐ a subject and verb in every statement

D REVISE YOUR WORK Read your sentences again. Can you improve your writing? Make changes if necessary.

UNIT 1 REVIEW

Test yourself on the grammar of the unit.

A Complete the sentences with *am*, *is*, or *are*.

1. My brother and I _____ baseball fans.

2. Our favorite sport _____ baseball.

3. I _____ a good baseball player.

4. My brother _____ a good baseball player, too.

5. We _____ athletes.

B Complete the sentences with *'m*, *'s*, or *'re*.

1. I_____ from Korea.

2. She_____ from Brazil.

3. We_____ basketball fans.

4. He_____ a good basketball player.

5. We_____ from Ohio, and LeBron James is from Ohio, too.

C Rewrite the sentences. Change the underlined words to pronouns and contractions of *be*.

1. <u>Lionel Messi is</u> not in Argentina now. _____

2. <u>Soccer and baseball are</u> exciting sports. _____

3. <u>My partner and I are</u> not baseball fans. _____

4. <u>Ms. Nagra is</u> the star of a movie. _____

D Correct the paragraph. There are six mistakes.

My father and mother are from India, but they're in Canada now. My parents are doctors. My father a sports doctor, and my mother she is a family doctor. My parents and I love sports. My father are a soccer fan, and my mother a baseball fan. I'm a soccer fan. My father and I am fans of Lionel Messi and Nuno Gomes. My sister no is good at sports. She's not a sports fan. She loves movies.

Now check your answers on page 445.

Present of *Be*: Questions
SCHOOL

OUTCOMES
- Ask and answer *yes/no* and *wh-* questions in the simple present
- Answer questions about details in a conversation
- Recognize main ideas and details in a conversation about two people
- Ask questions about a person and a place
- Write a list of questions about a place

STEP 1   GRAMMAR IN CONTEXT

BEFORE YOU READ

Work with a partner. Answer the questions.

1. Are you usually on time for school? For work? For parties? For family dinners?

2. Who in your family is often late?

READ

▶ 02|01   Read this conversation about the first day of an English class.

Are We Late?

AVA: Excuse me. Where's room 2?

AL: It's right here, next to the office.

AVA: Thanks. Are we late for class?

AL: No, we're right on time.

AVA: Whew! That's good. I hate to be late on the first day. Is the teacher here?

AL: Yes, he is.

AVA: How is he? Is he a good teacher?

AL: I think so. I'm Al. What's your name?

AVA: Ava.

AL: Nice to meet you. Are you new here?

AVA: Yes, I am.

AL: Where are you from? Are you from Latin America?

AVA: No, I'm from Spain. Hey, your English is so good! . . . Where are *you* from?

AL: I'm from Michigan.

AVA: Michigan? But that's in the United States.
Are you in the right class?

AL: Yes, I am.

AVA: Why are you here? Who are you?

AL: I'm not a new student. I'm a new *teacher*. I'm *your*
new teacher.

AVA: Oh . . . !

AFTER YOU READ

A VOCABULARY **Complete the sentences with the words from the box. Use a capital letter when necessary.**

excuse me	office	on time	right	room

1. A: _____, where's the elevator? B: It's around the corner.

2. A: Your class is in _____ 102, next to the stairs. B: Thanks.

3. A: Room 202 is _____ over there, near the elevator. B: Oh, I see it. Thanks.

4. A: We're _____. We're not late or early. B: Good.

5. A: Where's the director's _____? B: It's on the second floor.

B COMPREHENSION **Read the questions. Choose the correct answers.**

1. Are Ava and Al on time for class?
   a. Yes, they are. b. No, they're late. c. No, they're early.

2. Where is Ava from?
   a. Argentina b. Michigan c. Spain

3. Where is Michigan?
   a. in the United States b. in Argentina c. in Spain

4. Are Ava and Al students?
   a. She isn't a student, but he is. b. She's a student, but he isn't. c. Yes, they are.

5. What is true?
   a. Al is in the wrong class. b. Al isn't a good teacher. c. Al is Ava's teacher.

C DISCUSSION **Work with a partner. Compare your answers in B. Why do you think your answers are correct?**

STEP 2 GRAMMAR PRESENTATION

PRESENT OF *BE*: QUESTIONS

Yes/No Questions: Singular

Be	Subject	
Am	I	
Are	you	
	he	in room 2?
Is	she	
	it	

Short Answers: Singular

Yes		No	
	you **are**.		you're **not**. you **aren't**.
	I **am**.		I'm **not**.
Yes,	he **is**.	No,	he's **not**. he **isn't**.
	she **is**.		she's **not**. she **isn't**.
	it **is**.		it's **not**. it **isn't**.

Yes/No Questions: Plural

Be	Subject	
	we	
Are	you	on time?
	they	

Short Answers: Plural

Yes		No	
	you **are**.		you're **not**. you **aren't**.
Yes,	we **are**.	No,	we're **not**. we **aren't**.
	they **are**.		they're **not**. they **aren't**.

Wh- Questions

Wh- Word	Be	Subject	
Where	are	you	from?
Why			here?
What		your	name?
How	is	he?	
Who		she?	
When	am	I	in class?

Short Answers

Michigan.
I'm the teacher.
Al.
Good.
A student.
From 8:00 to 11:00.

Long Answers

I'm from Michigan.
I'm here because I'm the teacher.
My name is Al.
He's a good teacher.
She's a student.
You're in class from 8:00 to 11:00.

GRAMMAR NOTES

1 Yes/No and Wh- Questions

Yes/no **questions** usually have a *yes* or *no* answer.	A: Is he a student? B: **Yes**, he is. **or No**, he isn't.
Wh- **questions** ask for information.	A: **Who** is he? B: He's the teacher.

2 Yes/No Questions: Form

Use **am**, **is**, or **are** before the subject in yes/no questions.	**BE**	**SUBJECT**
	Am	I in English 2?
	Is	she a student?
	Are	we late?

3 Yes/No Questions and Answers

We usually give **short answers** to yes/no questions, but we can also give **long answers**.	A: Are you a new student? B: **Yes.** or **Yes, I am.** A: Are you a new student? B: **Yes, I'm new.** or **Yes, I'm a new student.**
BE CAREFUL! Do not use contractions in short answers with yes.	Yes, I am. NOT Yes, ~~I'm.~~ Yes, he is. NOT Yes, ~~he's.~~
USAGE NOTE When we do not know the answer to a question, we say, "I don't know."	A: Is he a new student? B: **I don't know.**
USAGE NOTE When someone asks a yes/no question that we think is true, we can say, "Yes, I think so."	A: Is he a new student? B: **Yes, I think so.**
USAGE NOTE If we think an answer is not true, we can say, "No, I don't think so."	A: Is he a new student? B: **No, I don't think so.**

4 Wh- Question Words

Wh- **question words** ask about the following:
- *Who* → people
- *What* → things
- *Where* → places
- *When* → time
- *How* → in what way
- *Why* → reason

QUESTIONS	SHORT ANSWERS
Who are they?	**My classmates.**
What is in your bag?	**My phone.**
Where is our classroom?	**In room 2.**
When is lunch?	**At noon.**
How is school?	**Good.**
Why are you late?	**My bus was late.**

In **long answers** to questions that start with **why**, use **because** before the reason.	A: **Why** are you late? B: I'm late **because** my bus was late.

5 Wh- Questions: Form

Use a **wh- word** before is or are in wh- questions.	**WH- WORD**	**BE**	
	What	**is**	your name?
	Where	**are**	the books?
USAGE NOTE We often use **contractions** (short forms) with wh- words + is in speaking and informal writing. We don't usually write contractions with wh- words + are.	**What's** your name? **How's** your class?		

6 Wh- Questions and Answers

We usually give **short answers** to wh- questions, but we can also give long answers.	A: Where are you from? B: **Mexico.** *(short answer)* A: Where are you from? B: **I'm from Mexico.** *(long answer)*
USAGE NOTE When we don't know the answer to a wh- question, we say, "I don't know."	A: Where is he from? B: **I don't know.**

STEP 3   FOCUSED PRACTICE

EXERCISE 1   DISCOVER THE GRAMMAR

GRAMMAR NOTES 1–6   Look at the picture. Circle the correct answers.

1. Are the students hungry?

    a. Yes, it is.   **b.** Yes, she is.   **c.** I don't know.

2. What time is it?

    a. It's September.   **b.** It's ten o'clock.   **c.** It's late.

3. Is the teacher a man?

    a. Yes, he is.   **b.** No, he's not.   **c.** Yes, she is.

4. Is the door open?

    a. Yes, she is.   **b.** No, it isn't.   **c.** Yes, it is.

5. Is the student at the door early?

   a. Yes, she's early.   **b.** No, she's late.   **c.** Yes, he is.

6. Is the student at the door unhappy?

   a. No, they aren't.   **b.** I think so.   **c.** Yes, he is.

7. Where is the teacher?

   a. Near the board.   **b.** At the door.   **c.** In September.

8. What month is it?

   a. It's September.   **b.** Yes, it is.   **c.** It's late.

EXERCISE 2 *YES / NO* QUESTIONS

GRAMMAR NOTE 2   Write *yes/no* questions about the statements in parentheses.

1. (The office is on this floor.)   *Is the office on this floor?* _____

2. (We are in the right building.)   _____

3. (You are a new student.)   _____

4. (Our teacher is from Canada.)   _____

5. (It's ten o'clock.)   _____

6. (Your classmates are friendly.)   _____

7. (Two students are absent today.)   _____

8. (I'm in the right room.)   _____

9. (This exercise is easy.)   _____

EXERCISE 3 *YES / NO* QUESTIONS AND SHORT ANSWERS

GRAMMAR NOTES 2–3   Write *yes/no* questions. Put the words in parentheses in the correct order. Then write true short answers with *yes*, *no*, *I don't know*, *I think so*, or *I don't think so*. Use contractions when possible.

1. (you / Are / usually early)

   A: *Are you usually early?* _____

   B: *Yes, I am. or No, I'm not.* _____

2. (your watch / fast / Is)

   A: _____

   B: _____

3. (from Italy / your jacket / Is)

A: _____

B: _____

4. (on this floor / the restroom / Is)

A: _____

B: _____

5. (your name / Is / easy to pronounce)

A: _____

B: _____

6. (different cities / Are / from / you and your classmates)

A: _____

B: _____

7. (busy / Are / your classmates / now)

A: _____

B: _____

EXERCISE 4 *WH-* QUESTIONS

GRAMMAR NOTES 4–5 **Read the answers. Then write *wh-* questions with the words in parentheses.**

1. A: (Who) *Who's Al Brown? or Who is Al Brown?* _____

B: Al Brown is the teacher.

2. A: (Where) _____

B: The computers are in room 304.

3. A: (What) _____

B: Today's date is September 3.

4. A: (Why) _____

B: We're late because we were in the wrong classroom.

5. A: (Why) _____

B: Diane is the teacher today because Al isn't here.

6. A: (How) _____

B: My computer class is great.

EXERCISE 5
YES / NO AND WH- QUESTIONS AND ANSWERS

GRAMMAR NOTES 1–6
Read this paragraph about Hao. Then complete the questions and answers.

Hao is a student in level 2. He's in his grammar class now. His grammar class is in room 201. His teacher is Diane. She's a wonderful teacher. The classroom is small, but comfortable. The students are great. They're from six different countries: China, Korea, Japan, Saudi Arabia, Argentina, and Italy.

1. A: _Is_ _____ Hao in level 2?

   B: _Yes, he is_ _____ .

2. A: _____ Hao's grammar class?

   B: It's in _____ .

3. A: _____ ?

   B: Diane.

4. A: _____ ?

   B: It's small, but _____ .

5. A: _____ ?

   B: _____ great.

6. A: _____ six different countries?

   B: Yes, _____ .

7. A: Where _____ ?

   B: China, Korea, Japan, Saudi Arabia,

   _____ , and _____ .

EXERCISE 6 QUESTIONS AND ANSWERS

A GRAMMAR NOTES 1–6 Read Alejandra's post on SmartGirl's blog. Write simple present questions with the words in parentheses. Then write short answers.

smart girl .com

Alejandra Suarez

Hey SmartGirl,

I have a great boyfriend, Oscar. He's fun and intelligent. We're a good match. But there's one problem. He's always late. He's late to school. He's late to work. He's late for me. Always.

Why?

Alejandra

1. (Oscar / fun)

   A: _Is Oscar fun?_ _____

   B: _Yes, he is._ _____

2. (Oscar / smart)

   A: _____

   B: _____

3. (Alejandra and Oscar / a good pair)

   A: _____

   B: _____

4. (Who / always late)

   A: _____

   B: _____

B Read SmartGirl's answer. Write simple present *yes/no* questions with the words in parentheses. Answer the questions with "*Yes, I think so,*" "*No, I don't think so,*" or "*I don't know.*"

smart
girl
.com

SmartGirl

Hey Alejandra,

OK, so your guy is great, but late. And you hate to wait. Why is he always late? Maybe he thinks, "I'm late. That means I'm important." Maybe he doesn't know it's a problem for you. He thinks it's no big deal. Tell him it is a big deal to you. Maybe he's just bad at planning his time. Try to help him.

Good luck.

SmartGirl

1. (Oscar / great)

A: *Is Oscar great?*

B: *No, I don't think so. or Yes, I think so.*

2. (Oscar / a bad boyfriend)

A: _____

B: _____

3. (Oscar / bad at planning time)

A: _____

B: _____

4. (SmartGirl's answer / good)

A: _____

B: _____

EXERCISE 7 EDITING

GRAMMAR NOTES 1–6 **Read the conversations. There are ten mistakes. The first mistake is already corrected. Find and correct nine more.**

1. A: Are you in the office?

 B: Yes, ~~I'm~~. *I am*

2. A: Is easy?

 B: No, it's hard.

3. A: He Korean?

 B: No, he's isn't.

4. A: Excuse me. Where's the office?

 B: Yes, it's in room 305.

5. A: Is this English 3?

 B: Yes, I think.

6. A: Is they in room 102?

 B: I don't know.

7. A: Where you from?

 B: I'm from Peru.

8. A: How your class is?

 B: It's very good.

9. A: What your nickname?

 B: Susie.

EXERCISE 8 LISTENING

02|02 **A** Listen to a conversation between Elena and Hugo. Check (✓) the people and countries that they talk about.

People	Countries
☐ Elena	☐ Canada
☐ Elena's classmates	☐ Chile
☐ Hao	☐ England
☐ Hugo's classmates	☐ Korea
☐ Hugo's cousins	☐ Portugal
☐ Hugo's teacher	☐ Saudi Arabia
☐ school director	☐ South Korea

02|02 **B** Listen again and answer the questions.

1. Is Hugo happy with school? _____

2. How's Hugo's teacher? _____

3. Where are his classmates from? _____

4. What are Hugo and Elena good at? _____

5. What is Hao good at? _____

C Work with a partner. Change the questions in B to questions about your partner, your teacher, and your classmates.

EXAMPLE: **A:** Are you happy with school?
B: Yes, I am, but English isn't easy. How about you?
A: I'm . . .

EXERCISE 9 ARE THE ANSWERS AT THE BACK?

A Q & A Work with a partner. Answer these questions about your textbook.

1. Where is a world map?
   EXAMPLE: It's on page 430.

2. Where is a map of the United States and Canada?

3. Are the answers to all the questions at the back of the book?

4. Where is the Glossary of Grammar Terms?

5. What's on page 42?

6. Is the Unit 1 Review on page 50?

7. What's the title of your book?

8. Is the cover of the book red?

B Write five new questions with your partner.

Is the cover interesting?
Is the photo on page…?

C Work in groups. Take turns. Ask and discuss the questions in B.

EXAMPLE: **A:** Is the cover interesting?
B: No, I don't think so.
C: I disagree. The colors are nice.

EXERCISE 10 HI, I'M . . .

ROLE PLAY Work in pairs. Imagine you and your partner are at a school party. Give yourself a new name, a new country, and a new occupation. Introduce yourself to your partner.

EXAMPLE: **A:** Hi, I'm Prince Harry.
B: Nice to meet you. I'm Princess Elsa. Are you from around here?
A: No, I'm from England. What about you?

EXERCISE 11 WHAT IS ULS?

A Q & A Work with a partner. Read the ad for University Language School. Write five *wh-* questions and five *yes/no* questions.

What's ULS?
Where is ULS?

B Work with another pair of partners. Read the ad again, and close your books. Ask and answer your questions from A. Take turns.

EXAMPLE: **A:** Where is ULS?
C: It's in New York.
B: What can you learn at ULS?
D: English.

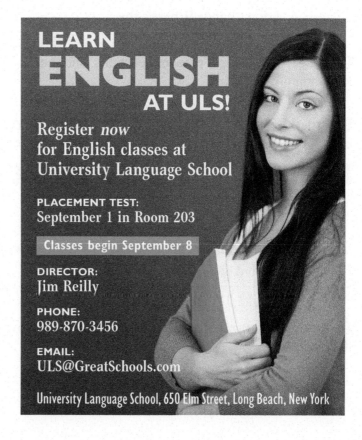

LEARN
ENGLISH
AT ULS!

Register *now*
for English classes at
University Language School

PLACEMENT TEST:
September 1 in Room 203

Classes begin September 8

DIRECTOR:
Jim Reilly

PHONE:
989-870-3456

EMAIL:
ULS@GreatSchools.com

University Language School, 650 Elm Street, Long Beach, New York

A BEFORE YOU WRITE Work with a partner. Ask and answer questions about your school. Use the ideas below or your own ideas. Take turns.

School Calendar
- the next school holiday
- the winter break
- the last day of class

School Staff
- your teacher
- the school director
- office assistant

Places in the School
- the school library
- the computer room
- the registration office
- the cafeteria
- the rest rooms
- the staircase

EXAMPLE: A: Is May 23 the last day of class?
          B: Yes, it is. Who's the school director?
          A: I don't know. Where's the . . . ?

B WRITE Write simple present questions with the verb *be* about your school. Use your ideas from A.

C CHECK YOUR WORK Read your questions in B. Underline the verb *be* in your questions. Use the Editing Checklist to check your work.

Editing Checklist
Did you . . . ?
☐ use *is* with *he/she/it* and *are* with *you/we/they*
☐ put *am*, *is*, or *are* before the subject in *yes/no* questions
☐ use a *wh-* word before *is* or *are* in *wh-* questions

D REVISE Read your questions again. Can you improve your writing? Make changes if necessary.

UNIT 2 REVIEW

Test yourself on the grammar of the unit.

Ⓐ Complete A's questions. Circle the correct words.

1. A: Where's / What's the library?   B: In room 3.

2. A: Who's / How's your class?   B: It's great.

3. A: What's / How's your name?   B: Jin-Hee Lee.

4. A: Is / Are you from Seoul?   B: Yes, I am.

5. A: Is / Are it cold in Seoul now?   B: No, it isn't.

Ⓑ Complete the short answers.

1. A: Are you home?   B: Yes, _____ .

2. A: Is your nickname JD?   B: No, _____ .

3. A: Are they late?   B: No, _____ .

4. A: Are we in the right room? B: Yes, _____ .

5. A: Am I late?   B: No, _____ .

Ⓒ Write questions. Use the words in parentheses and the simple present of *be*.

1. (What / today's date)   _____

2. (Where / the men's room)   _____

3. (Why / he / absent)   _____

4. (When / your first class)   _____

5. (Who / your teacher)   _____

Ⓓ Correct the questions. There are five mistakes.

1. She your teacher?

2. What your name?

3. Where your class?

4. Is Bob and Molly good friends?

5. Why you late?

Now check your answers on page 445.

Past of *Be*

A FIRST DAY

OUTCOMES
- Use the verb *be* in the simple past
- Ask and answer questions about the past with *was/were*
- Correct false statements from an article
- Recognize detailed information in phone messages
- Talk about the weather
- Talk about the first day of school
- Write a paragraph about your first day of school

STEP 1   GRAMMAR IN CONTEXT

BEFORE YOU READ

Work with a partner. Answer the questions.

1. How was your first day at school?

2. Were you happy? Were you nervous? Were you excited?

READ

○ 03|01   Read this article about Sarah's first day at a new school.

Sarah's First Day

The first day at a new place is sometimes difficult and sometimes scary. We're often afraid of new people and places. Sometimes we're nervous and excited at the same time. How was your first day at a new school? Do you remember it? Was it good? Were you nervous? Was it difficult? Were your classmates friendly?

    There is a wonderful children's book called *First Day Jitters*[1] by Julie

---

1 *jitters:* a nervous, uneasy feeling

Danneberg. It's about Sarah Jane Hartwell's first day at a new school. Sarah was frightened. She was nervous. Mr. Hartwell said, "Sarah. Wake up. It's time for school."

Sarah said, "I'm sick. My hands are cold. I don't want to go to a new school."

Mr. Hartwell was kind and patient.[2] He drove Sarah to school. The school principal took Sarah to the classroom. The children were all there. They weren't nervous. They were happy. Sarah was not happy, but the principal smiled and said, "Don't worry, Sarah."

Then the principal turned to the class and said, "Class, I want you to meet your new teacher, Mrs. Sarah Jane Hartwell."

Young children like the story. They like the surprise ending. They also like to learn that sometimes teachers are nervous, too.

---

2 *patient:* calm, slow to get angry

AFTER YOU READ

A VOCABULARY Complete the paragraph with the words from the box.

afraid of	difficult	nervous	principal	surprise

1. Last year, Ms. Rogers was the _____ .

2. She was never in her office. It was _____ to find her.

3. She wasn't kind to the students or the teachers. Many teachers and children were

    _____ her.

4. She complained a lot. Children were _____ when they were in her office.

5. One day, she was gone. It was a _____ , but no one was sad. In fact, it was a very good thing since our new principal is great.

B COMPREHENSION All the statements are false. Correct them. There is more than one correct answer.

1. People are never afraid of new places and new things.

2. *First Day Jitters* is a book for teenagers.

3. Sarah was in school before the children.

4. Sarah was a new student.

5. Teachers are never nervous.

C DISCUSSION Work with a partner. Compare your answers in B. Then discuss: Was the ending of the story a surprise to you?

PAST OF *BE*: AFFIRMATIVE STATEMENTS

Singular

Subject	*Be*		Time Marker
I	was	a student	last year.
You	were		
He She	was		
It		in Asia	

Plural

Subject	*Be*		Time Marker
We You They	were	in New York	two weeks ago.

PAST OF *BE*: NEGATIVE STATEMENTS

Singular

Subject	*Be* + *not*		Time Marker
I	was not wasn't	at school	last night.
You	were not weren't		
He She It	was not wasn't		

Plural

Subject	*Be* + *not*		Time Marker
We You They	were not weren't	at work	last week.

PAST OF *BE*: *YES*/*NO* QUESTIONS

Singular

Be	Subject		Time Marker
Was	I	in class	yesterday?
Were	you		
Was	he she it		

Plural

Be	Subject		Time Marker
Were	we	in class	last week?
	you		
	they		

SHORT ANSWERS

Singular

Yes	Subject	*Be*		No	Subject	*Be* + not
	you	were.			you	weren't.
Yes,	I	was.		No,	I	wasn't.
	he she it				he she it	

Plural

Yes	Subject	*Be*		No	Subject	*Be* + not
	you				you	
Yes,	we	were.		No,	we	weren't.
	they				they	

PAST OF *BE*: *WH-* QUESTIONS

Wh- questions			Long Answers
Wh- Word	*Be*		
What		your first job?	I was a server.
Where	was	the restaurant?	It was in New York.
When		that?	It was in 2005.
How		the job?	It was fun.
Who	were	the other servers?	They were my brothers and my cousin.
Why		you in New York?	My parents were there.

GRAMMAR NOTES

1 Past Forms of *Be*

The past of *be* has two forms: ***was*** and ***were***.

• *was*	I **was** excited.
• *were*	They **were** happy.

2 Negative Statements

Use ***not*** after a form of ***was*** or ***were*** to make a negative statement.

• *was not*	I **was not** in school.
• *were not*	We **were not** late.

3 Contractions

In informal writing and speaking, use the contractions ***wasn't*** and ***weren't*** in negative statements and negative short answers.

• *wasn't*	He **wasn't** at the interview. No, he **wasn't**.
• *weren't*	They **weren't** in class. No, they **weren't**.

4 *Yes/No* Questions

To ask a *yes/no* question, put ***was*** or ***were*** before the subject.	**Was**	he	a student?
	Were	they	nervous?

5 Wh- Questions

Use a **wh- question word** before *was* or *were* in *wh-* questions.	**When was** he a salesman? **Where were** they students? **How was** your first day at school?
USAGE NOTE The answer to *Who was...?* can be singular or plural.	Who **was** absent yesterday? Suna **was**. Who **was** absent on Monday? Suna and Paul **were**.

6 Time Markers

Time markers say when something happened. Examples of past time markers are: *yesterday, last week, two years ago,* and *in the past.*

Time markers are often at the **end of statements**.	We were in class **yesterday**. John wasn't in class **last week**.
Time markers are sometimes at the **beginning of statements**.	**Yesterday**, we were in class. **Last week**, he wasn't in class.
Time markers are at the **end of a question**.	Were you in high school **two years ago**? Were they servers **in the past**?
BE CAREFUL! Do not put a time marker in the middle of a statement or question.	We were in class **yesterday**. NOT We were ~~yesterday~~ in class. Were they servers **in the past**? NOT Were they ~~in the past~~ servers?
BE CAREFUL! Use *ago* after a time period in the past. Do not use *before* + a time period.	Were you in high school **two years ago**? NOT Were you in high school ~~before two years~~?

EXERCISE 1 DISCOVER THE GRAMMAR

Ⓐ GRAMMAR NOTES 1–6 Read this article about the first jobs of famous people.
Underline *was*, *wasn't*, *were*, and *weren't*.

Chris Rock   Lady Gaga   George Clooney   Madonna   Patrick Dempsey

A first job is very exciting. A first boss and a first paycheck are hard to forget. But a first job is not always the job of your dreams. Here are the first jobs of some famous people.

• In the past, Chris Rock, the comedian, <u>was</u> a busser at a restaurant.

• George Clooney was a shoe salesman.

• Lady Gaga and Madonna weren't always singers. Many years before they were famous, they worked in restaurants: Madonna was a server and Lady Gaga was a busser.

• Patrick Dempsey, the actor, was a juggler.

So maybe you're not happy with your job today. Maybe it isn't the job you really want. Don't feel bad. Just keep looking.

Ⓑ Look at the article in A again. Answer the questions. Circle the correct answers.

1. Were Chris Rock and Lady Gaga jugglers?
   a. Yes, they were.   **b.** No, they weren't.

2. Was George Clooney a busser?
   a. Yes, he was.   **b.** No, he wasn't.

3. Who was a server?
   a. Madonna was.   **b.** Lady Gaga was.

4. Who was a shoe salesman?
   a. Patrick Dempsey was.   **b.** George Clooney was.

EXERCISE 2 *WAS* AND *WERE*

GRAMMAR NOTE 1 Complete the sentences with *was* or *were*.

1. My first day at school ____was____ fun. The students _____ friendly, and the teacher _____ great.

2. Pablo and Maria _____ absent on the first day of school. They _____ in a different class.

3. Our first test _____ difficult, and it _____ long.

4. My first-grade teacher _____ a young, new teacher. She _____ tough, and my classmates and I _____ afraid of her.

5. My first job _____ in a restaurant. I _____ a server. The other servers _____ helpful. The job _____ great. I'm a doctor now. My first days at work in the hospital _____ scary. I _____ nervous and unsure of everything.

EXERCISE 3 AFFIRMATIVE AND NEGATIVE FORMS

GRAMMAR NOTES 1–3 Complete the sentences with *was*, *wasn't*, *were*, or *weren't*.
Use contractions.

1. My first day at school was great. The students ____were____ helpful and kind.

2. My first day at work _____ good. My boss was angry and my co-workers weren't helpful.

3. My two interviews _____ long. They were over two hours.

4. His interview _____ long. It was only fifteen minutes.

5. My first month at work was very easy. There was very little work. I _____ busy, and the work _____ hard.

6. *First Day Jitters* was Julie Danneberg's first book. It _____ a big success, and it's still popular today.

7. The weather was terrible on my first day of school. It _____ cold and windy.

8. In July, the classroom _____ hot. The air conditioner was broken.

9. Yesterday the classroom _____ hot. The air conditioner was good.

10. My first months in college _____ very difficult. I was up until 1 a.m. every night.

EXERCISE 4 WORD ORDER OF QUESTIONS AND ANSWERS

Ⓐ GRAMMAR NOTES 1–3, 5–6 Complete the conversation. Put the words in parentheses in the correct order. Use a capital letter when necessary.

ANA: Hey, look at this. It's a photo of me on my first day at work at Lacey's.

CHAD: _____ *When were you there* _____?
      1. (when / you / there / were)

ANA: _____.
      2. (was / it / five years ago)

CHAD: So, _____? Do you remember it?
      3. (your first day / how / was / at work)

ANA: Uh-huh. _____. I was nervous,
      4. (it / hard / was)

_____, and _____.
5. (busy / were / my co-workers)   **6.** (afraid of / was / my boss / I)

_____.
7. (wasn't / sure of anything / I)

CHAD: And now?

ANA: I like my job. What about you? _____?
      8. (your first day / was / how / at work)

CHAD: Great! _____. My boss was
      9. (I / relaxed / was / and happy)

wonderful. But _____.
      10. (wasn't / my second month / good)

ANA: Why?

CHAD: My boss and a co-worker were let go. _____.
      11. (my new boss and new co-worker / helpful / weren't)

_____, but now it's OK.
12. (was / for a few weeks / hard / it)

Ⓑ **LISTEN AND CHECK** Listen to the conversation and check your answers in A.

EXERCISE 5 PRESENT AND PAST OF *BE*

GRAMMAR NOTE 1 Complete the sentences with *is*, *are*, *was*, or *were*.

1. The weather ____ *was* ____ terrible on the first day of our vacation. Now the weather

____ *is* ____ great.

2. My father _____ the CEO of his company today. He _____ an assistant in 2001.

3. Bob and Steve _____ absent yesterday, but they _____ in class now.

4. The class _____ easy at first. Now it _____ very hard.

5. She _____ a great manager now, but she _____ terrible the first month

on the job.

6. We _____ nervous on our first plane trip, but now we _____ relaxed.

EXERCISE 6 EDITING

GRAMMAR NOTES 1–6

Read the email. There are six mistakes. The first mistake is already corrected. Find and correct five more.

Hi Victor,

was
How your weekend ~~was~~? You were busy?

I was yesterday at a job interview. It was for a sales job at a drugstore. The interviewer be friendly. The questions no were easy, but I think my answers was good. I hope I get the job. It's not my dream job, but it's a job with a paycheck.

Write soon.
Ella

STEP 4   COMMUNICATION PRACTICE

EXERCISE 7 LISTENING

▶ 03|03 **A** Listen to five phone messages. Who is each message from? Check (✓) the correct column.

	Friend	Family Member	Business Contact			Friend	Family Member	Business Contact
1.	☐	☐	☐		**4.**	☐	☐	☐
2.	☐	☐	☐		**5.**	☐	☐	☐
3.	☐	☐	☐					

▶ 03|03 **B** Listen again. Discuss each statement. Then check (✓) *True*, *False*, or *No Information*.

	True	False	No Information
1. Ella's interview was at a drugstore.	☑	☐	☐
2. Emiko was at a party with Ella.	☐	☐	☐
3. Ella and Emiko are classmates.	☐	☐	☐
4. Mr. Hess is Ella's friend.	☐	☐	☐
5. Ella's parents were out with Aunt Mona.	☐	☐	☐
6. Dave was in Ottawa on a vacation.	☐	☐	☐
7. Dave was stuck in Ottawa.	☐	☐	☐
8. Dave wasn't at the party for Emiko.	☐	☐	☐

C Work with a partner. Make guesses about the people in the messages in A.

EXAMPLE: I think Ella and Dave are close friends because . . .
I think Ella's interview was good because . . .

EXERCISE 8 HOW'S THE WEATHER?

A GUIDED CONVERSATION Prepare for the conversation in B. Study the weather words.

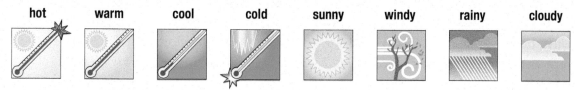

| hot | warm | cool | cold | sunny | windy | rainy | cloudy |

B Imagine it is the second day of your vacation in a new city. A friend calls you. Use the chart below to have a conversation about the weather.

EXAMPLE: A: Hi, Maria. How's Bangkok?
B: It's great.
A: How's the weather?
B: Well, it's cloudy today, but yesterday it was sunny and warm.

City	Yesterday		Today
Bangkok	☀	🌡	☁
Beijing	☁	🌡	☀
Budapest	☁	🌡	☀
Istanbul	☀	🌡	🌧

City	Yesterday		Today
Rio de Janeiro	☀	🌡	☁
Seoul	🌧	🌡	☁
Vancouver	🌬	🌡	☁
Washington	☀	🌡	🌬

EXERCISE 9 ON THE FIRST DAY OF CLASS . . .

GAME Work in groups. Say one true thing and one false thing about the first day of class. The next person repeats the true statement and corrects the false statement. Use *was, wasn't, were,* and *weren't* in your sentences. Take turns.

EXAMPLE: A: On the first day of class, Boris was late and it was warm and sunny.
B: Boris was late, but it wasn't warm and sunny. It was cool and cloudy.
A: Right! Your turn.
B: Ali and Iota were absent, and the classroom was dirty.
C: . . .

FROM GRAMMAR TO WRITING

A BEFORE YOU WRITE Read about Mario's first day at a school. Then work with a partner. Think about a first day at one of your schools. Your partner asks you five questions about your first day. Write notes on your answers in the chart.

Mario's First Day

My first day at high school was ten years ago. It was a bad day for me. The weather was awful. It was rainy, and my bus was late. My umbrella was broken. I'm usually early, but I was late that day. All the students were there. My clothes and books were wet. My hair and shoes were wet. I was very unhappy. My teacher was unhappy, too. I wasn't late again.

	Mario's First Day at School	Your First Day at School
What school was it?	High school	
When was it?	10 years ago	
How was the weather?	Awful	
How was your day?	Bad day!	
Why?	Umbrella broken, late, wet, teacher unhappy	

B WRITE Write a paragraph about your first day at a school. Use the paragraph in A and your chart. Use *was*, *were*, *wasn't*, or *weren't*.

C CHECK YOUR WORK Read your paragraph in B. Underline examples of the past of *be*. Use the Editing Checklist to check your work.

Editing Checklist

Did you . . . ?

☐ use *was* with *I/he/she/it* and *were* with *you/we/they*

☐ use past time markers at the beginning or end of sentences

☐ use *ago* after time periods

D REVISE YOUR WORK Read your paragraph again. Can you improve your writing? Make changes if necessary.

UNIT 3 REVIEW

Test yourself on the grammar of the unit.

Ⓐ Complete the questions. Use *was* or *were*.

1. When _____ your interview?

2. Where _____ your interview?

3. _____ you nervous?

4. How _____ the questions?

5. _____ she at a job interview, too?

Ⓑ Match the questions and answers.

_____ 1. How was the weather?   **a.** Yes, I was.

_____ 2. Who was there?   **b.** Jon and Sri.

_____ 3. Were they home all evening?   **c.** Warm and sunny.

_____ 4. Were you late last week?   **d.** No, they weren't.

Ⓒ Complete the conversation with *was*, *wasn't*, *were*, or *weren't*.

A: How _____ your weekend?
            1.

B: Great. I _____ at the park all day Saturday.
              2.

A: _____ you with Ali?
     3.

B: Yes, I _____. We _____ together all day Saturday and Sunday.
              4.   5.

A: Ali _____ in class this morning. Where _____ he?
              6.   7.

B: I don't know.

Ⓓ Correct the paragraph. There are four mistakes.

John is at a job interview yesterday. It were for a job at a bank. The questions no were easy, but John's answers were good. He was happy. It a good day for John.

Now check your answers on page 445.

Nouns, Adjectives, and Prepositions

PART 2

OUTCOMES
- Use count nouns, proper nouns, and common irregular nouns
- Recognize details in a short biography
- Recognize main ideas and details in a short lecture
- Talk about favorite people, places, and things
- Write a paragraph about a family member

OUTCOMES
- Use adjectives to describe nouns
- Recognize details in an article about a place
- Recognize details in a conversation about an interesting place
- Talk about interesting places, using adjectives
- Write a paragraph about an interesting place

OUTCOMES
- Describe locations with prepositions of place
- Recognize important details in a short article
- Locate places on a map from recorded descriptions
- Give directions to help others find places
- Write a short invitation to a party or an event

Count Nouns and Proper Nouns

PHOTOGRAPHS AND PHOTOGRAPHERS

OUTCOMES
• Use count nouns, proper nouns, and common irregular nouns
• Recognize details in a short biography
• Recognize main ideas and details in a short lecture
• Talk about favorite people, places, and things
• Write a paragraph about a family member

STEP 1   **GRAMMAR IN CONTEXT**

BEFORE YOU READ

Look at the black and white photo. Work with a partner. Answer the questions. Make guesses and give your opinion.

1. Who are the people?
   Where are they?

2. What year was it?

READ

▶ 04|01   Read this article about Henri Cartier-Bresson and one of his photographs.

A Photographer and a Photo

Henri Cartier-Bresson was a photographer and an artist. He was born in France in 1908 and died in 2004. At that time, he was almost ninety-six years old. Cartier-Bresson

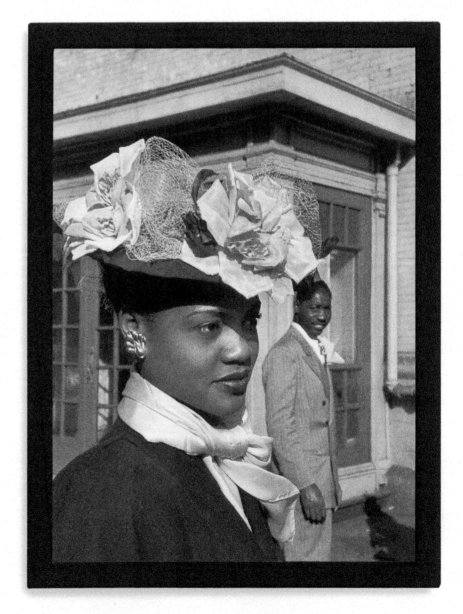

traveled the world. He was in West Africa, the United States, India, China, Egypt, and Russia. His photos are from all over the world.

Cartier-Bresson is famous for "street" photography. Street photographs are about people in the street or other public places such as parks and beaches. They are sometimes about a special moment in time.

Look at this photo by Cartier-Bresson. It's a photo of a woman and a man on a special occasion. They are both wearing fine clothes. The woman is wearing a big hat with many flowers. The man is wearing a suit. The man is looking at the woman. They are in Harlem, in New York City. It's 1947. People say photos by Cartier-Bresson are striking. What do you think? Is this a striking photo?

AFTER YOU READ

A VOCABULARY Match the words in **bold** with their meanings.

1. Henri Cartier-Bresson **was born** in France.
   a. came into the world   **b.** lived

2. His photos are from **all over** the world.
   a. some parts of   **b.** everywhere in

3. It's open to **the public**.
   a. everyone   **b.** only some people

4. His photos are **striking**.
   a. dangerous and hurtful   **b.** unusual and attractive

5. It's a big **occasion**.
   a. special day   **b.** usual day

B COMPREHENSION Read the statements. Check (✓) *True* or *False*.

	True	False
1. Henri Cartier-Bresson was almost 69 years old when he died.	☐	☐
2. Almost all of Cartier-Bresson's photos were of Europe.	☐	☐
3. Cartier-Bresson was in many countries during his life.	☐	☐
4. Cartier-Bresson is famous for "holiday" photography.	☐	☐
5. Street photography shows people in places like parks or beaches.	☐	☐
6. Harlem is not in New York.	☐	☐

C DISCUSSION Work with a partner. Compare your answers in B. Change the false statements to true ones. Then look at the black and white photo on page 42 again. Do you like it? Why or why not?

COUNT NOUNS AND PROPER NOUNS

Singular Nouns
He is **a photographer**.
He is **an artist**.

Plural Nouns
They are **photographers**.
They are **artists**.

Irregular Plural Nouns

Singular	Plural
a man	men
a woman	women
a child	children
a foot	feet
a tooth	teeth
a person	people

Proper Nouns

Harlem is in **New York City**.
The singer **Harry Belafonte** was born in **Harlem**.

GRAMMAR NOTES

1 Nouns

Nouns are the names of: • people • places • animals • things	**Cartier-Bresson** was a photographer. He was born in **France**. A **bird** is in the photo. His **camera** is in his hands.

2 Singular Count Nouns

Count nouns are nouns that **you can count**: *one photo, two photos, three photos.*	
Use *a* before **singular count nouns** that begin with a **consonant sound** like /n/, /b/, or /h/.	She's **a** nurse. He's **a b**aker. It's **a h**ouse.
Use *an* before singular count nouns that begin with a **vowel sound**.	She's **an** artist. He's **an e**ngineer. It's **an u**mbrella.
BE CAREFUL! Use *a* before a *u* that sounds like *yew*.	This is **a u**nit about nouns.
BE CAREFUL! Use *an* before an *h* that is silent.	It's **an h**our too early. *(Hour sounds like our.)*

3 Plural Count Nouns

To form the **plural** of most **count nouns**, add -*s* or -*es*.	one **park** three **parks** one **watch** three **watches**
Some nouns have **irregular** plurals.	one **man** two **men** one **tooth** two **teeth**
Some nouns such as *clothes*, *glasses*, *jeans*, and *scissors* are always plural.	My **jeans** are blue.
BE CAREFUL! Do not put *a* or *an* before plural nouns.	They are friends. **NOT** They are a̶ friends.

4 Proper Nouns

Names of specific people and places are **proper nouns**. Begin these nouns with a capital letter.	**Harlem** is in **New York City**. **Harry Belafonte** is a singer.
BE CAREFUL! Do not put *a* or *an* before proper nouns.	Harry Belafonte was born in Harlem. **NOT** A̶ Harry Belafonte was born in a̶ Harlem.

PRONUNCIATION NOTE

▶04|02 **Plural Noun Endings**

When **nouns are plural**, the **ending** can have one of three sounds: /**s**/, /**z**/, or /**ɪz**/.	
• /s/	students
• /z/	teachers
• /ɪz/	buses

REFERENCE NOTES

For information on **non-count nouns** and *the* (the definite article), see Unit 26 on page 310.

For a list of **spelling and pronunciation rules for plural nouns**, see Appendices 8 and 10 on page 434.

For a list of **irregular nouns**, see Appendix 9 on page 434.

For a list of **rules of capitalization**, see Appendix 20 on page 439.

STEP 3   FOCUSED PRACTICE

EXERCISE 1
DISCOVER THE GRAMMAR

A GRAMMAR NOTES 1–4
Read the conversation. Underline all the proper nouns and count nouns.

MIKE: So Doug, who's that with you in the photo?

DOUG: That's me with friends from college.

MIKE: Where are they now?

DOUG: Well, the woman next to me, Jasmine, is in Brazil.

MIKE: Really?

DOUG: Uh-huh. She's a teacher there. And the guy on the left, Bob, is here in New York. He's an accountant.

MIKE: Who's the other woman?

DOUG: That's Amy. She's a street photographer. She always has a camera with her. What a life! She travels all over the world. Last month, she was in India. Before that, she was in Central America. Now her photos are in a show at the library here.

MIKE: I'd love to see them.

DOUG: Them? Or her?

B Look at the conversation in A again. Find these nouns and write them.

1. One noun that begin with a vowel sound: _____*accountant*_____

2. Three singular nouns that begin with a consonant sound:

   _____ , _____ , _____

3. Two proper nouns: _____ , _____

4. Two plural nouns: _____ , _____

EXERCISE 2 *A* AND *AN*

A GRAMMAR NOTE 2 Write *a* or *an* before each word.

1. __*a*__ man   5. _____ flower   9. _____ lip

2. _____ hand   6. _____ suit   10. _____ woman

3. _____ hat   7. _____ eye

4. _____ earring   8. _____ ear

B Look at the photo, *Harlem, 1947*. Label the parts of the photo with the words from A.

_____ hat _____

_____

_____

_____

_____

EXERCISE 3 *A, AN,* AND *Ø*

GRAMMAR NOTES 1–3 **Complete the sentences with *a* or *an*. Write *Ø* (no article) before plural nouns.**

1. Henri Cartier-Bresson was _____a_____ photographer.

2. Cartier-Bresson and Ansel Adams were _____Ø_____ photographers.

3. Cartier-Bresson was _____ artist, too.

4. All good photographers are _____ artists.

5. Adams was _____ pianist before he was _____ photographer.

6. Adams was also _____ environmentalist.

7. Adams was born in California. Photography began for Adams with _____ trip to Yosemite National Park.

8. Adams said, "It's easy to take _____ photograph, but hard to make _____ masterpiece."

EXERCISE 4 REGULAR AND IRREGULAR PLURAL NOUNS

GRAMMAR NOTE 3 Complete the sentences with the plural form of the nouns in the box. See Appendix 8 (Regular Plural Nouns: Spelling Rules) and Appendix 9 (Irregular Nouns) on page 434 for help.

artist	class	eye	flower	man	person
~~city~~	country	fish	life	museum	watch

1. San Francisco and Los Angeles are _____*cities*_____ in California.

2. Brazil and France are _____.

3. The Louvre and the Prado are _____.

4. Seiko and Rolex are kinds of _____.

5. Your photos of _____ in the water are striking.

6. There are two _____, a man and a woman, in the photo *Harlem, 1947*.

7. The woman in *Harlem, 1947* has a hat with _____.

8. Her face is beautiful, especially her _____.

9. Many _____ and photographers live in New York City.

10. The _____ of famous artists are interesting to read about.

11. I'm taking two photography _____ at The New School in New York.

12. Six _____ and four women are in my "Street Photography" class.

EXERCISE 5 PROPER NOUNS

GRAMMAR NOTE 4 Change small letters to capital letters where necessary. See Appendix 20 (Capitalization and Punctuation Rules) on page 439 for help.

MIKE: Hi, are you ~~amy~~ *Amy* lin?

AMY: Yes, I am.

MIKE: I'm mike cho. I work with Doug.

AMY: Nice to meet you, mike.

MIKE: It's nice to meet you. Your photos are great.

AMY: Thanks. So, mike, are you from phoenix?

MIKE: No, I'm not. I'm from san francisco. I'm here for the Labor Day holiday.

AMY: Oh, san francisco is beautiful. I was there last year.

MIKE: Doug says you travel a lot.

AMY: Yes, I do. I was in india last year, and the year before that I was in almost every country in Central America.

MIKE: That's great.

AMY: Do you travel?

MIKE: When I can. I was in mexico last november during the thanksgiving vacation, and I was in canada with my family for a week last summer.

AMY: Any photos?

MIKE: No. My dad's brother sam is the photographer in our family.

EXERCISE 6 PLURAL NOUN ENDINGS

04|03 **A** PRONUNCIATION NOTE Listen and complete each sentence with the correct word from the box. Then listen again and check the noun ending sounds that you hear.

| artists | books | boxes | classes | glasses | ~~photos~~ | scissors |

	/s/	/z/	/ɪz/
1. The ___photos___ are ready.	☐	☑	☐
2. Her art _____ are from 10:00 to 1:00.	☐	☐	☐
3. Be careful. The _____ are sharp.	☐	☐	☐
4. The _____ are full of old photos.	☐	☐	☐
5. The paintings are by different _____.	☐	☐	☐
6. I need my _____ to see the names of the artists.	☐	☐	☐
7. I have some interesting _____ about African art in that bookcase.	☐	☐	☐

04|03 **B** Listen again and repeat the sentences.

EXERCISE 7
EDITING

GRAMMAR NOTES 1–4
Read the sentences. There are eight mistakes. The first mistake is already corrected. Find and correct seven more.

Matisse and His Doves, 1944

1. Henri Cartier-Bresson's photos are often of famous ~~person~~ *people*.

2. This is photo of Henri Matisse.

3. Henri Matisse was great artist.

4. Before Matisse was artist, he was lawyer.

5. Matisse's paintings are in museum all over the world.

6. In this photo, Matisse is in the south of france.

7. We see four bird outside their cages.

STEP 4   COMMUNICATION PRACTICE

EXERCISE 8   LISTENING

04|04   **A** Listen to a talk about a famous artist. Then circle the correct answers.

1. Born: **a.** 1928   **b.** 1958

2. Place of birth: **a.** Transylvania   **b.** Pennsylvania

3. Father's occupation: **a.** a photographer   **b.** a construction worker

4. First job after college: **a.** a photographer   **b.** a commercial artist

5. Famous things he painted: **a.** soup cans   **b.** paint cans

6. Person he painted: **a.** Jack Kennedy   **b.** Jackie Kennedy

B Listen again. Make up the beginnings of three sentences about the artist. Then work with a partner. Say the beginnings of your sentences. Your partner finishes the sentences. Take turns.

EXAMPLE: A: He was a famous . . .

B: painter and photographer.

B: He was born in . . .

A: . . .

C Work in groups. Close your books. Take turns. Say things about the artist. Continue as long as you can.

EXAMPLE: A: He was a famous painter and photographer.

B: He was born in . . .

EXERCISE 9 A FEW OF MY FAVORITE THINGS

A PRESENTATION Prepare for your presentation in B. Draw a picture or find photos of places, people, or things you like. Choose pictures that show at least one proper noun, one singular noun, and one plural noun.

B Work in groups. Talk about your pictures. Take turns. When it's your turn to listen, write down your classmates' favorite people, places, and things.

EXAMPLE: This is a photo of my favorite park. It's Yosemite Park in California.

And this is a photo of my good friend. Her name is Margot Stram.

This is a photo of my car.

C Discuss: Do you and your classmates like the same things?

EXERCISE 10 WHAT'S IN YOUR BAG?

A GAME Work in groups. You have ten minutes. Look around the room or find things in your pockets, handbags, and book bags. Try and list one thing for each letter of the alphabet. The group with the most things wins.

EXAMPLE: A: an apple

B: a book

C: a comb

B Look at one other group's things. Can you name everything?

A BEFORE YOU WRITE Read about a photo. Then find a photo of one of your relatives. Complete the chart about your photo.

> This is a photo of my grandmother, Chanda Patel. She was born in India in 1935. She's in Los Angeles now. She was an artist. In this photo, she's in a park. There are flowers and trees in the park. My grandmother is old. She is over eighty years old, but I think she's still a striking woman.

	Chanda Patel	Person in my photo:
Relative	grandmother	
Date and place of birth	India, 1935	
Profession	artist	
Age of person in photo	over 80	
Place of photo	in a park	

B WRITE Write a paragraph about your photo. Use the paragraph in A and your chart. Use count nouns and proper nouns. Use capital letters when necessary. See Appendix 20 on page 439 for help.

C CHECK YOUR WORK Read your paragraph. Underline count nouns and proper nouns. Use the Editing Checklist to check your work.

Editing Checklist
Did you . . . ?
☐ use *a* before singular count nouns that begin with consonant sounds
☐ use *an* before singular count nouns that begin with vowel sounds
☐ use Ø before plural count nouns
☐ add *-s* or *-es* to plural count nouns
☐ use a capital letter for proper nouns

D REVISE YOUR WORK Read your paragraph again. Can you improve your writing? Make changes if necessary.

UNIT 4 REVIEW

Test yourself on the grammar of the unit.

A Complete the sentences. Use *a*, *an*, or Ø (no article).

1. This is _____ photo of my best friend.

2. He is _____ actor.

3. He is _____ from Ireland.

4. His friends are _____ actors, too.

5. They are _____ servers, too.

B Complete the sentences with the words from the box. Use the plural form.

city	clothes	fish	person	watch

1. My favorite _____ are Venice and Rio de Janeiro.

2. The two _____ in the photograph show midnight.

3. The woman is wearing _____ from the 1950s.

4. We take photos of the _____ in the sea with our underwater camera.

5. We see three _____ in the photo: a man and two women.

C Add capital letters where necessary.

A: Hi, are you the photographer?

B: Yes, I'm Amy lin.

A: Nice to meet you. I'm ali Mohammed.

B: Are you from london?

A: Yes, I am. I'm here for your thanksgiving Day holiday.

D Correct the paragraph. There are six mistakes.

    Melanie Einzig is artist and an photographer. She was born in Minnesota, but lives in New york. Einzig captures moments in time. Her photograph are striking. They are in museum in San francisco, Chicago, and Princeton.

Now check your answers on page 445.

Descriptive Adjectives
INTERESTING AND UNUSUAL PLACES

OUTCOMES
- Use adjectives to describe nouns
- Recognize details in an article about a place
- Recognize details in a conversation about an interesting place
- Talk about interesting places, using adjectives
- Write a paragraph about an interesting place

STEP 1   GRAMMAR IN CONTEXT

BEFORE YOU READ

Look at the photo of the rock formations. Work with a partner. Answer the questions.

1. What words describe the rock formations?

   beautiful   dangerous   exciting   relaxing   scary   unusual   usual

2. Are there unusual rock formations in your country? Where?

READ

05|01   Read this article about an interesting place.

Cappadocia, a Place of Mystery

This place is like another world, but it is here on Earth. What is this place? It's Cappadocia, in Turkey. Why is it so different? What's so unusual about it? Beautiful underground cities and formations of rock make it a very special place.

Cappadocia has a long history. Many people lived in the underground cities to be safe from enemies.[1] These cities were big.

Underground cities

---

1 *enemies:* people who want to hurt you

Rock formations

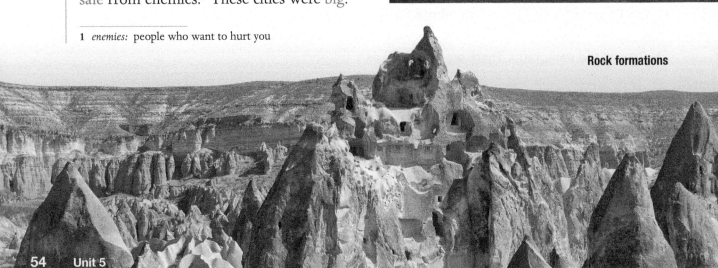

One city, Derinkuyu, had room for more than 30,000 people.

Today only a few people live in cave homes in these cities. But many people from all over the world visit them. From above, Cappadocia looks like another world.

The climate in Cappadocia changes. The weather is comfortable during the long, dry summers, but cold and snowy in the winters. In the late spring and fall, the weather is usually great.

Awesome underground cities, beautiful formations, and an interesting history—these things make Cappadocia a special place to see.

AFTER YOU READ

A VOCABULARY **Complete the sentences with the words from the box.**

climate	comfortable	dry	safe	unusual

1. Be careful. It is not _____ to walk there.

2. Bring water. It is hot and _____ there.

3. My shoes are _____. I can walk in them for hours.

4. I bought a(n) _____ bowl. It's very different from other bowls.

5. The _____ changes each season.

B COMPREHENSION **Circle the correct words to complete the sentences.**

1. Cappadocia has amazing formations of <u>rock</u> / <u>snow</u>.

2. Underground cities were <u>dangerous</u> / <u>safe</u> places to stay.

3. Cave homes were <u>unusual</u> / <u>usual</u> in Cappadocia long ago.

4. Cappadocia has a <u>short</u> / <u>long</u> history.

5. Cappadocia is <u>dry</u> / <u>wet</u> in the summer.

C DISCUSSION **Work with a partner. Compare your answers in B. Then tell your partner three things about Cappadocia.**

DESCRIPTIVE ADJECTIVES

Adjective After *Be*

Noun	*Be*	Adjective
The room	is	**small**.
The rooms	are	

Adjective Before Noun

	Adjective	Noun
It is a	**small**	room.
They are		rooms.

GRAMMAR NOTES

1 Adjectives: Meaning and Placement

Adjectives describe nouns.	NOUN ADJECTIVE **Cappadocia** is **beautiful**.
Adjectives can come **before** a **noun**.	ADJECTIVE NOUN It's a **big** **room**. **NOT** It's a ~~room big~~.
Adjectives can also come **after** the verb *be*.	BE ADJECTIVE The room **is** **big**.
When two adjectives come after *be*, we use *and* or *but* to connect them. *And* adds information. *But* shows a contrast or a surprise.	I am hungry **and** tired. He was happy **but** tired.
BE CAREFUL! Do not add *-s* to adjectives. They have the **same form** before singular and plural nouns.	It was a **hot** *summer*. They were **hot** *summers*. **NOT** They were ~~hots~~ summers.
A **noun** can also describe a noun. Like adjectives, these modifying nouns have the **same form** before singular and plural nouns.	MODIFYING NOUN NOUN Our **hotel** *room* was big. *(singular)* Our **hotel** *rooms* were big. *(plural)*

2 *A* or *an* Before an Adjective

When an adjective comes before a singular count noun, use *a* or *an* before the adjective.

Use *a* before the adjective if it begins with a **consonant sound**.	It's **a beautiful** place. It's **a modern** hotel.
Use *an* before the adjective if it begins with a **vowel sound**.	It's **an unusual** place. It's **an old** city.

3 Adjective Endings

Some adjectives end in *-ing*, *-ed*, or *-ly*. Don't confuse them with verbs or adverbs.	It's **interesting**. We're **tired**. They're **friendly**.

EXERCISE 1   DISCOVER THE GRAMMAR

A GRAMMAR NOTES 1–3   Maria is visiting Turkey. Read her travel blog about her hotel in Cappadocia. Underline the adjectives.

This area is <u>magical</u>. Where am I? I'm at Gamirasu Cave Hotel in the center of Cappadocia. The hotel is in a small, traditional village. It's in a cave. In the past, it was a home. Now it's a hotel. My room is fun. It's old, but has a modern bathroom. The rooms are not expensive. The price of the room includes a delicious breakfast and dinner. The service is good too—the people are helpful and friendly. Also, it's easy to visit all of Cappadocia from the hotel. It was a great choice.

B How does Maria describe each of the following?

1. the village: _____*small*_____, _____

2. the bathroom: _____

3. the price of the rooms: _____

4. the breakfast and dinner: _____

5. people: _____, _____

6. the choice of hotel: _____

EXERCISE 2   PLACEMENT OF ADJECTIVES

GRAMMAR NOTES 1–3   Complete the telephone conversation. Put the words in parentheses in the correct order. Use a capital letter at the start of a sentence.

LISA: Where are you?

BEN: _____*We're at an outdoor market*_____ in Cappadocia.
　　　　　　　　1. (market / at / we're / outdoor / an)

　　　　_____.
　　　　　　　2. (the / awesome / carpets / are)

LISA: Are they for sale?

BEN: Yes, they are. _____ .
3. (reasonable / prices / the / are)

LISA: How's the weather?

BEN: _____ .
4. (warm / it's / and / sunny)

LISA: You're lucky. _____ here.
5. (cold / windy / and / it's)

How are you and Al?

BEN: _____ .
6. (tired / happy / we're / but)

EXERCISE 3 SENTENCES WITH ADJECTIVES

GRAMMAR NOTES 1–3 Complete the sentences with the words in parentheses. Add the correct form of the verb *be*. Add *a* or *an* if necessary.

1. We are at Gamirasu Cave Hotel. _____ *It is a comfortable hotel* _____ .
(It / comfortable / hotel)

_____ .
(The rooms / not / expensive)

2. Our guide says, "_____
(Topdeck / good / restaurant)

in Cappodacia. _____ ,
(the food / delicious)

and _____ ."
(the waiters / friendly / and / helpful)

3. _____ .
(Yesterday / we / at / outdoor / market)

_____ .
(The vegetables / fresh / and / delicious)

EXERCISE 4 EDITING

GRAMMAR NOTES 1–3 Read the conversation. There are six mistakes. The first mistake is already corrected. Find and correct five more.

          new lamp
RITA: Is that a ~~lamp new~~?

TED: Yes, it is. It's from Turkey.

RITA: The colors are beautifuls.

TED: Thanks. I got it at old market in Cappadocia near our hotel.

RITA: Were there many things interesting to buy?

TED: Yes. These bowls colorful are from the market, too.

RITA: The colors unusual. I like them a lot.

TED: Here. This one is for you.

EXERCISE 5 LISTENING

▶05|02 Ⓐ Listen to the telephone conversation between Sun Hi and her friend Russ. What are they talking about? Circle the correct answer.

a. Russ and Sun Hi's vacation   b. Sun Hi's visit to a national park   c. unusual places

▶05|02 Ⓑ Listen to the conversation again. Complete the sentences. Circle the correct words. Explain your answer to a partner.

1. Sun Hi says Mesa Verde is (awesome) / awful.

2. The homes in the mountains are very cold / old.

3. Spruce Tree House was home to 130 people / 80 people.

4. The hotel is clean / nice.

5. The weather is warm / cold.

6. The park is crowded / not crowded.

▶05|02 Ⓒ Work with a partner. Listen again. Sun Hi uses the words in the box to talk about her vacation. What does she say? Ask questions. Take turns.

awesome	cold	different	reasonable
clean	convenient	huge	unusual

EXAMPLE: A: What's awesome?
          B: Sun Hi says Mesa Verde National Park is awesome. What's clean?
          A: She says . . .

EXERCISE 6 MY FAVORITE PLACE

Ⓐ Q & A Prepare for a Q & A exercise in B. Work with a partner. Find adjectives on the left that can describe the nouns on the right.

Adjectives			Nouns
cheap	delicious	modern	climate
cold	expensive	safe	food
comfortable	friendly	traditional	people
crowded	hot	unfriendly	shops
dangerous	interesting	unusual	transportation

EXAMPLE: A: Let's see. You can say a cold climate and a hot climate. Anything else?
          B: I think you can also say a comfortable climate.

B Work with a partner. Ask and answer questions about places that you know well. Take turns. Use the nouns and adjectives from the chart in A and your own ideas.

EXAMPLE: A: I know about Mesa Verde.

B: What is it?

A: It's a national park in Colorado.

B: How's the climate?

A: Summers are hot, but winters are cold.

B: Is the food delicious?

A: . . .

EXERCISE 7 POSITIVE OR NEGATIVE?

A WORD PLAY Work in small groups. Complete the chart. Add *a* or *an* and as many adjectives as you can.

A / AN	ADJECTIVE	NOUN	A / AN	ADJECTIVE	NOUN
a an	huge unusual	city			hotel
a an	big expensive	restaurant			park

B Write your phrases from A on the board. Then read other groups' phrases and talk about them. Are they positive (good)? Are they negative (bad)? Are they both positive and negative (good and bad)?

POSITIVE (+)	NEGATIVE (−)	BOTH (+/−)
an interesting city	an expensive city	a huge city

EXAMPLE: A: I think "a huge city" is both good and bad.

B: I agree. A huge city is good when you need a job.

A: But sometimes huge cities are dangerous. That's bad.

FROM GRAMMAR TO WRITING

A BEFORE YOU WRITE
Read about Jeju Island. Then complete the chart about an interesting place you know. Tell your partner about your place. Is your place like Jeju Island?

Jeju Island is a beautiful island in South Korea. Many Koreans go to this island on their honeymoon. The people are friendly. The climate is warm and comfortable, but windy. There are awesome beaches, high mountains, and cold, dark caves. One unusual thing to see is the hardworking, older women of Jeju Island. They dive in the water and they, not the men, catch the fish.

LOCATION	Jeju Island, South Korea	My place:
CLIMATE	warm, comfortable, windy	
PLACES TO SEE	awesome beaches high mountains cold, dark caves	
PEOPLE	friendly hardworking, older women divers	

B WRITE Write a paragraph about an interesting place you know. Use the paragraph in A and your chart. Use adjectives.

C CHECK YOUR WORK Read your paragraph. Underline the adjectives. Use the Editing Checklist to check your work.

Editing Checklist
Did you . . . ?
☐ remember not to add -s to adjectives
☐ put an adjective right before a noun, not right after a noun
☐ use a or an before an adjective + count noun
☐ use and or but to connect two adjectives

D REVISE YOUR WORK Read your paragraph again. Can you improve your paragraph? Make changes if necessary.

UNIT 5 REVIEW

Test yourself on the grammar of the unit.

Ⓐ Complete the sentences. Add *a*, *an*, or Ø (Ø = no article).

1. San Francisco is _____ big city.

2. We like to visit _____ cities.

3. Miami has _____ hot, humid summers.

4. It is _____ interesting place.

5. The Grand Canyon has _____ beautiful rock formations.

Ⓑ Circle the correct words to complete each sentence.

1. We are at a hotel small / a small hotel.

2. The hotel has an interesting garden / a interesting garden.

3. Our hotel room is big and comfortable / a big and comfortable.

4. The people here are kinds and helpful / kind and helpful.

5. It was a great choice / great choice.

Ⓒ Put the words in parentheses in the correct order.

1. (museum / I'm / the / at / new)   _____ .

2. (things / interesting / It has)   _____ to see.

3. (bowls / unusual / It has)   _____ from long ago.

4. (has / It / carpets / beautiful)   _____ too.

5. (place / is / The museum / a / great)   _____ .

Ⓓ Correct the paragraph. There are five mistakes.

The Grand Canyon National Park in Arizona is a awesome place to visit. Almost five million people visit the park every year. It is a park beautiful. The weather is good in the late spring and summer, but the park crowded is during those months. There are seven differents places to stay in the park. I like El Tovar. It is a old hotel with a great view.

Now check your answers on page 445.

UNIT 6

Prepositions of Place
LOCATIONS

OUTCOMES
- Describe locations with prepositions of place
- Recognize important details in a short article
- Locate places on a map from recorded descriptions
- Give directions to help others find places
- Write a short invitation to a party or an event

STEP 1 GRAMMAR IN CONTEXT

BEFORE YOU READ

Work with a partner. Answer the questions.

1. What's your favorite museum?
2. Where is it?
3. Why do you like it?

READ

06|01 Read this article about the American Museum of Natural History.

The American Museum of Natural History

Two teens are in front of the four-foot-long (one-meter-long) jaw of a dinosaur. A little boy is next to a 94-foot (29-meter) whale. Three young women are near the Star of India—a very big, blue gem.[1] I'm in a room with butterflies in front of me, in back of me, and above me. Butterflies are everywhere. Where are we? We're all at the American Museum of Natural History. This awesome museum is located in New York City on Central Park West between 77th Street and 81st Street. It's home to an amazing collection.

Do you like to study animals and plants? Are you interested in dinosaurs and butterflies? Do you want to find out more about beautiful gems or the stars in

---

1 *gem:* a stone used to make jewelry

the sky? If you do, this museum is for you. It's huge. There are four floors and a lower level. The 94-foot (29-meter) whale and the blue sapphire are on the first floor. The dinosaur skeleton[2] is on the fourth floor. There are free tours and a free app with a GPS. For a special visit, you can spend a night at the museum and sleep under the whale.

So the next time you're in New York City, visit the American Museum of Natural History. Go to AMNH.org and read about the different sections, but choose only one or two parts to see. Save the rest for other visits.

_____

2 *skeleton:* all the bones of a human or animal

AFTER YOU READ

A VOCABULARY **Complete the sentences with the words from the box.**

| app | dinosaur | huge | interested | located | tour |

1. The museum is _____ on Central Park West across the street from Central Park.

2. Blue whales are _____. Some blue whales are 100 feet (30 meters) long and weigh 200 tons (181 metric tons).

3. She is _____ in the Star of India because she works at a jewelry store.

4. The _____ was one hour. The guide was very good.

5. You can download a(n) _____ for the American Museum of Natural History.

6. The _____ lived between 230 and 65 million years ago.

B COMPREHENSION **Answer the questions.**

1. In what city is the American Museum of Natural History? _____

2. Between what streets is the museum? _____

3. Where is the Star of India? _____

4. Where is the big dinosaur? _____

5. What two things can you find on the first floor? _____

C DISCUSSION **Work with a partner. Say three false things about the American Museum of Natural History. Your partner corrects you.**

PREPOSITIONS OF PLACE

The glasses are **between** the book and the watch.

The glasses are **next to** the newspaper.

The glasses are **behind** the box.

The glasses are **under** the table.

The glasses are **in** his pocket.

The glasses are **on** the table **near** the window.

The man is **on the left**. He is **in back of** the woman.

The man is **on the right**. He is **in front of** the woman.

GRAMMAR NOTES

1 Prepositions of Place

Prepositions of place tell **where something is**. Below are some common **one-word prepositions**.

• *at*	Two students are **at** the door.
• *behind*	Ali is **behind** Olga.
• *between*	Our classroom is **between** room 205 and 209.
• *in*	We're **in** room 207.
• *inside*	Our jackets are **inside** the closet.
• *near*	Our school is **near** the museum.
• *on*	The paintings are **on** the second floor.
• *outside*	My friend is **outside** the museum.
• *over*	The sign **over** the door says, "Exit."
• *under*	A book bag is **under** the bench.

2 Prepositions of Place with Two or More Words

Some prepositions of place have two or more words.

• *across from*	The museum is **across from** a park.
• *in back of*	A garden is **in back of** the art museum.
• *in front of*	A fountain is **in front of** the art museum.
• *next to*	A bookstore is **next to** the art museum.

3 Common Prepositional Phrases

Prepositional phrases have three or more words.

• *on the right*	My father is **on the right**.
• *on the left*	My uncle is **on the left**.
• *in the middle*	I am **in the middle**.
• *in the world*	The Star of India is the biggest sapphire **in the world**.
• *on the corner of*	An art store is **on the corner of** Main Street and Mott Avenue.

4 Prepositions of Place Before *Work*, *Home*, and *School*

Use *at* before *work*.	I'm **at** work now.
Use *at* or no preposition before *home*.	I'm **at home**. or I'm **home**.
Use *at* or *in* before *school*.	I'm **at school**. or I'm **in school**.
BE CAREFUL! We can say "I'm in school," and "I'm at school," but *in* and *at* can mean something very different. *In* means inside. *At* means at that location.	I'm **in** the car. *(I'm inside the car.)* I'm **at** the car. *(I'm outside, next to the car.)*

5 Prepositions in Addresses

For prepositions in **addresses**, use *in*, *on*, and *at*.	
Use *in* before a country, a state, a province, or a city.	He's **in** Canada. *(country)* He's **in** British Columbia. *(province)* He's **in** Vancouver. *(city)*
Use *on* before a street, an avenue, a road, or the floor of a building.	My apartment is **on** Tenth *Avenue*. It's **on** the third *floor*.
Use *at* for the number of the building.	We're **at** 78 Main Street.
BE CAREFUL! Use **ordinal numbers** (*first, second, third*) with streets and avenues and the floors of a building. Do not use cardinal numbers (*one, two, three*).	It's on **Seventh** Street. It's on the **fourth** floor. NOT It's on ~~Seven~~ Street. It's on the ~~four~~ floor.
BE CAREFUL! Remember to use *the* before the ordinal number for the floor of a building.	I live **on the** fourth floor. NOT I live ~~on fourth~~ floor.
USAGE NOTE In informal conversation, when we say that a building is on the corner of two streets, we often drop the words *Street* or *Avenue*.	It's on the corner of Main and Fourth.

REFERENCE NOTE

For lists of **ordinal numbers** (*first, second, third*, etc.) and **cardinal numbers** (*one, two, three*), see Appendix 4 on page 432.

EXERCISE 1 DISCOVER THE GRAMMAR

GRAMMAR NOTES 1–2, 5 **Read about these museums. Underline the prepositions of place. Then match the descriptions with the photos below.**

___C___ **1.** The National Anthropology Museum of Mexico is <u>in</u> a park in Mexico City. It has things from the Olmec, Maya, and Aztec cultures. Before you enter the museum, you walk under a huge concrete umbrella.

_____ **2.** This red brick museum is in Amsterdam, Holland. It's the Rijksmuseum and it's located at Museumstraat 1. In front of the museum, you can see a beautiful canal. The museum has a collection of Dutch and other European art.

_____ **3.** The State Hermitage was a palace, but now it is a museum. This green and white section of the museum is on the bank of the Neva River. It is in St. Petersburg in Russia.

_____ **4.** The Guggenheim Museum Bilbao is in Bilbao, Spain. The architect was Frank Gehry. The curves of the building catch the light. It is located on the bank of the Nervión River. Inside the museum, there is a huge area with views of Bilbao's water and the hills of the Basque country.

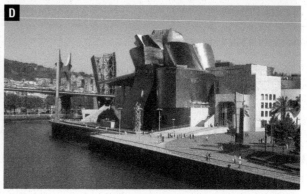

EXERCISE 2 PREPOSITIONS FOR PLACES ON A MAP

GRAMMAR NOTES 1–3, 5 Look at the map. Complete the sentences with the words from the box. You can use some words more than once.

| at | between | next to | on | on the | on the corner of | under |

1. Tiny Toys is _____ *on* _____ Third Avenue.

2. Paul's Hair Salon is _____ Sam's Shoes.

3. Da Vinci's Bakery is _____ Third Avenue and Fifth Street.

4. Café Z is _____ DJ Drugstore and Tiny Toys.

5. Paul lives _____ 25 Second Avenue.

6. His apartment is _____ fourth floor.

7. Café Z and DJ Drugstore are _____ Joe's Gym.

8. Fred's Flowers is _____ Second Avenue and Fifth Street.

9. Star Restaurant is _____ Fred's Flowers and Paul's Hair Salon.

10. Harvest Bank is _____ 15 Second Avenue.

EXERCISE 3 MORE PREPOSITIONS OF PLACE

GRAMMAR NOTES 1–5 **Complete the sentences with the words from the box. You can use some words more than once.**

| at | between | in | in front of | on |

1. My best friend lives in an apartment _____*in*_____ Lakeville.

2. He lives _____ 435 East Water Street.

3. He lives _____ the third floor.

4. His apartment is _____ a library and a bank.

5. The bank is _____ the corner of Lexington Avenue and 77th Street.

6. We need a taxi. . . . Look! There's a taxi _____ that bus.

7. My friend isn't _____ work today.

8. He's _____ home because it's a holiday.

EXERCISE 4 EDITING

GRAMMAR NOTES 1–5 **Read the conversations. There are six mistakes. The first mistake is already corrected. Find and correct five more.**

1. A: Where's the museum?

   B: It's ~~in~~ Five Avenue between Eight and Ninth Streets.
      on

2. A: Excuse me, are the dinosaurs the third floor?

   B: I'm not sure. Ask at the Information Booth.

   A: Where's the Information Booth?

   B: It's in front the stairs.

3. A: Is Jeff at the museum?

   B: No. He's in home right now.

EXERCISE 5 LISTENING

06|02 **A** Look at the world map in Appendix 2 on page 430. Listen to the descriptions. Find each country on the map and write its name.

1. _K o r e a_   4. __ __ __ __ __

2. __ __ __ __ __ __ __   5. __ __ __ __

3. __ __ __ __ __ __ __ __ __   6. __ __ __ __ __ __ __ __

06|02 **B** Listen again and check your answers.

C Work with a partner. Look at the world map in Appendix 2 again. Write sentences about a country's location. Use the prepositions *between*, *near*, *next to*, and *in*. Ask your classmates to guess the country.

EXAMPLE: **A:** This country is between Mexico and Canada. What country is it?
             B: It's the United States.
             A: Right.

EXERCISE 6 IT'S ON THE SECOND FLOOR

GAME Work in a group. Study the World Art Museum map. Ask and answer questions about places on the map. Try to use as many prepositions as possible in your answers. Take turns.

EXAMPLE: **A:** Where is the Chinese garden?
             B: It's on the second floor.
             C: It's next to a restroom.
             D: It's between a restroom and the Photographs of India.

EXERCISE 7 WHERE IS IT?

A BRAINSTORMING The class decides on a well-known place in your city. Then work in a group. Use prepositions to describe the location of the place.

EXAMPLE: **Central Park:**

    A: It's between Fifth Avenue and Central Park West.
    B: It's across from the American Museum of Natural History on the West Side.
    C: And it's in Midtown.
    D: It's between 60th Street and 110th Street.

B Write your group's sentences on the board. Compare the sentences of the different groups. Decide which group has the best description and the most correct sentences.

EXAMPLE: A: I think there's a mistake is Group 2's last sentence. The grammar is correct, but the park is not between 60th Street and 110th Street. It's between 59th Street and 110th Street.
    B: Oh, you're right. Thanks.
    A: And I think there's a grammar mistake in . . .

EXERCISE 8
WHERE'S THE BUTTERFLY?

A PICTURE DISCUSSION Add the things in the box to picture A. Do not show your picture to your partner.

butterfly   glasses   book   star   clock

Picture A   Picture B

B Work with a partner. Use prepositions to tell your partner about your picture. Do not show the picture. Your partner draws your picture in picture B. Then compare your pictures.

EXAMPLE: In my picture, the butterfly is under the table. The book is inside the desk. The glasses are on the table. The star is next to the glasses. The clock is on the wall on the right above the desk.

FROM GRAMMAR TO WRITING

A BEFORE YOU WRITE
Read George's invitation to his wife's birthday. Then complete the chart with information about a party you are planning.

● ● ●

GEORGE RAMI shared a message

You're invited to a birthday party for Martha at 12 p.m. on Sunday, June 18 at Bridgeport Café.

Bridgeport Café is at 2 Market Street. It's on the corner of Market and Pine Street. It's across from Pine Park. The party is on the second floor.

Shh! It's a surprise! Hope to see you there!

	George's invitation	Your invitation
Party for	Martha	
Type of party	Birthday	
Given by	George	
Location	Bridgeport Café	
Address	2 Market Street	
Date	Sunday, June 18	
Start time	Noon	

B WRITE Write an invitation to your party. Use George's message in A and your chart to help you. Use prepositions of place.

C CHECK YOUR WORK Read your message. Underline the prepositions. Then use the Editing Checklist to check your work.

Editing Checklist

Did you . . . ?

- [ ] use *to* after *next*
- [ ] use *from* after *across*
- [ ] use *of* after *in front* and *in back*
- [ ] use *on* before a street
- [ ] use *at* before a building number

D REVISE Read your message again. Can you improve your writing? Make changes if necessary.

UNIT 6 **REVIEW**

Test yourself on the grammar of the unit.

Ⓐ Look at the picture. Complete the sentences with the words from the box.

behind	in front of	next to	on	under

1. The book is _____ the table.

2. The glasses are _____ the table.

3. The cup is _____ the book.

4. The watch is _____ the book.

5. The pencil is _____ the book.

Ⓑ Complete the sentences. Circle the correct answers.

1. Al's <u>at / on</u> work. His office is <u>on / across</u> the street from the big bank.

2. His apartment is <u>in / at</u> 235 West Second Street. It's <u>on / between</u> the corner of Second and Oak Avenue.

Ⓒ Look at the picture of a circle, a square, and a triangle. Complete the sentences with the words from the box. You can use some words more than once.

above	inside	in the	on the	under

1. The circle is _____ left. The square is _____ middle.

   The triangle is _____ right.

2. The star is _____ the square. The butterfly is _____ the circle.

   The glasses are _____ the triangle.

Ⓓ Correct the conversation. There are five mistakes.

A: Is Jon on school?

B: No. He's in home.

A: Where does he live?

B: He lives at Oak Street at New City.

A: Does he live in an apartment?

B: Yes. He lives in the third floor.

Now check your answers on page 446.

Imperatives and the Simple Present

PART 3

OUTCOMES

- Make offers and suggestions
- Give directions, orders, advice, and requests
- Recognize the advice given in a short article
- Recognize important details in a radio ad
- Discuss what to do and where to go, and make arrangements to meet
- Give advice about everyday problems
- Write an ad for a place to stay

OUTCOMES

- Talk about habits, routines, feelings, and thoughts
- Talk about how often something happens with adverbs of frequency
- Recognize details in a short article about customs
- Recognize details in a conversation about cultural traditions
- Talk about customs and traditions
- Write a paragraph about a holiday or tradition

OUTCOMES

- Ask and answer *yes/no* questions in the simple present
- Answer questions about a questionnaire
- Recognize important details in a conversation
- Complete a questionnaire and discuss results
- Ask and answer questions about objects, interests, likes, and dislikes
- Write an email about yourself

OUTCOMES

- Ask for information, using *wh-* questions in the simple present
- Answer questions about information in a talk show transcript
- Answer questions about details in a conversation
- Talk about dreams and sleep habits
- Ask questions about someone's life and write an interview transcript with the answers

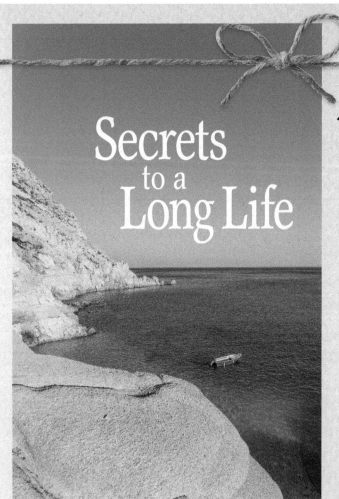

Imperatives;
Suggestions with
Let's, Why don't we...?
LONG LIFE

OUTCOMES
- Make offers and suggestions
- Give directions, orders, advice, and requests
- Recognize the advice given in a short article
- Recognize important details in a radio ad
- Discuss what to do and where to go, and make arrangements to meet
- Give advice about everyday problems
- Write an ad for a place to stay

STEP 1   GRAMMAR IN CONTEXT

BEFORE YOU READ

Work with a partner. Answer the questions.

1. Who is the oldest person you know? How old is he or she?

2. What do you think is important for a long life?

READ

07|01   Read this article. Then read the conversation between Joe and Mary.

Secrets to a Long Life

Yiannis Karimalis was forty years old. He was a bridge painter in the United States. He was sick. His doctor said, "I'm sorry. You have stomach cancer.[1] It is very bad." Yiannis moved back to his hometown on the island of Ikaria in Greece.

Yiannis is over eighty and is still alive today. His doctor is dead.

Many people on the island of Ikaria live long lives. What are their secrets?

---

1 *cancer:* a serious disease in which cells in the body divide uncontrollably

Scientist Dan Buettner studies the lifestyle[2] of older people in different parts of the world. As a result of his studies in Ikaria, he offers this advice:

- **Eat** a lot of green vegetables, fresh fruit, olive oil, fish, and Greek honey.
- **Drink** herbal tea and goat milk.
- **Don't worry.**
- **Take** naps.
- **Walk. Don't use** a car, a bus, or a train.
- **Call** friends often.
- **Pray.**

_____
2 *lifestyle:* the way you live

Conversation:

JOE: Interesting article. But I don't have time to nap or think about the food I eat.

MARY: Come on, Joe, these suggestions are easy to follow. Let's try some of them.

JOE: I have a better idea. Let's move to Ikaria!

MARY: Um, why don't we just take a trip to Greece?

JOE: Stop right there. I'm looking up flights to Ikaria.

AFTER YOU READ

A VOCABULARY Complete the sentences with the words from the box.

advice	dead	island	nap	pray	secret

1. You look very tired. Why don't you take a(n) _____?

2. Don't tell him. It's a(n) _____.

3. The plant is _____. Throw it away.

4. The doctor's _____ to Mark was, "Walk more. Eat less."

5. Some people _____ in a church, mosque, or temple, but you can do it anywhere.

6. Why don't we visit a Greek _____ on our next vacation?

B COMPREHENSION What advice does Dan Buettner give in "Secrets of a Long Life"? Read the statements. Check (✓) *True, False,* or *No Information*.

	True	False	No Information
1. Don't eat oil.	☐	☐	☐
2. Don't sleep during the day.	☐	☐	☐
3. Don't listen to your doctor.	☐	☐	☐
4. Take walks.	☐	☐	☐
5. Drink juice.	☐	☐	☐

C DISCUSSION Work with a partner. Look at the article. Study the advice. Close your book. Tell your partner the secrets of a long life. Take turns.

THE IMPERATIVE

Affirmative Statements	
Base Form of Verb	
Walk	to work.

Negative Statements		
Don't	Base Form of Verb	
Don't	take	a bus.

SUGGESTIONS

Affirmative Statements		
Let's	Base Form of Verb	
Let's	use	olive oil.

Negative Statements			
Let's	Not	Base Form of Verb	
Let's	not	use	butter.

Suggestions for You and Another Person		
Why don't we	Base Form of Verb	
Why don't we	go	on a bike tour?

Suggestions for Another Person		
Why don't you	Base Form of Verb	
Why don't you	get	the cameras?

RESPONSES TO SUGGESTIONS

Agree
That's a good idea. **or** Good idea.
That sounds good to me. **or** Sounds good to me.

Disagree
Why don't we . . . instead?
Sorry, I can't. I need to . . .

GRAMMAR NOTES

1 Imperatives: Uses

We use the **imperative** to give **directions**, **orders**, **advice**, **warnings**, and **requests**.

• give directions and instructions	**Turn** right.
• give orders	**Stand** there.
• give advice	**Use** olive oil. **Don't use** butter.
• give warnings	**Be** careful! It's hot.
• make polite requests	Please **call** before noon.

2 Affirmative and Negative Forms

The imperative uses the **base form of the verb**.	**Take** the train.
To make a negative imperative statement, use *don't* + **base form** of the verb.	**Don't worry.** **Don't be** late.

3 The Subject of an Imperative Statement

In an imperative statement, the **subject is always** *you*, but we usually don't say it or write it. The subject can be singular or plural.	Be careful. *(one person)* Be careful. *(two or more people)*

4 *Please* with Imperatives

Use *please* to make orders, warnings, and requests more polite.	**Please stand** there. **Please be** careful.
Please can come **at the beginning** or **the end** of the sentence.	**Please call** before noon. **Call** before noon, **please**.

5 Suggestions with *Let's* and *Let's not*

Use *Let's* or *Let's not* + **base form** for suggestions that include you and another person.	**Let's go.** **Let's not eat** there.

6 Suggestions with *Why don't we . . . ?* and *Why don't you . . . ?*

Use *Why don't we* + **base form** to make a suggestion for you and another person.	**Why don't we go** to the gym?
Use *Why don't you* to make a suggestion or give advice to another person.	**Why don't you look** on the Internet?
IN WRITING Remember to put a question mark (?) at the end of sentences with *Why don't we* and *Why don't you*.	**Why don't we meet** at the gym? **Why don't you drink** herbal tea?

EXERCISE 1 DISCOVER THE GRAMMAR

A GRAMMAR NOTES 1–6 Match each sentence with its purpose.

___d___ **1.** Take the number 4 bus to the gym.

_____ **2.** Be careful. Don't take more than two pills a day.

_____ **3.** Please don't use your phone in the doctor's office.

_____ **4.** Stop!

_____ **5.** Why don't we get goat milk for a change?

_____ **6.** Why don't you eat honey? It's good for a sore throat.

a. Advice for someone

b. Polite request

c. Warning

d. Directions

e. Order

f. Suggestion for you and me

B Read the sentences in A again. Circle three affirmative imperative forms and two negative imperative forms. Underline two suggestions.

EXERCISE 2 IMPERATIVES AND SUGGESTIONS

GRAMMAR NOTES 1–6 Complete the conversations. Circle the correct words.

1. **A:** Let's to buy / (buy) chicken.

   B: I don't like chicken. And I'm tired of cooking. Why don't we eat / eats out today?

2. **A:** Please not get / don't get more broccoli. It isn't good.

   B: OK. How about kale?

3. **A:** Let's no take / not take the train to school. Let's walk. The weather is great.

   B: But it's late. Let's to walk / walk after school.

4. **A:** Let's call / calls Roberto and invite / to invite him to dinner.

   B: Good idea. What's his number?

5. **A:** Why don't you take / takes some time off? You look tired.

   B: Don't be worry / worry. I'm fine.

EXERCISE 3 AFFIRMATIVE AND NEGATIVE STATEMENTS

GRAMMAR NOTES 1–6 Complete the sentences. Use the affirmative or negative imperative forms of the verbs in parentheses.

1. The bread is still hot. Wait a few minutes. _____*Don't eat*_____ it now.
                                                            (eat)

2. It's cold here. Please _____ the window.
                                     (close)

3. It's a secret. Please _____ your brother about my plan.
(tell)

4. For information about Dan Buettner, _____ the Internet.
(check)

5. Let's _____ to the store. It's not far and we need the exercise.
(walk)

6. Let's _____ those doughnuts. They're not very healthy.
(buy)

7. Please _____ me directions to the gym. I want to go there today.
(give)

8. _____ this herbal tea. It's delicious.
(try)

9. _____ a nap now. Help me prepare dinner.
(take)

10. _____ that island in July. The weather is usually awful then.
(visit)

EXERCISE 4 IMPERATIVES FOR DIRECTIONS

🅐 GRAMMAR NOTES 1–2 **Joe is giving Mary directions to Olivia's gym. Read their conversation. Then look at the map and put an X on the gym.**

MARY: Excuse me. . . . Where's Olivia's Gym?

JOE: Um, sure. . . . The gym is on Second Avenue between 70th and 71st Street. We're on Third Avenue at 73rd Street. Walk down Third Avenue to 71st Street. That's two blocks from here. Turn left at 71st Street. Walk one block to Second Avenue. Then turn right on Second Avenue. It's right there, on your right.

🅑 **Look at the map again. You are at the drugstore. Complete the directions to the library.**

Walk down 71st Street to _____

_____

EXERCISE 5 EDITING

GRAMMAR NOTES 1–6 **Read the conversation. There are six mistakes. The first mistake is already corrected. Find and correct five more.**

JOE: Let's ~~to~~ go to the movies.

MARY: Why we don't go to the park first? It's a beautiful day.

JOE: OK. But first let have lunch. I'm hungry.

MARY: I'm hungry, too. Why don't we have a fruit salad with yogurt and nuts?

JOE: Good idea.

MARY: But you don't use those apples. They're bad. Throws them away.

JOE: OK.

MARY: And why you don't add honey to the yogurt? It's delicious that way.

JOE: You're right. This *is* really good.

STEP 4   COMMUNICATION PRACTICE

EXERCISE 6 LISTENING

07|02   **A** **Listen to the ad. What is it for? Circle the correct letter.**

a. a spa   **b.** exercise classes   **c.** healthy meals

07|02   **B** **Listen again. Complete the chart.**

Name of business	Mia's Health Spot
Kind of class	
Breakfast foods	
Drinks	
Kind of massage	
Number of free weeks	

C Work with a partner. Imagine you are at Mia's Health Spot. Name a time. Your partner makes a suggestion with *Let's* or *Why don't we*. Take turns.

EXAMPLE: A: It's 6:00 a.m.

B: Let's take a yoga class. The yoga class is always fun.

A: Sounds good to me.

B: It's 7:00.

A: Why don't we . . .

EXERCISE 7 GIVE ADVICE

PROBLEM SOLVING Work with a partner. Imagine you have a small problem. For example, you're thirsty, tired, or bored. Tell your partner your problem. Your partner makes a suggestion starting with *Why don't you . . .* Agree or disagree. Tell why. Take turns.

EXAMPLE: A: I'm thirsty.

B: Why don't you have a soda?

A: Soda? That's not healthy.

B: Well, why don't you have some water?

A: OK. That's a good idea.

EXERCISE 8 LET'S WORK OUT

CONVERSATION Work with a partner. You want to do something healthy today. Student A, make a suggestion. Student B, disagree and make another suggestion. Give a reason why. Take turns.

EXAMPLE: A: Let's work out at the gym.

B: Why don't we take a walk instead? I don't want to be indoors.

A: OK. Let's take a walk in Woods Park.

B: Woods Park? Let's not walk there. Let's walk in . . .

EXERCISE 9 PUT YOUR ARMS IN THE AIR!

A PRESENTATION Prepare an exercise routine for your classmates. Use the ideas in the box or your own ideas.

Hop on one foot.	Put your arms in the air.	Touch your toes.
Jump up and down.	Touch your knees.	Wave your arms.

B Lead your class. They follow your instructions.

EXAMPLE: OK, everyone. Put your arms in the air. Good. Now wave your arms like this. No, Lia, not like that, like this. OK. Now . . .

A BEFORE YOU WRITE Read this ad for a hotel on the island of Ikaria. Write the imperative verbs on the lines below. Then compare answers with a partner.

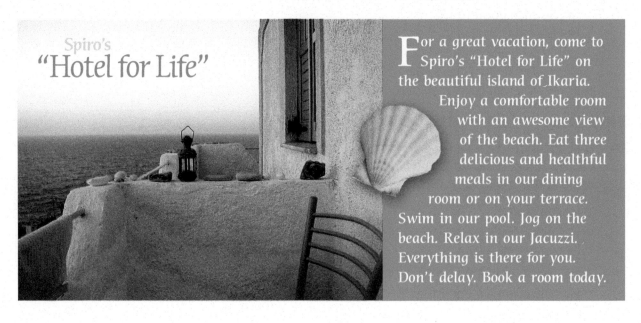

Spiro's
"Hotel for Life"

For a great vacation, come to Spiro's "Hotel for Life" on the beautiful island of Ikaria. Enjoy a comfortable room with an awesome view of the beach. Eat three delicious and healthful meals in our dining room or on your terrace. Swim in our pool. Jog on the beach. Relax in our Jacuzzi. Everything is there for you. Don't delay. Book a room today.

come

B WRITE Write an ad for your own hotel. It can be anywhere in the world, under the water, or in outer space. Use your imagination. Use the imperative verbs in A and your own verbs.

C CHECK YOUR WORK Read your ad. Underline all the imperatives. Then use the Editing Checklist to check your work.

Editing Checklist
Did you . . . ?
☐ use the base form of the verb for the imperative
☐ use *don't* + the base form for the negative imperative

D REVISE Read your ad again. Can you improve your writing? Make changes if necessary.

UNIT 7 REVIEW

Test yourself on the grammar of the unit.

Ⓐ Complete the sentences. Circle the correct words.

1. Let's get / Let's not get ice cream. It's on sale this week.

2. Why don't we / Let's not invite Bob? He's really nice.

3. Please buy / Don't buy peppers. I don't like them.

4. Let's meet / Let's not meet inside the restaurant. It's cold and windy outside.

5. Touch / Don't touch the wall. The paint is still wet.

Ⓑ Complete the instructions with the imperative forms of the verbs in parentheses. Use the affirmative or negative.

1. _____ comfortable clothes to yoga class. We want you to feel good.
   (wear)

2. _____ heavy clothes. It's warm in the classroom.
   (wear)

3. _____ a mat and water.
   (bring)

4. _____ coffee or soda inside the classroom. You can have those drinks
   (bring)
   after class.

5. Please _____ by check or cash. We don't accept credit cards.
   (pay)

Ⓒ Complete the conversations with *Let's*, *don't we*, or *don't you*.

1. A: _____ go to the gym.   B: Good idea.

2. A: Why _____ take a trip together?   B: OK. Where do you want to go?

3. A: I'm hungry.   B: Why _____ eat a sandwich?

4. A: _____ visit Grandma Millie.   B: That sounds like a great idea.

Ⓓ Correct the sentences. There are six mistakes.

1. Why you don't ask Andrij for help?

2. You look really tired. You take a short nap.

3. Let's to walk to work. Let's not drive.

4. Don't ask Boris to fix the car. Asks Mickey.

5. I'm on a diet, so buy please yogurt. Don't to get sour cream.

Now check your answers on page 446.

Simple Present: Affirmative and Negative Statements

HOLIDAYS

OUTCOMES
- Talk about habits, routines, feelings, and thoughts
- Talk about how often something happens with adverbs of frequency
- Recognize details in a short article about customs
- Recognize details in a conversation about cultural traditions
- Talk about customs and traditions
- Write a paragraph about a holiday or tradition

STEP 1 · GRAMMAR IN CONTEXT

BEFORE YOU READ

Work with a partner. Answer the questions.

1. What is a holiday?

2. Do you like holidays? Do you have a favorite holiday?

READ

08|01 Read this article about New Year traditions around the world.

New Year Traditions Around the World

People all around the world observe the New Year. Most people don't work or go to school. They frequently get together with family and friends. In some cultures, the New Year is a serious occasion. In other cultures, it is more festive. Every culture does something to mark the beginning of the year, but the New Year comes at different times in different cultures.

The Chinese New Year is a very important time. It lasts fifteen days. Families gather for a big feast. They often eat special food such as dumplings, spring rolls, and a whole fish for a prosperous[1] year. They watch parades, set off firecrackers, and give children red envelopes with money in them. The envelopes are red because red is a lucky color.

In one European country, every December 31 just before midnight, radios and TV stations play a waltz, and everyone dances at the stroke of midnight. It's the country of Strauss, Mozart, Wiener schnitzel, and Sacher torte. Do you know the country? It's Austria.

---

1 *prosperous:* successful and rich

In a country in South America, people often decorate their homes and wear something yellow for luck and happiness. Sometimes they make a bath of flowers. They also follow a Spanish tradition. They eat twelve grapes at midnight. Can you guess the country? It's Peru.

Why do people always mark the New Year? It's a time to remember the past, look ahead to the future and wish everyone a happy, healthy, and prosperous year.

AFTER YOU READ

A VOCABULARY Complete the sentences with the words from the box.

| at the stroke of | culture | eve | get together | look ahead | tradition |

1. _____ midnight, all over Japan, Buddhist temples ring their bells 108 times.

2. Not every _____ follows the same calendar, so New Year's Day comes at different times of the year.

3. A Cuban New Year _____ is to throw water out the window. People want to wash away bad things from the year before.

4. In the United States, friends often _____ for a party on New Year's Eve.

5. New Year's Day is a time of hope for a better future. People everywhere _____ to the new year.

6. The night before New Year's Day is New Year's _____.

B COMPREHENSION Match the beginnings of the sentences with the endings.

_____ 1. People in China eat

_____ 2. On New Year's Eve, people in Spain often

_____ 3. People see the New Year

_____ 4. People often get together with

_____ 5. On New Year's Eve at midnight, people in Austria

a. family and friends.

b. dance the waltz.

c. as a time to look back and look ahead.

d. dumplings and spring rolls.

e. eat twelve grapes at midnight.

C DISCUSSION Work with a partner. Compare your answers in B. Then tell your partner three things that you remember from the article "New Year Traditions Around the World."

EXAMPLE: The Chinese New Year lasts fifteen days. People frequently get together with their family on New Year's Day. In Peru, . . .

SIMPLE PRESENT: AFFIRMATIVE AND NEGATIVE STATEMENTS

Affirmative Statements		
Subject	Verb	
I You* We They	eat like	noodles.
He She It	has	

Negative Statements			
Subject	Do not / Does not	Base Form of Verb	
I You We They	do not don't	eat like have	noodles.
He She It	does not doesn't		

* *You* can be singular or plural.

ADVERBS AND EXPRESSIONS OF FREQUENCY

Adverbs of Frequency			
Subject	Adverb	Verb	
I You We They	usually almost never	cook	on holidays.
He She		cooks	
It		rains.	

Adverbs of Frequency with *Be*			
Subject	*Be*	Adverb	
I	am	usually almost never	busy.
You We They	are		
He She It	is		

Adverbs of Frequency	
always	100%
almost always	↑
frequently	
usually	
often	
sometimes	50%
rarely / seldom	
almost never	↓
never	0%

Expressions of Frequency	
Emiko cooks	**every** day. **twice a** week. **three times a** month. **several times a** year. **once in a while**.

GRAMMAR NOTES

1 Simple Present for Things That Happen Again and Again

Use the simple present to talk about **habits**, **regular occurrences**, **customs**, and **routines**.

• habits	She **drinks** tea every morning.
• regular occurrences	They **visit** their parents on most holidays.
• customs	They **dance** the waltz on New Year's Eve.
• routines	He **gets up** at seven.

Past   **Now**   Future

They dance on New Year's Eve.

2 Simple Present for Facts

Use the simple present to express **facts**.	It **rains** a lot in San Francisco.

3 Simple Present for Feelings, Thoughts, and Possessions

Use the simple present to express **feelings**, **thoughts**, and **possessions** such as *love, be, need, want, understand, know,* and *have*.

• feelings	I **love** you.
• thoughts	We **understand** him.
• possessions	She **has** a car.

4 Affirmative Statements

In **affirmative statements**, use the **base form** of the verb for *I, we, you, they,* and **plural nouns**.	**I cook** on New Year's Eve. **They play** cards on New Year's Day. **We wear** traditional clothes on New Year's Day.
Add **-s** or **-es** to the base form of the verb when the subject is *he, she, it,* or a singular noun.	**She dances** the waltz. **Jon watches** TV. **It starts** at 10:00.
BE CAREFUL! *Everyone, everybody, no one, nobody,* and *family* are singular.	**Everyone likes** my mother's cooking. NOT Everyone ~~like~~ my mother's cooking.
The **third-person singular affirmative** forms of *have, do,* and *go* have irregular spelling and pronunciation. • has /**hæz**/ • does /**dʌz**/ • goes /**goʊz**/	 She **has** a new dress for the holiday. He **does** his homework the day before the holiday. He **goes** to his uncle's home on New Year's Eve.

5 Simple Present of the Verb *Be*

The simple present of the verb *be* is irregular. (See Units 1 and 2.)	I **am** tired. He **is** hungry. We **are** tired.
BE CAREFUL! Do not use *be* + another simple present verb after the subject.	I am tired. **or** I feel tired. **NOT** I am ~~feel~~ tired. **NOT** I ~~am~~ feel tired. He is from Italy. **or** He comes from Italy. **NOT** He is ~~comes~~ from Italy. **NOT** He ~~is~~ comes from Italy.

6 Negative Statements

In **negative statements**, use *does not* or *do not* before the base form of the verb.	He **does not work** on New Year's Day. We **do not go** to school on New Year's Day.
USAGE NOTE Use the contractions *doesn't* or *don't* in speaking or in informal writing.	He **doesn't work** on New Year's Day. We **don't go** to school on New Year's Day.
BE CAREFUL! Do not use *no* before the base form of the verb to make a negative statement.	He doesn't work. **NOT** He ~~no~~ work.
BE CAREFUL! When *or* connects verbs in a negative statement, do not repeat *don't* or *doesn't*.	I **don't smoke** or **drink** coffee. **NOT** I don't smoke or ~~don't~~ drink coffee.

7 Adverbs of Frequency and Their Placement

Adverbs of frequency tell **how often** something happens. They include: *always, almost always, frequently, usually, often, sometimes, rarely, seldom, almost never, never*.	
Adverbs of frequency usually come **after the verb** *be*.	That store *is* **usually** open on holidays. It *is* **rarely** closed.
Adverbs of frequency usually come **before other verbs**.	We **often** *go* to the park. We **sometimes** *have* a picnic.
Some adverbs of frequency can go at the start or the end of a sentence.	**Sometimes** we have a picnic. We go there very **often**.
BE CAREFUL! Don't begin or end a sentence with *never, seldom, rarely,* or *always* followed by the subject + verb.	I never cook. I always wash the dishes. **NOT** ~~Never~~ I cook. I wash the dishes ~~always~~.

8 Expressions of Frequency

Expressions of frequency are time markers. They say **how often** something happens.	
Expressions of frequency usually come **at the beginning** or **at the end** of a sentence.	**Every Sunday**, she bakes a cake. She bakes a cake **every Sunday**.

PRONUNCIATION NOTE

08|02 **Third-Person Singular Verbs**

The pronunciation of verbs that end in -*s* is /**s**/ or /**z**/. The pronunciation of verbs that end in -*es* is /**ɪz**/.

- verbs ending in /**s**/
- verbs ending in /**z**/
- verbs ending in /**ɪz**/

like**s**	eat**s**	cook**s**	visit**s**
play**s**	buy**s**	throw**s**	clean**s**
watch**es**	wish**es**	us**es**	exchang**es**

REFERENCE NOTES

For more information on **non-action verbs** such as *like, want, have,* see Unit 17 on page 196.

For **spelling and pronunciation rules** for the **third-person singular** in the **simple present**, see Appendices 13 and 14 on page 436.

For more information on the **present tense of the verb** *be*, see Unit 1 on page 6 and Unit 2 on page 17.

STEP 3   FOCUSED PRACTICE

EXERCISE 1   DISCOVER THE GRAMMAR

GRAMMAR NOTES 1–5, 7–8 **Read the sentences. Circle the simple present verbs. Underline the adverbs and expressions of frequency.**

Songkran (is) the name of the traditional Thai New Year celebration. Every year, people celebrate Songkran in April. On this holiday, Thais throw water at each other. They often use water guns. Sometimes they use containers. Once in a while, they use garden hoses. Thailand is hot and dry, and the water feels good. Gan loves the holiday. He says, "The water feels great, and Songkran is a lot of fun."

EXERCISE 2 AFFIRMATIVE SENTENCES

GRAMMAR NOTES 1–4 Complete the sentences. Circle the correct answers.

1. My brother live /(lives) in Sydney, Australia. On New Year's Eve, he always watch / watches the New Year celebration at Sydney Harbor. I live in Florida. I see / sees the Sydney fireworks on TV in the United States the following day.

2. In the United States, Canada, and the Netherlands, some people jump / jumps into a cold lake, sea, or ocean on New Year's Day. My cousin belong / belongs to a "polar bear club." He swim / swims in the ocean every New Year's Day. Our family think / thinks he's strange.

3. Denmark has / have an unusual New Year tradition. People visit / visits friends at midnight on New Year's Eve and throw / throws plates at their door. Popular people in Denmark has / have many broken plates at their doorsteps on New Year's Day.

4. In Saudi Arabia, people follow / follows the Muslim lunar calendar. New Year come / comes at different times of the year.

EXERCISE 3 NEGATIVE SENTENCES

GRAMMAR NOTE 6 Complete the sentences. Use the simple present forms of the verbs in parentheses. Use contractions.

1. My mother _____*doesn't clean*_____ on New Year's Day. She always cleans the house
   (not / clean)
   before the holiday.

2. On New Year's Day, we open the door and windows. We _____ bad
   (not / want)
   things to stay with us.

3. My brother _____ to bed on New Year's Eve. He stays up all night long.
   (not / go)

4. In my family, the women and girls wear traditional clothes, but the men and boys

   _____ traditional clothes.
   (not / wear)

5. Yael _____ to school on New Year's Day. Relatives visit and the
 (not / go)
family enjoys a delicious meal together.

6. We _____ on New Year's Eve or New Year's Day. We prepare for the
 (not / work)
holiday on the day of New Year's Eve, and celebrate that night and the whole next day.

EXERCISE 4 ADVERBS OF FREQUENCY

GRAMMAR NOTES 7–8 Write sentences. Put the words in parentheses in the correct
order. Start with a capital letter.

1. (often / watches / he / parades)

He often watches parades.

2. (goes / he / rarely / football games / to)

_____

3. (a lot / eat / every Thanksgiving Day / we)

_____

4. (my grandparents / visit / I / every holiday)

_____

5. (that store / always / crowded/ is)

_____

6. (we / once in a while / wear / traditional clothes)

_____

EXERCISE 5 THIRD-PERSON SINGULAR VERBS

08|03 PRONUNCIATION NOTE Underline the verb in each sentence. Then listen to each
sentence and check (✓) the sound of the verb ending.

	/s/	/z/	/ɪz/
1. He <u>cooks</u> for the holidays.	☑	☐	☐
2. He uses a lot of spices.	☐	☐	☐
3. He buys food at the green market.	☐	☐	☐
4. The food costs a lot of money.	☐	☐	☐
5. She knows about different traditions.	☐	☐	☐
6. She watches the fireworks on TV.	☐	☐	☐
7. She misses her family.	☐	☐	☐
8. She thinks about the past.	☐	☐	☐

EXERCISE 6
EDITING

GRAMMAR NOTES 1–7

Correct the paragraph. There are eight mistakes. The first mistake is already corrected. Find and correct seven more.

usually start
In the United States, people ~~start usually~~ the New Year holiday on New Year's Eve. Many people plans celebrations weeks in advance. My cousin always invite friends to a party. My parents usually goes to a restaurant with friends. Many people watch an event on TV just before midnight. On New Year's Day, people usually am relax from the night before. My brother watches football games on TV, and my sister is go to her friend's home. I sleeps all day long and not do anything.

| STEP 4 | COMMUNICATION PRACTICE |

EXERCISE 7 LISTENING

▶08|04 **A** Listen to a conversation about Independence Day celebrations. Then write the name of the country and the date of its Independence Day.

Country	Independence Day	Notes
1. India	August 15th	white, green, orange decorations—colors of flag
2.		
3.		
4.		

▶08|04 **B** Listen to the conversation again. Take notes about the traditions in the different countries in the chart in A.

C Work with a partner. Talk about the traditions in the four countries.

EXAMPLE: A: On Independence Day in India, they decorate everything in white, green, and orange.

B: That's right. White, green, and orange are the colors of the Indian flag.

EXERCISE 8 TRADITION, TRADITION

A DISCUSSION Work in a group. Talk about traditions in six countries. One student takes notes.

EXAMPLE: A: In the Netherlands, some people jump in the sea on New Year's Day.

B: That's right. And in India, students celebrate Teacher's Day. The students perform for their teachers and dress like their teachers.

A: How do you know? You're not from India.

B: My friend is from India.

C: In Saudi Arabia, some people don't eat on our New Year. New Year's Day isn't a big occasion.

D: In Poland, we always eat babka on . . .

B Tell the class about the traditions.

EXERCISE 9 THAT'S NOT TRUE!

GAME Work in a group. Say three things about different holidays. Two are true and one is false. The other groups guess the false statement.

EXAMPLE: GROUP A: On Labor Day in the United States, most people don't work. On Chinese New Year, children get red envelopes. On Thanksgiving Day, most Americans eat a lot of seafood.

GROUP B: The third sentence is false. Americans eat a lot of *turkey* on Thanksgiving. They don't eat a lot of seafood.

EXERCISE 10 LET'S CELEBRATE!

A PRESENTATION Prepare for a presentation. Tell your partner about your favorite holiday. When is it? What do you do on the holiday? Use ideas from the box to tell about the holiday.

clean	don't work	get together with family
cook	eat special food	pray
don't go to school	exchange gifts	wear traditional clothes

EXAMPLE: A: My favorite holiday is Labor Day. I never work on Labor Day. I get together with my family.

B: Oh. My favorite holiday is Thanksgiving. I don't work. I cook a lot of special food, and I eat the food with my family . . .

B Give a presentation about your favorite holiday to the class.

EXAMPLE: I'd like to tell you about Labor Day. On Labor Day, people don't work . . .

A BEFORE YOU WRITE Read the information about an Independence Day celebration in the United States. Then choose a holiday that your family celebrates and complete the chart. Work with a partner. Tell your partner about the holiday.

July 4th is Independence Day in the United States. On this holiday, my family usually gets together for a barbecue. My older sister bakes a pie, and my older brother bakes cookies. My aunt doesn't bake anything, but she always helps my mother. They prepare different salads. My father barbecues hamburgers and hot dogs. The holiday is usually fun, but sometimes my brother teases my sister. They act like little children. At the end of the day, we're all tired and full, but happy.

Independence Day		Your holiday:	
Family Member	**What does he or she do?**	**Family Member**	**What does he or she do?**
sister	bakes a pie		
brother	bakes cookies, teases sister		
aunt and mother	prepare salads		
father	barbecues		

B WRITE Write a paragraph about your holiday. Use the paragraph in A and your chart. Use the simple present tense and adverbs of frequency.

C CHECK YOUR WORK Read your paragraph. Underline the simple present and adverbs of frequency. Use the Editing Checklist to check your work.

Editing Checklist
Did you...?
☐ add -*s* or -*es* to the third-person singular
☐ put adverbs of frequency before all verbs except *be*
☐ put adverbs of frequency after the verb *be*
☐ put expressions of frequency at the start or the end of a sentence

D REVISE YOUR WORK Read your paragraph again. Can you improve your writing? Make changes if necessary.

UNIT 8 **REVIEW**

Test yourself on the grammar of the unit.

A Complete the sentences. Circle the correct answers.

1. My father love / loves to celebrate his birthday.

2. He no have / doesn't have brothers, but he has four sisters.

3. He invite / invites all his sisters to our home.

4. We not give / don't give him expensive presents. We give him funny little presents.

5. We have / has a great time.

B Complete the sentences with the correct forms of the words in parentheses. Use the correct word order.

1. Students in India _____ Teacher's Day on September 5.
   (always / celebrate)

2. A student _____ the clothes of a teacher.
   (sometimes / wear)

3. A teacher _____ in the class and pretends to be a student.
   (often / sit)

4. Children _____ in a school performance.
   (usually / dance)

5. Teachers _____ happy on Teacher's Day.
   (usually / be)

C Complete the sentences. Circle the correct answers.

1. Everyone think / thinks about workers on this holiday.

2. Most people don't work / doesn't work on this holiday.

3. In the United States, this holiday come / comes at the end of the summer.

4. The name of this holiday is / are Labor Day.

D Correct the paragraph. There are six mistakes.

Some people don't enjoys holidays and family gatherings. Bill Jones visits usually his wife's sister on holidays. He likes his wife's sister, but he don't like her husband. Mary Brown doesn't like holidays because she lives far from her family. She have a very important job, but she doesn't have close friends. She usually watches movies and wait for the holiday to be over. Always she is happy to return to work.

Now check your answers on page 446.

Simple Present: *Yes/No* Questions and Short Answers

ROOMMATES

OUTCOMES
- Ask and answer *yes/no* questions in the simple present
- Answer questions about a questionnaire
- Recognize important details in a conversation
- Complete a questionnaire and discuss results
- Ask and answer questions about objects, interests, likes, and dislikes
- Write an email about yourself

STEP 1 **GRAMMAR IN CONTEXT**

BEFORE YOU READ

Work with a partner. Answer the questions.

1. Do you live alone or do you have a roommate?

2. Imagine you are looking for a roommate. What do you want to know about the person?

READ

▶09|01 Colleges often use questionnaires to help students find the right roommate. Read this roommate questionnaire.

Roommate Questionnaire[1]

Name: **Dan**   ame: **Jon**

		Dan YES	Dan NO	Jon YES	Jon NO
1.	Do you wake up early?	☐	☑	☐	☑
2.	Do you stay up late?	☑	☐	☑	☐
3.	Are you neat?	☑	☐	☑	☐
4.	Does a messy room bother you?	☑	☐	☑	☐
5.	Are you quiet?	☐	☑	☑	☐
6.	Are you talkative?	☑	☐	☐	☑
7.	Are you outgoing?	☑	☐	☐	☑
8.	Are you a private person?	☑	☐	☐	☑
9.	Are you easygoing?	☐	☑	☑	☐
10.	Does noise bother you?	☐	☑	☐	☑
11.	Do you listen to loud music?	☑	☐	☑	☐
12.	Do you watch a lot of TV?	☑	☐	☑	☐
13.	Do you study and listen to music at the same time?	☑	☐	☑	☐
14.	Do you study with the TV on?	☑	☐	☑	☐

1 *questionnaire:* a list of questions

AFTER YOU READ

Ⓐ VOCABULARY **Complete the sentences with the words from the box.**

| bother | easygoing | messy | outgoing | private | stay up |

1. Is her room always so _____? She needs to put things away.

2. Does that smell _____ you? I feel a little sick from it.

3. Do you usually _____ late? Your lights are always on after midnight.

4. Nothing upsets your brother. Is your sister _____, too?

5. Is your friend's daughter always _____? She wasn't afraid to talk to anyone at the party.

6. My parents don't say much about themselves. Are your parents _____ people, too?

Ⓑ COMPREHENSION **Read the questions. Choose the correct answers.**

1. Do Dan and Jon wake up late?   **a.** Yes, they do.   **b.** No, they don't.

2. Are Dan and Jon neat?   **a.** Yes, they are.   **b.** No, they aren't.

3. Is Dan quiet?   **a.** Yes, he is.   **b.** No, he isn't.

4. Are Dan and Jon outgoing?   **a.** Dan is, but Jon isn't.   **b.** Dan isn't, but Jon is.

5. Is Dan a private person?   **a.** Yes, he is.   **b.** No, he isn't.

6. Is Jon easygoing?   **a.** Yes, he is.   **b.** No, he isn't.

7. Do Dan and Jon dislike loud music?   **a.** Yes, they do.   **b.** No, they don't.

8. Does Dan study and listen to music at the same time?   **a.** Yes, he does.   **b.** No, he doesn't.

Ⓒ DISCUSSION **Work with a partner. Compare your answers in B. Then discuss: Are Dan and Jon a good match? Give reasons for your answer.**

SIMPLE PRESENT: *YES/NO* QUESTIONS AND SHORT ANSWERS

Yes/No Questions			Short Answers						

Do/Does	Subject	Base Form of Verb
Do	I you we they	**work?**
Does	he she it	

Affirmative				Negative			
Yes,	you I/we you they	**do.**		**No,**	you I/we you they	**don't.**
	he she it	**does.**			he she it	**doesn't.**

GRAMMAR NOTES

1 Simple Present: Form of *Yes/No* Questions

For *yes/no questions* in the **simple present**, use *do* or *does* before the subject. Use the base form of the verb after the subject.	**SUBJECT** **Do** you need a roommate? **Does** he have a roommate?
BE CAREFUL! Do not use *do* or *does* for *yes/no* questions with *be*.	**Are** you from Ecuador? **Is** he from France? NOT ~~Do you be~~ from Ecuador? NOT ~~Does he is~~ from France?

2 Simple Present: Answers to *Yes/No* Questions

We usually use **short answers** in conversation, but we can also use **long answers**.	A: Do you need a roommate? B: **Yes.** or **Yes, I do.** (*short answers*) or B: **Yes, I need a roommate.** (*long answer*)

REFERENCE NOTE

For information on *yes/no* questions with *be*, see Unit 2 on page 17.

EXERCISE 1   DISCOVER THE GRAMMAR

GRAMMAR NOTES 1–2
Read about Dan and Jon.
Then match the questions
and answers.

In many ways, Dan and
Jon are alike. Both Dan
and Jon like music and
sports, but Dan likes
pop music, and Jon
likes hip-hop. Both Dan
and Jon like basketball,
but Jon likes soccer and Dan doesn't. Dan
and Jon are both neat. They don't like a
messy room. They both like to go to bed
late—after midnight. They watch about two
hours of TV at night, and they study with
the TV on. But in one way Dan and Jon are
completely different. Dan is talkative, but Jon
is quiet. Dan says, "We're lucky about that.
It works out nicely. I talk, he listens." Jon
says, "Uh-huh."

___b___ **1.** Do Dan and Jon both like music and sports?   **a.** It doesn't say.

_____ **2.** Do Dan and Jon like to go to bed early?   ~~**b.**~~ Yes, they do.

_____ **3.** Does Dan like pop music?   **c.** Yes, he does.

_____ **4.** Is Jon talkative?   **d.** No, they don't.

_____ **5.** Do Dan and Jon like movies?   **e.** Yes, they are.

_____ **6.** Are Dan and Jon neat?   **f.** No, he isn't.

EXERCISE 2   *YES/NO* QUESTIONS AND SHORT ANSWERS

GRAMMAR NOTES 1–2   Complete the questions with *Do* or *Does* and the verbs in
parentheses. Then complete the short answers.

1. (listen)   A: _____*Do*_____ you _____*listen*_____ to music?

            B: Yes, _____*we do*_____ . **or** Yes, _____*I do*_____ .

2. (have)   A: _____ your roommate _____ a TV?

            B: No, she _____ .

3. (wake up)   A: _____ he _____ early?

            B: No, _____ .

4. (stay up)   A: _____ they _____ late?

                 B: Yes, _____ .

5. (bother)   A: _____ the TV _____ you?

                 B: No, _____ .

6. (have)   A: _____ your room _____ a big window?

                 B: Yes, _____ .

7. (like)   A: _____ you _____ a cool room?

                 B: No, _____ .

8. (have)   A: _____ the room _____ Wi-Fi?

                 B: Yes, _____ .

9. (go)   A: _____ she _____ to parties all the time?

                 B: No, _____ .

10. (need)   A: _____ we _____ more light?

                 B: Yes, _____ .

11. (sell)   A: _____ they _____ lamps on campus?

                 B: Yes, _____ .

EXERCISE 3   *YES/NO* QUESTIONS WITH *DO* AND *BE*

GRAMMAR NOTES 1–2   Complete the *yes/no* questions with *Do, Does, Am, Is,* or *Are.*
Then complete the short answers.

1. A: ___*Am*___ I late?   B: No, ___*you aren't*___ .

2. A: ___*Does*___ he come home late?   B: Yes, ___*he does*___ .

3. A: _____ you busy?   B: Yes, we _____ .

4. A: _____ they have a lot of work?   B: No, _____ .

5. A: _____ they roommates?   B: No, _____ .

6. A: _____ they live in a dormitory?   B: Yes, _____ .

7. A: _____ she your sister?   B: No, _____ .

8. A: _____ you live at home?   B: Yes, I _____ .

9. A: _____ your roommate play baseball?   B: No, he _____ .

10. A: _____ we in the right room?   B: Yes, you _____ .

11. A: _____ you friends?   B: Yes, _____ .

12. A: _____ you cook well?   B: No, I _____ .

EXERCISE 4 *YES/NO* QUESTIONS AND SHORT ANSWERS

GRAMMAR NOTES 1–2 **Complete the conversation. Write questions with the correct forms of the words in parentheses. Then write short answers with** *do, does, don't,* **or** *doesn't.*

YURI: So tell me about your new roommate, Edward. <u>Do you like</u> him?
1. (you / like)

SHEN: <u>Yes, I do</u>. He's a really nice guy.
2.

YURI: Where is he from? He sounds like a native speaker. _____ from
3. (he / come)

England?

SHEN: _____. He comes from Australia.
4.

YURI: Cool. What's he studying?

SHEN: Music.

YURI: Oh, he's a music major. _____ an instrument?
5. (he / play)

SHEN: Of course. He plays three instruments: violin, cello, and piano.

YURI: Wow. _____ with him?
6. (you / play)

SHEN: _____. I'm not a good musician. But sometimes his cousin plays
7.

with him.

YURI: _____ family close by?
8. (he / have)

SHEN: _____. His uncle, his aunt, three cousins, and his grandmother are
9.

ten minutes away. I was at their home last night.

YURI: Really? _____ them often?
10. (you / see)

SHEN: _____. They invite us for a meal at least once a month. They all
11.

play music, and they're interesting people. His uncle is a

conductor, and his cousin is an opera singer.

YURI: _____ them a small gift when you visit?
12. (you / bring)

SHEN: _____. I'm a poor student.
13.

YURI: Hey, you're not that poor.

EXERCISE 5 EDITING

GRAMMAR NOTES 1–2 **Correct the conversations. There are nine mistakes. The first mistake is already corrected. Find and correct eight more.**

1. A: Does she ~~goes~~ *go* to school?

   B: Yes, she goes.

2. A: Does he needs help?

   B: Yes, he does.

3. A: Do they are like rock music?

   B: Yes, they do.

4. A: Do she live near the university?

   B: Yes, she lives.

5. A: Does he has a roommate?

   B: Yes, he has.

6. A: Are you friends?

   B: Yes, we do.

STEP 4 COMMUNICATION PRACTICE

EXERCISE 6 LISTENING

09|02 **A** Listen to the conversation. Why is Andrea talking to Valentina Gold?

a. to find a roommate   **b.** to work out a problem with her roommate

09|02 **B** Listen to the conversation again and complete the chart with Andrea's answers.

	Andrea	Leyla
Parties		*likes parties*
Music		*likes rock*
Sports		*plays basketball, soccer, swims*
Study habits		*studies at night in her room*

C Work with a partner. Discuss: Are Andrea and Leyla a good match? Why or why not?

EXAMPLE: **A:** I think Andrea and Leyla are a bad match because Andrea doesn't like parties, but Leyla likes them.

B: Really? I disagree. I think they're a good match because . . .

EXERCISE 7 COMPARING HABITS AND PERSONALITY

A QUESTIONNAIRE Answer the roommate questionnaire.

Roommate Questionnaire   Name: _____

		YES	NO
1.	Do you wake up early?	☐	☐
2.	Do you stay up late?	☐	☐
3.	Are you neat?	☐	☐
4.	Does a messy room bother you?	☐	☐
5.	Are you quiet?	☐	☐
6.	Are you talkative?	☐	☐
7.	Does noise bother you?	☐	☐
8.	Are you outgoing?	☐	☐
9.	Are you a private person?	☐	☐
10.	Are you easygoing?	☐	☐
11.	Do you listen to loud music?	☐	☐
12.	Do you watch a lot of TV?	☐	☐
13.	Do you study and listen to music at the same time?	☐	☐
14.	Do you study with the TV on?	☐	☐

B Compare your questionnaire answers with your partner. Are you and your partner a good match?

C Work with a partner. Think of one more question for the questionnaire. Ask your partner the question. Then answer it yourself.

EXAMPLE: **A:** What's your question?

B: My question is, "Do you keep a lot of stuff?"

A: No. I don't like to hold on to things. What about you?

B: I keep a lot of stuff. What's your question?

A: . . .

EXERCISE 8 FIND SOMEONE WHO . . .

A GAME Walk around your classroom. Ask your classmates *yes/no* questions in order to fill out the chart. When a classmate answers "yes," write his or her name in the chart. The first person to complete the chart wins.

EXAMPLE: A: Mattias, do you cook well?

B: Yes, I do. I cook every day.

A: Are you a soccer fan?

B: No, . . .

Find someone who . . .	Name
cooks well	*Mattias*
is a soccer fan	
texts every day	
plays a musical instrument	
is athletic	
is an only child	
has more than three brothers and sisters	
is interested in science	
is interested in business	
has a pet	
listens to the news every day	
is a good dancer	

B Report back to the class.

EXAMPLE: Mattias is a good cook. He isn't a soccer fan . . .

EXERCISE 9 ROOM FOR RENT

ROLE PLAY Work with a partner. You are Student A. You are looking for a room to rent. Your partner, Student B, has a room to rent. Ask your partner questions about the room. Your partner answers your questions and asks you questions about yourself. You can use the ideas in the boxes.

EXAMPLE: A: I have a few questions about the room for rent. First of all, is it near the university?

B: Yes. It's only two blocks away.

A: Good. Does the room have furniture?

B: It has . . .

STUDENT A

a window?
a closet?
a bed? a desk?
Wi-Fi?
a view?

STUDENT B

listen to music?
play an instrument?
have any pets?

FROM GRAMMAR TO WRITING

A BEFORE YOU WRITE Read this email to you from a future roommate at an English language school. Work with a partner. What do you want to know about Sammy? Write questions.

● ○ ○

Hi,

I'm Sammy Morales from Colombia. I am going to be your roommate. I'm excited about our English language school, but I'm also a little nervous. Maybe you feel the same way.

I'm nineteen years old, and I'm from Fusagasugá, a town near Bogotá, Colombia. I come from a large family. I have five brothers and two sisters. Do you have any brothers and sisters?

I love sports and music. How about you? Do you have a favorite music group? Do you have a favorite sport? Please tell me about yourself.

I look forward to meeting you next month.

All the best,
Sammy

B WRITE Write an email to Sammy. Answer Sammy's questions and ask Sammy your questions from A. Use the simple present.

C CHECK YOUR WORK Read your email. Underline *yes/no* questions in the simple present. Then use the Editing Checklist to check your work.

Editing Checklist
Did you . . . ?
☐ use *do* in simple present *yes/no* questions with *I, you, we,* or *they*
☐ use *does* in simple present *yes/no* questions with *he, she,* or *it*

D REVISE YOUR WORK Read your email again. Can you improve your writing? Make changes if necessary.

UNIT 9 **REVIEW**

Test yourself on the grammar of the unit.

Ⓐ Complete the sentences with the words from the box.

Am	Are	Do	Does	Is

1. _____ you know his brother?

2. _____ his brother messy?

3. _____ he have a lot of friends?

4. _____ they easygoing?

5. _____ I your best friend?

Ⓑ Complete the questions with the correct forms of the words in parentheses.

1. _____ a roommate?
   (you / have)

2. _____ English fluently?
   (his roommate / speak)

3. _____ TV at night?
   (your roommate / watch)

4. _____ talkative?
   (be / your roommate)

5. _____ in the United States?
   (be / your roommate's parents)

Ⓒ Write questions about an apartment. Use the correct forms of the words in parentheses.

1. (be / the neighbors / noisy) _____

2. (the building / have / an elevator) _____

3. (be / the apartment / near buses) _____

4. (the bedroom / have / two closets) _____

5. (be / the bedroom / big) _____

Ⓓ Correct the conversations. There are five mistakes.

1. A: Does he have a big TV in his room?   B: Yes, he has.

2. A: Does she needs help?   B: No, she don't.

3. A: Do you are friends?   B: Yes, we aren't.

Now check your answers on page 446.

OUTCOMES
- Ask for information, using *wh-* questions in the simple present
- Answer questions about information in a talk show transcript
- Answer questions about details in a conversation
- Talk about dreams and sleep habits
- Ask questions about someone's life and write an interview transcript with the answers

STEP 1	GRAMMAR IN CONTEXT

BEFORE YOU READ

Work with a partner. Answer the questions.

1. Do you dream?

2. Do you remember your dreams?

3. What do you dream about?

READ

▶ 10|01   *Ask the Expert* is a radio talk show. Today Mike Stevens is talking to dream expert Ella Lam. Read their conversation about dreams.

Dreams

MIKE: Good afternoon. I'm Mike Stevens. Welcome to *Ask the Expert*. This afternoon my guest is Ella Lam. She's the author of *Sleep and Dreams*. Thank you for coming.

ELLA: Thanks, Mike. It's great to be here.

MIKE: Ella, we have a lot of questions about dreams. Our first question is from Carolina Gomes. She asks, "Why do we dream?"

ELLA: Actually, nobody really knows why. But I think dreams help us understand our feelings.

MIKE: OK. Our next question is from Jonathan Evans. He asks, "Who dreams? Does everyone dream?"

ELLA: Yes, everyone dreams. And what's more, scientists believe animals dream, too.

MIKE: Wow! That's really interesting. How do we know?

ELLA: Machines show when people or animals dream. But, of course, no one knows what animals dream about.

MIKE: Interesting. OK. Our next question is from Pablo Ortiz. He writes, "People don't remember *all* their dreams. What dreams do they remember?"

ELLA: People remember their unusual dreams. And, unfortunately, they remember their nightmares.

MIKE: Beata Green says, "I have the same dream again and again. What does that mean?"

ELLA: That dream has special meaning for you. You need to think about it.

MIKE: Here's a question from Samuel Diaz. "When do people dream?"

ELLA: They dream during REM or deep sleep. REM means *rapid*[1] *eye movement*.

MIKE: I hear REM sleep is important. Why do we need it?

ELLA: It *is* important. Without it, we can't remember or think clearly.

MIKE: Ron Morgan writes, "Why do I remember my dreams? My roommate doesn't."

ELLA: Well, a University of Iowa professor says, "Creative[2] people remember their dreams."

MIKE: Really? . . . Thank you so much, Ella. We look forward to reading your new book.

---

1 *rapid:* fast
2 *creative:* able to see things in a new way

AFTER YOU READ

Ⓐ VOCABULARY **Complete the sentences with the words from the box.**

author	guest	nightmare	remember	unfortunately

1. Who is the _____ of *Sleep and Dreams*?

2. What is the name of the _____ on tonight's *Ask the Expert*?

3. Do you _____ your dreams?

4. A very bad dream is called a(n) _____ .

5. This book about dreams sounds interesting. _____, it's over a thousand pages long, so I don't have time to read it!

Ⓑ COMPREHENSION **Answer the questions.**

1. Who dreams? _____

2. What do animals dream about? _____

3. Why do people dream? _____

4. What does REM stand for? _____

5. Who remembers dreams? _____

Ⓒ DISCUSSION **Work with a partner. Compare your answers in B. Give reasons for your answers. Then discuss: What else do you want to know about dreams?**

SIMPLE PRESENT: *WH-* QUESTIONS; SHORT AND LONG ANSWERS

Wh- Questions

Wh- Word	Do/Does	Subject	Base Form of Verb
When	do	I	
Where	do	you	**sleep?**
Why	do	we	
What	do	they	**need?**
Who	does	she	**know?**
How	does	it	**feel?**
How often	does	he	**get up?**

Answers

Short	Long
From 10:00 p.m. to 5:00 a.m.	You sleep from 10:00 p.m. to 5:00 a.m.
On the futon.	I sleep on the futon.
Because we're tired.	We sleep because we're tired.
Two pillows.	They need two pillows.
My brother.	She knows my brother.
Good.	The blanket feels good.
Three times a night.	He gets up three times a night.

Wh- Questions About the Subject

Wh- Word	Verb	
Who	sleeps	in that bedroom?
Who	sleeps	in this bedroom?

Answers

My brother does.
My parents do.

GRAMMAR NOTES

1 Wh- Questions

Wh- **questions** ask for information. They are sometimes called **information questions**.

The form of a *Wh-* question is usually:
Wh- word + *do/does* + subject + base form

WH- WORD	DO/DOES	SUBJECT	BASE FORM	
When	**do**	you	**go**	to bed?
What	**does**	he	**dream**	about?

2 Wh- Questions About a Subject

We use *who* to ask about a person who does something (the subject).

Questions about a **subject** follow this form:
Who + third-person-singular verb

A: **Who wakes** Felix?
B: **Inez** wakes him. *(Inez = the subject)*

BE CAREFUL! Do not use *do* or *does* with questions about a subject. Do not use the base form of the verb.

Who wakes Feliz?
NOT Who does wakes Felix?
NOT Who do wakes Felix?
NOT Who wake Felix?

We use *who* (or *whom*) to ask about a person who is the object of the question.

| Questions about an **object** follow this form: | A: **Who does Inez wake**? |
| *Who(m)* + *do/does* + **subject** + **base form** | B: Inez wakes **Felix**. *(Felix = the object)* |

| **USAGE NOTE** *Whom* can be used instead of *who* in questions about an object, but *whom* is very formal so most people don't use it. | **Who does** Dr. Chen **visit**?
 Whom does Dr. Chen **visit**? *(very formal and not common)* |

REFERENCE NOTE

For more information about *who*, *what*, *where*, *when*, and *why*, see Unit 2 on page 17.

STEP 3 FOCUSED PRACTICE

EXERCISE 1
DISCOVER THE GRAMMAR

GRAMMAR NOTES 1–2 Night owls like to stay up late at night. Early birds get up early. Read about a night owl and an early bird. Then match the questions and answers.

> Felix is a night owl. He hates to get up in the morning. On weekends, he goes to bed at 1:00 a.m. and gets up at noon. Unfortunately for Felix, during the week his first class starts at 8:15, and he needs to get up early.
>
> At 7:00 a.m., Felix's alarm rings. He wakes up, but he doesn't get up. He stays in bed and daydreams. At 7:20, his mom comes in. She has a big smile. She says, "Felix, it's time to get up."
>
> Inez is Felix's mother. She's an early bird. She's up at 6:00 a.m. even when she's on vacation. When she wakes Felix up, he says, "Leave me alone. I'm tired."
>
> Finally, at about 7:30, Felix gets up. He jumps out of bed, showers, and gets dressed. At 7:50, he drinks a big glass of juice and runs to the bus stop. The bus comes at 8:00.

_g_ 1. Who hates to get up in the morning?

____ 2. How does Felix feel in the morning?

____ 3. Who does Inez wake up on school days?

____ 4. Why does Felix run to the bus stop?

____ 5. What does Felix have for breakfast?

____ 6. When does Felix sleep late?

____ 7. What happens at 7:00?

____ 8. When does Inez wake up?

a. On weekends.

b. Tired.

c. At 6:00 a.m.

d. Felix's alarm rings.

e. A glass of juice.

f. Because he doesn't want to be late.

g. Felix does.

h. She wakes Felix up.

EXERCISE 2 WORD ORDER OF *WH-* QUESTIONS

GRAMMAR NOTE 1 Complete the conversations. Read the answers. Then write questions. Put the words in parentheses in the correct order.

1. (do / you / usually get up / When)

   A: *When do you usually get up?*

   B: At 7:00 on weekdays.

2. (Where / come from / your guest / does)

   A: _____

   B: She's from Sydney.

3. (at night / they / How / do / feel)

   A: _____

   B: They're never tired at night. They're night owls.

4. (does / Who / he / dream about)

   A: _____

   B: He dreams about me.

5. (What / she / dream about / does)

   A: _____

   B: Actually, she never remembers her dreams.

6. (wake up / your mother/ does / What time)

   A: _____

   B: She wakes up at 6:00 a.m.

EXERCISE 3 *WH-* QUESTIONS ABOUT THE SUBJECT

GRAMMAR NOTES 2–3 Complete the conversations. Read B's answers. Then write A's questions. Use the correct forms of the words in parentheses.

1. (Who / daydream)

   A: *Who daydreams?*

   B: John does.

2. (Who / have / nightmares)

   A: _____

   B: Her brother Sam does.

3. (Who / get up / before 6:00 a.m.)

   A: _____

   B: Grandma Ilene does.

4. (Who / hate / early morning classes)

A: _____

B: Bob, Emiko, and Jill do.

5. (Who / need / more than eight hours of sleep)

A: _____

B: Feng does.

EXERCISE 4 *WH-* QUESTIONS

GRAMMAR NOTES 1–3 **Read the answers. Then ask questions about the underlined words.**

1. Sabrina daydreams.

Who *daydreams?* _____

2. Sabrina daydreams during her math class.

When _____

3. Sabrina daydreams about her boyfriend.

Who _____

4. Sabrina daydreams during her math class because she doesn't like the class.

Why _____

5. Sabrina's boyfriend is 3,000 miles away in Alaska.

Where _____

6. Sabrina feels lonely.

How _____

7. Sabrina's boyfriend has a good job.

Who _____

8. Sabrina's boyfriend works for an oil company.

What _____

EXERCISE 5 *WH-* QUESTIONS: SUBJECT AND OBJECT

GRAMMAR NOTES 2–3 Underline and label the subject (*S*) and object (*O*) in each sentence. Then write one question about the subject and one question about the object. Begin with *who*.

1. My mother calls me every day.
       S   O

   Q: *Who calls you every day?*

   A: My mother does.

   Q: *Who does your mother call every day?*

   A: My mother calls me.

2. In a dream, Jake meets his boss at a party.

   Q: _____

   A: Jake does.

   Q: _____

   A: He meets his boss.

3. In a nightmare, two men push Maya.

   Q: _____

   A: Two men do.

   Q: _____

   A: They push Maya.

4. In my dream, my grandfather visits my friends.

   Q: _____

   A: My grandfather does.

   Q: _____

   A: My friends.

EXERCISE 6 EDITING

GRAMMAR NOTES 1–3 There are ten mistakes. The first mistake is already corrected. Find and correct nine more.

1. Where do they ~~sleeps~~? *sleep*

2. Why they need two pillows?

3. Who sleep on the sofa?

4. When does she goes to bed?

5. Who wake you?

6. Who does you dream about?

7. How he feels about that?

8. What you dream about?

9. How long does she sleeps at night?

10. Where he sleep?

EXERCISE 7 LISTENING

⏵10|02 **A** Mia often has the same dream. She tells a doctor about her dream. Listen to their conversation. What is she looking for in the dream?

_____

⏵10|02 **B** Listen again. Answer the questions. Then work with a partner and compare your answers.

1. What important event does Mia have in her dream?

   *She has an important test.*_____

2. What does the man in the dream say? _____

3. What does Dr. Fox think Mia has? _____

4. What are the two paths Dr. Fox talks about? _____

5. What does Mia's father want her to study? _____

EXERCISE 8 SNORING, DREAMING, AND SLEEP

A PRESENTATION Prepare for a presentation in B. Answer the questions. Then work with a partner. Ask your partner the questions.

	You	Your Partner
Are you an early bird or a night owl?		
What time do you go to bed?		
What days do you sleep late?		
Does anyone wake you up? If so, who?		
Do you dream? If so, what do you dream about?		
Do you walk or talk in your sleep?		
Do you snore?		
Do you need a lot of sleep? Do you ever have trouble sleeping?		

B Tell the class about your partner's sleep habits. The class asks your partner more questions.

EXAMPLE: **A:** Ali is a night owl. He usually goes to bed at 2:00 a.m.
B: Ali, what do you do at night?
C: I usually read at night.
D: Are you tired in the morning?
C: I'm always tired in the morning!

EXERCISE 9 DREAMS

INFORMATION GAP Work with a partner. Student A, follow the instructions below. Student B, follow the instructions on page 455.

STUDENT A

• Student B has a dream again and again. Find out about the dream. Ask Student B the questions below. Write down his or her answers.

1. Where are you in your dream? _____

2. Who do you see? _____

3. Is the person big? Little? _____

4. Are you big? Little? _____

5. What does the person say? _____

6. What do you do? _____

• You have a dream again and again. Read about your dream below. Student B will ask you questions about this dream. Answer Student B's questions.

You are on an airplane. The pilot comes to you. He says, "I need your help." You go with the pilot. You fly the plane. You land the plane. Everyone claps. You feel good. You wake up.

• Talk about your dreams. What do they mean?

FROM GRAMMAR TO WRITING

A BEFORE YOU WRITE Read the interview between Todd Jones and Ella Lam, best-selling author of the book *Sleep and Dreams*. Then work with a partner. Imagine your partner is famous. Ask your partner questions about his or her life. Take notes. Then switch roles.

TODD: How is your life different now that you are famous?

ELLA: People think I'm smarter.

TODD: What do you do in your free time?

ELLA: I travel. I was in South Africa last month, and next month I plan to go to Thailand.

TODD: Where do you live?

ELLA: I live in New York City.

TODD: Do you dream?

ELLA: Yes, I do. And I remember my dreams. Sometimes, I write them down.

TODD: What do you dream about?

ELLA: I dream about horses. I . . .

B WRITE Write an interview between you and your partner. Use the interview in A and your notes. Use the simple present for all your questions.

C CHECK YOUR WORK Read your interview. Underline simple present questions. Use the Editing Checklist to check your work.

Editing Checklist
Did you . . . ?
☐ use a *wh-* word + *do/does* + subject + base form for most simple present *wh-* questions
☐ remember NOT to use *do/does* in questions about a subject
☐ remember to use *do/does* in questions about an object

D REVISE YOUR WORK Read your questions and answers again. Can you improve your writing? Make changes if necessary.

UNIT 10 REVIEW

Test yourself on the grammar of the unit.

A Complete the *wh-* questions with the words from the box.

how	when	where	who	why

1. A: _____ does she snore? B: I don't know why.

2. A: _____ do they get up? B: At about 9:00 or 10:00.

3. A: _____ sleeps in that room? B: Their uncle does.

4. A: _____ do you feel? B: Sleepy.

5. A: _____ do you buy sheets? B: At Bloom's department store.

B Write questions with the correct forms of the words in parentheses.

1. (What / you / dream about) _____

2. (What time / your mother / get up) _____

3. (What time / you / go to bed) _____

4. (Where / your brother / sleep) _____

5. (Who / snore / in your family) _____

C Read the statement and answers. Then write the questions.

John meets his uncle at the diner on Saturdays.

1. A: _____ B: John does.

2. A: _____ B: His uncle.

3. A: _____ B: At the diner.

4. A: _____ B: On Saturdays.

D Correct the questions. There are six mistakes.

1. Where you live?

2. Why he daydreams in class?

3. When does she gets up?

4. How they feel about sleeping pills?

5. Who does you dream about?

6. What time he wake up?

Now check your answers on page 446.

There Is / There Are; Possessives

PART 4

OUTCOMES

- Use *there is / are* to introduce people or things
- Use *there is / are* to tell the location of people or things or the time of events
- Recognize details in a short article about a famous place
- Recognize details about a place in a conversation
- Talk about places in your town
- Write a paragraph about a place to shop

OUTCOMES

- Talk about possessions
- Recognize details in a conversation transcript
- Recognize details in a conversation about possessions
- Ask and answer questions about objects and describe them in detail
- Write a paragraph about people in your family

There is / There are

PLACES TO SHOP

OUTCOMES
- Use *there is / are* to introduce people or things
- Use *there is / are* to tell the location of people or things or the time of events
- Recognize details in a short article about a famous place
- Recognize details about a place in a conversation
- Talk about places in your town
- Write a paragraph about a place to shop

STEP 1   GRAMMAR IN CONTEXT

BEFORE YOU READ

Work with a partner. Discuss the questions.

1. Do you like shopping malls? Why or why not?

2. Where is the nearest mall? Do you go there? Why or why not?

READ

▶11|01   Read this page from a guidebook about the Dubai Mall.

For a wonderful time, join the 750,000 weekly shoppers at the Dubai Mall. There are more than 1,200 stores including "Candylicious," the world's largest candy store. But the mall has a lot more than just the stores. There's a luxury hotel, twenty-two cinema screens, and 120 restaurants and cafés.

Are there things for kids to do? Yes, lots. There's an aquarium, an underground zoo, and an ice rink[1] on the first level. And on the second level, there's the Sega indoor theme park.

What about parking? There are 14,000 parking spaces. And it's easy to find your car. Your parking ticket includes a computer system to help you locate[2] your car.

So make your plans now. There isn't a better place to shop.

---

1 *ice rink:* a place where people can skate on ice
2 *locate:* find

AFTER YOU READ

A VOCABULARY **Complete the sentences with the words from the box.**

aquarium	including	indoor	join	luxury	parking spaces

1. He drives a(n) _____ car with leather seats and a great stereo system.

2. There are _____ for only a few cars, so you may need to leave your car at home.

3. There's a(n) _____ garage, so your car stays cool when it is hot outside.

4. There are hundreds of different fish in the _____.

5. Please _____ us for a tour of the new shopping center.

6. The total bill comes to a thousand dollars _____ tax.

B COMPREHENSION **Complete the sentences. Circle the correct words.**

1. Candylicious is a huge store for sweet / spicy treats.

2. There aren't any restaurants / museums at the Dubai Mall.

3. There are / aren't activities for children at the Dubai Mall.

4. There's a car-locating system / car wash at the Dubai Mall.

5. There's a hotel / an apartment building at the Dubai Mall.

6. Every week, there are more than 7,500 / 750,000 shoppers at the Dubai Mall.

C DISCUSSION **Work with a partner. Compare your answers in B. Explain why you think your answers are correct. Then answer the question: Would you like to go to the Dubai Mall? Why or why not?**

THERE IS / THERE ARE

Affirmative Statements

There	*Be*	Subject	Place/Time
There	is	a restaurant	on this level.
		a movie	at 6:30.
There	are	two restaurants	near the entrance.
		shows	at 7:00 and 9:00.

Contractions

there is	→	**there's**
there is not	→	**there isn't**
there are not	→	**there aren't**

Negative Statements

There	*Be + not*	Subject	Place/Time
There	isn't	a restaurant	on the second level.
There	aren't	any movies	at 8:00.

Yes/No Questions

Be	*There*	Subject	Place
Is	there	a pizza place	on Second Street?
Are	there	any banks	nearby?

Short Answers

Affirmative		Negative	
Yes,	there is.	No,	there isn't.
	there are.		there aren't.

GRAMMAR NOTES

1   *There is / There are*

There is and *There are* **introduce** people or things into a conversation or a piece of writing.

We use *there is* to tell about the existence of:
- a person
- a thing

There is *a salesperson* near the door.
There is *a shoe store* at the mall.

We use *there are* to tell about the existence of:
- people
- things

There are *two women* in the store.
There are *restaurants* on the third level.

USAGE NOTE We often use *there are* to tell about the number of people or things that exist.

There are **14,000** parking spaces at the mall.
There are **two** Thai restaurants in that mall.

USAGE NOTE It is very common to use the contraction *there's* with singular nouns. However, we almost never use the contraction *there're* with plural nouns.

There's a salesperson near the door.
There are two women in the store.
NOT ~~There're~~ two women in the store.

There in *there is* and *there are* is different from *there* on its own. *There* on its own is an adverb of place. It means "in that place."

There are two salespeople **there**.

2 *There is/There are* for Location or Time

We often use *there is* or *there are* to tell the **location** of people or things or the **time** of events.

• location	There's an aquarium **on the first floor.**
• time	There are concerts **on Friday and Saturday nights.**

3 Negative Forms

In the negative, use *there isn't* and *there aren't*. USAGE NOTE We don't often use the full forms *there is not* or *there are not*.	**There isn't** a school in the mall. **There aren't** any malls near our home.

4 *Yes/No* Questions

Begin *yes/no* questions with *Is there* or *Are there*.	**Is there** a mall nearby?

5 Agreement

When two nouns follow *there is* or *there are*, the verb usually agrees with the **first noun**.	**There's a shoe store** and two hair salons. **There are two hair salons** and a shoe store.

6 *There is* and *It is*, *He is*, and *She is*; *There are* and *They are*

We often use *there is* or *there are* the first time we introduce people or things. We use *he, she, it,* or *they* to tell more about the people or things.	**There's a Thai restaurant** across the street. *It's* next to the shoe store. **There's a salesman** over there. *He's* next to the cash register. **There are three little girls** in the dress store. *They're* excited about all the beautiful dresses.

REFERENCE NOTE

For more information about *any*, see Unit 27 on page 324.

EXERCISE 1   DISCOVER THE GRAMMAR

A GRAMMAR NOTES 1–5 **Look at the mall directory. Write** *T* (*True*) **or** *F* (*False*) **for each statement.**

BURLINGTON MALL DIRECTORY

THIRD LEVEL	House of Kebab	Chinese food	Burgers	Sushi bar	Café	Restrooms
SECOND LEVEL	Women's clothes	Shoe store	Art supply store	Furniture store	Children's clothes	Cosmetics store
FIRST LEVEL	Restrooms	Gift shop	Bookstore	Flower shop	Electronics store	Women's clothes

_T_ **1.** There's a flower shop on the first level.

____ **2.** There's a café on the second level.

____ **3.** There aren't any toy stores.

____ **4.** There are five places to eat.

____ **5.** There isn't a restroom on the second level.

____ **6.** There's a bookstore and an electronics store on the second level.

B **Look at the mall directory again. Circle the correct answers.**

1. A: Are there any office supply stores at the mall?

  B: Yes, there are. / No, there aren't.

2. A: Are there any jewelry stores at the mall?

  B: Yes, there are. / No, there aren't.

3. A: Is there an amusement park at the mall?

  B: Yes, there is. / No, there isn't.

4. A: Is there an art supply store at the mall?

  B: Yes, there is. / No, there isn't.

EXERCISE 2 *THERE IS / THERE ARE*

GRAMMAR NOTES 1–2 Complete the sentences about the Burlington Mall with *There is* or *There are*.

1. ____*There are*____ two women's clothes stores at the mall.

2. _____ a good electronics store on the first level.

3. _____ a shoe store next to the art supply store.

4. _____ a lot of places to eat at the mall.

5. _____ restrooms on the first and the third levels.

6. _____ a cosmetics store at the mall.

EXERCISE 3 AFFIRMATIVE AND NEGATIVE STATEMENTS

GRAMMAR NOTES 1–3 Find the incorrect sentences. Rewrite them with the correct word order.

1. There's a mall in the Chinese restaurant. *There's a Chinese restaurant in the mall.*

2. There's a second level on the shoe store. _____

3. There are two women's clothing stores at the mall. _____

4. There's an electronics store on the first level. _____

5. There isn't a mall at the men's clothing store. _____

6. There aren't any classrooms in the desks. _____

EXERCISE 4 AFFIRMATIVE AND NEGATIVE STATEMENTS

Ⓐ GRAMMAR NOTES 1–3, 6 Complete the conversation. Use *there's, there are, there isn't, there aren't, they're,* or *they aren't.*

AL: This pizza place is awful. ____*There aren't*____ any tablecloths, and the placemats are dirty.
       _{1.}

KATE: You're right. _____ any napkins either. _____ a busboy here
                           _{2.}   _{3.}
       somewhere, but I don't see him now.

AL: Well, I need a knife and fork.

KATE: _____ knives and forks on that table. Oh, no. _____ clean.
             _{4.}   _{5.}

AL: Boy, it's hot in here. _____ even a fan.
                                   _{6.}

KATE: Oh, my gosh! You won't believe this.

AL: What is it?

KATE: Well, _____ a mouse over there, near the wall!
                   _{7.}

AL: What? Ugh, _____ two mice! Let's leave!
8.

KATE: What about our food?

AL: Let the mice have it. _____ hungry, too!
9.

▶11|02 **B** LISTEN AND CHECK Listen to the conversation and check your answers in A.

EXERCISE 5 *THERE IS / THERE ARE, THERE,* AND *THEY ARE*

A GRAMMAR NOTES 1–2, 6 Complete the conversation. Use *there's, there are, there,* and *they're*.

NICK: How about some Chinese food?

TINA: Well, ____*there's*____ only one Chinese food restaurant nearby. But it's expensive.
1.

_____ a lot of other restaurants, though.
2.

NICK: Today is Sunday. Are they open?

TINA: _____ all open seven days a week.
3.

NICK: Well, _____ a nice Mexican place over _____.
4.   5.

TINA: Where?

NICK: Over _____ next to the diner.
6.

TINA: I know the place. It's good and not expensive. Let's go.

▶11|03 **B** LISTEN AND CHECK Listen to the conversation and check your answers in A.

EXERCISE 6 *THERE IS / THERE ARE* AND SUBJECT PRONOUNS

GRAMMAR NOTES 1–2, 5–6 Complete the sentences. Use *There's* or *There are* in the first sentence. Use *He's, She's, It's,* or *They're* in the second sentence.

1. _____*There's*_____ a good café over there. _____*It's*_____ next to the bookstore.

2. _____ a salesman behind the counter. _____ talking to that woman.

3. _____ a lot of wool sweaters. _____ in the back of the store.

4. _____ a scarf on the floor. _____ your new one, isn't it?

5. _____ some indoor parking spaces over there. _____ near the exit.

6. _____ a small mall on Route 4. _____ next to the amusement park.

7. _____ a lot of people in that line. _____ buying tickets for the movie.

8. _____ a pizza place and two restaurants here. _____ open now.

9. _____ a woman in a blue dress. _____ the owner of the pizza place.

EXERCISE 7 YES/NO QUESTIONS AND ANSWERS

GRAMMAR NOTES 1–4, 6 Look at the calendar. Complete the questions with *Is there* or *Are there*. Then write answers.

FIND THINGS TO DO *This week*

TODAY

Carmen
Columbia College
Tonight at 8:00

FRIDAY

Buyers Flea Market
4545 West Street
8:00–5:00
Cheap clothing!

SATURDAY

The Misfits
Great Drama with
Marilyn Monroe!
Main Street Cinema
4:30, 6:30, 8:30

SUNDAY

Chicago Symphony Orchestra
All Beethoven
Chicago Cultural Center
8:00 p.m.

1. A: _____*Is there*_____ a performance tonight? What is it?

   B: _____

2. A: _____ any movies or concerts this weekend? When?

   B: _____

3. A: How many showings of the movie _____?

   B: _____

4. A: _____ a flea market? When and where is it?

   B: _____

EXERCISE 8 EDITING

GRAMMAR NOTES 1–6 Read the sentences about pizza places. There are eight mistakes. The first mistake is already corrected. Find and correct seven more.

there
1. Is ~~they~~ a pizza place near you?

2. There not are any pizza places on my street. There is one on the next street and four

   in my town.

3. There be pizza places at almost every mall in the United States. The pizzas come in all shapes and sizes.

4. Are traditional pizzas with mushrooms, pepperoni, and broccoli.

5. There is also pizzas with curry, fish, and coconut.

6. In the United States, they are over 70,000 pizza places. There sell lots of pizzas.

7. Pizzas are popular with everyone. There are popular with both young and old people.

STEP 4   COMMUNICATION PRACTICE

EXERCISE 9 LISTENING

▶11|04 **A** Listen to the conversation. Then choose the correct answer to each question.

1. Where's the mall?
   a. two miles north   **b.** two miles south   **c.** two miles west

2. How are the prices at the mall?
   a. Everything is expensive.   **b.** Everything is inexpensive.   **c.** They vary by store.

3. Is there an Italian restaurant?
   a. Yes, there is.   **b.** No, there isn't.   **c.** Maybe.

4. Where's the food court?
   a. on the second level   **b.** on the third level   **c.** on the ground level

5. Why is there traffic on the drive to the mall?
   a. People are walking in the road.   **b.** There's road construction.   **c.** There's an accident.

B Work with a partner. Use the list below to ask questions about the mall in the listening. Your partner answers them.

EXAMPLE: A: Is there a department store at the mall?
          B: Yes, there is. There are two department stores.

• a department store   • parking spaces
• a movie theater   • good prices
• places to eat   • a place to buy towels

EXERCISE 10 HOW ARE THEY DIFFERENT?

GAME Work with a partner. Find ten differences between Picture A and Picture B.

EXAMPLE: In Picture A, there's a shoe repair shop between the bakery and the pizza place.
In Picture B, there isn't a shoe repair shop between the bakery and the pizza
place. The shoe repair shop is between the pizza place and the flower shop.

Picture A

Picture B

EXERCISE 11 GREAT PLACES TO SHOP

Ⓐ DISCUSSION Work in groups. Talk about good places to shop in your area or online.

EXAMPLE: **A:** There's a great place to get running shoes on 3rd Street.
   B: Where on 3rd Street?
   A: It's between Elm and Oak. It's next to the bank.
   C: How are the prices?
   A: Not bad.

Ⓑ Tell the class about four places your group likes to shop. Use *there is* or *there are* in your report.

EXERCISE 12 TIC TAC TOE

GAME Walk around the class. Use the phrases in the boxes to ask your classmates questions. Begin with *Is there* or *Are there any*. If a student answers "yes," write his or her name in the box. The first person to have three names across, down, or diagonally calls out "Tic Tac Toe."

EXAMPLE: **ALI:** Is there a big mall near your home?
   BORIS: Yes, there is. It's on Glendale Avenue. *(Ali writes Boris's name in the box.)*

a big mall near your home[1]	a bakery near your home	shops on your street
a park near your home	two or more credit cards in your purse or pocket	a pet in your home
a pizza place near your home	a bus stop near your home	flowers in your home

---

1 *near your home:* you can walk there in ten minutes or less

FROM GRAMMAR TO WRITING

A | BEFORE YOU WRITE
Read about a store called "Village Gifts." Underline *there's*, *there are*, and *there aren't*. Then take notes in the chart below about a store that you like to shop at and why. Work with a partner. Tell your partner about the place you shop.

There's a small store near my home. It's called "Village Gifts." It's on a street with two other small shops. The owners are a husband and wife. Their gifts include unusual crafts from all over the world. There are some great things to buy—colorful pottery from Mexico, beautiful jewelry from Thailand, traditional rugs from China, and baskets from Jamaica. The owners love the things they sell. There's a story behind every item. That's why I like to shop there. There aren't many shops like that.

My Store

B | WRITE Write a paragraph about a place you like to shop. Give reasons why you like to shop there. Use the paragraph in A and your chart. Use *there is* and *there are*.

C | CHECK YOUR WORK Read your paragraph in B. Underline *there is* and *there are*. Use the Editing Checklist to check your work.

Editing Checklist

Did you . . . ?
- [ ] use *there is* for singular nouns and *there are* for plural nouns
- [ ] check your spelling

D | REVISE YOUR WORK Read your paragraph again. Can you improve your writing? Make changes if necessary.

UNIT 11 REVIEW

Test yourself on the grammar of the unit.

Ⓐ Complete the sentences with *There's*, *There are*, *There isn't*, or *There aren't*.

1. _____ any restrooms on this level, but there's one on the next level.

2. _____ a great bakery on Elm Street. It sells delicious cakes and cookies.

3. _____ three Mexican restaurants on West Street. They're all very good.

4. Sorry. _____ a pool in this hotel, but there's a fitness center.

5. _____ a mouse in the corner. Let's get out of here. I don't like mice.

6. _____ two big malls in that town. I often shop in them.

Ⓑ Circle the correct words to complete the *yes/no* questions and short answers.

1. A: Are there / Are they any soda machines in the building?

   B: Yes, there are / they are.

2. A: Is it / Is she the teacher?

   B: Yes, she's / she is.

3. A: Are there / Are they new students?

   B: No, they aren't / she isn't.

4: A: Are there / Is there a men's room on this floor?

   B: No, they aren't / there isn't.

Ⓒ Complete the sentences with *There's*, *There are*, *She's*, *It's*, or *They're*.

1. _____ a new pizza place on Elm Street. _____ next to the post office.

2. _____ a lot of people outside the pizza place. _____ in a long line.

3. _____ a great pizza chef there. _____ funny, and her pizzas are delicious.

Ⓓ Correct the paragraph. There are four mistakes.

Visit the new Shopper's Mall on Route 290. There's over 100 stores. There a movie

theater, and they are ten great places to eat. Come early. Every morning at 10:30, there are

a free show for children. The mall is three miles from the Tappan Bridge on Route 290.

Check your answers on page 446.

Possessive Nouns and Adjectives; Pronouns; Questions with *Whose*
POSSESSIONS

OUTCOMES
- Talk about possessions
- Recognize details in a conversation transcript
- Recognize details in a conversation about possessions
- Ask and answer questions about objects and describe them in detail
- Write a paragraph about people in your family

STEP 1   GRAMMAR IN CONTEXT

BEFORE YOU READ

Work with a partner. Answer the questions.

1. Is your handwriting neat? Is it difficult to read?

2. Look at Michelle and Rick's handwriting. Whose handwriting is neat? Whose is messy?

My name is Michelle Young.

READ

▶12|01 Read this conversation between a teacher and her students.

Whose Composition Is This?

TEACHER: Whose composition is this?

BORIS: Is it a good paper?

TEACHER: It's excellent.

BORIS: It's my composition.

YOLANDA: No, that's not your handwriting. It's Kim's composition. Her name is right there. She's absent today.

TEACHER: Thanks, Yolanda. Whose paper is *this*?

BORIS: Is it a good paper?

TEACHER: It's OK.

BORIS: Then it's mine.

JUAN: It's not yours. It's mine. See, my name is on the back.

TEACHER: You're right, Juan. I recognize your handwriting. Here, Boris. *This* is your composition.

BORIS: Is it a good paper?

TEACHER: It needs some work.

BORIS: I don't think it's mine.

TEACHER: Uh . . . I think it is yours. All the other compositions have a name on them.

AFTER YOU READ

A VOCABULARY **Complete the sentences with the words from the box.**

| back | composition | excellent | grade | recognize |

1. He has a new hairstyle and is wearing a new suit. It's hard to _____ him.

2. We had to write a _____ about a favorite childhood possession. Mine was about my blue blanket.

3. Are the answers in the _____ of the book?

4. What was your _____ in English? Mine was an A+.

5. Her writing is _____. It is clear, organized, and interesting.

B COMPREHENSION **Write short answers to the following questions.**

1. Whose composition is very good? _____

2. Who's absent? _____

3. Whose composition has a name on the back? _____

4. Whose composition needs work? _____

C DISCUSSION **Work with a partner. Compare your answers in B. Then look at the compositions below. Which composition is Kim's, Juan's, and Boris's? Explain your answers.**

1. _____   2. _____   3. _____

POSSESSIVES; PRONOUNS; QUESTIONS WITH *WHOSE*

Possessive Nouns

Singular Nouns	Plural Nouns
John's last name is Tamez. **Russ's** last name is Stram.	The **girls'** gym is on this floor.
My **mother's** name is Rita. The **woman's** name is Carmen.	My **parents'** car is in the garage. The **women's** restroom is on the first floor.

Subject Pronoun	Possessive Adjective	Possessive Pronoun	
I	**my**	**mine**	That is **my** book. That book is **mine**.
You	**your**	**yours**	Do you have **your** key? Do you have **yours**?
He	**his**	**his**	This is **his** car. This car is **his**.
She	**her**	**hers**	That's **her** house. That house is **hers**.
It	**its**		Look at that bird. **Its** feathers are red and gold.
We	**our**	**ours**	We lost **our** notes. We lost **ours**.
They	**their**	**theirs**	They can't find **their** tickets. They can't find **theirs**.

	Object Pronoun (Singular)
	me.
	you.
Raul likes	**him**.
	her.
	it.

	Object Pronoun (Plural)
	us.
Sarah knows	**you**.
	them.

Questions with *Whose*

Questions	Answers
Whose book report is long?	Carmen**'s**. Carmen**'s** book report is long.
Whose eyes are green?	Igor**'s**. Igor**'s** eyes are green.
Whose compositions are finished?	Yoko**'s** and Kaori**'s**. Yoko**'s** and Kaori**'s** compositions.

GRAMMAR NOTES

1 Possessive Nouns and Possessive Adjectives

Possessive nouns and possessive adjectives show that something belongs to someone.

• a possessive noun	This is **Kim's** car. *(the car belongs to Kim)*
• a possessive adjective	It is **her** car.

2 Possessive Nouns

We use **an apostrophe** (') to show possession.	
Add an apostrophe (') + *s* to a **singular noun**.	That's **Juan's** composition.
Add an apostrophe (') to a **plural noun** ending in -*s*.	My **parents'** home is near my home.
Add an apostrophe (') + *s* to an **irregular plural noun**.	The **women's** restroom is on the first floor.
BE CAREFUL! Remember to say or write the *'s* ending on possessive nouns.	That's Maria's book. **NOT** That's ~~Maria~~ book.
BE CAREFUL! A noun + apostrophe (') + *s* may also be a contraction of a noun + *is* in conversation and informal writing.	**Anna's** late. *(= Anna **is** late.)*

3 Possessive Adjectives

A **noun** follows a possessive adjective.	**His** *sister* is in Busan.
Possessive adjectives replace **possessive nouns**.	A: Where's your *father's* sister? B: **His** sister is in Busan. A: Where's your *mother's* sister? B: **Her** sister is in Seoul.
BE CAREFUL! Possessive adjectives agree with the nouns they replace.	A: Where's your *father's* sister? B: **His** sister is in Busan. **NOT** ~~Her~~ sister is in Busan. *(Sister is feminine, but the possessive adjective agrees with the noun it replaces—father—who is masculine.)*
BE CAREFUL! Do not confuse *its* and *it's*. **Its** is a possessive adjective; *it's* = *it is*.	This is my turtle. **Its** name is Tubby. **It's** a hot day.

4 Possessive Pronouns

A **possessive pronoun** can replace a **possessive adjective** and **noun**.	This isn't *my umbrella*. **Mine** is blue. *(My umbrella is blue.)*
BE CAREFUL! A noun never follows a possessive pronoun.	This is my hat. This is **mine**. **NOT** This is ~~mine~~ hat.

5 *Whose*

Use **whose** to ask questions about possessions.	A: **Whose** car is that?
We often answer questions with *whose* with a possessive noun, a possessive adjective + a noun, or a possessive pronoun.	B: It's **Kim's** car. **or** It's **her** car. **or** It's **hers**.
BE CAREFUL! *Who's* sounds like *whose*, but it is short for *Who is*.	**Whose** book is this? **NOT** ~~Who's~~ book is this?

6 Subject Pronouns and Object Pronouns

Remember that all sentences must have **a subject + a verb**. (See Unit 1.)	**Kim works.** *(Kim = subject; works = verb)*
A sentence can also have **a subject + a verb + an object**.	SUBJECT NOUN VERB OBJECT NOUN **Kim** **loves** **Ron.**
We can replace a subject noun with a subject pronoun. We can replace an object noun with an object pronoun.	SUBJECT PRONOUN OBJECT PRONOUN **She** loves **him.** *(She replaces Kim and him replaces Ron)*

REFERENCE NOTES

For more about **irregular plural nouns**, see Appendix 9 on page 434.

EXERCISE 1 DISCOVER THE GRAMMAR

GRAMMAR NOTES 1–6 Read the conversation. Then look at the words in bold and put them into the chart below. The first one in each category is done for you.

Possessive Nouns	Possessive Pronouns	Possessive Adjectives	Object Pronouns
Marco's	mine	your	it

BEN: Whose book is on the table next to the printer? Is it **Marco's** book?

LI: No, it's **mine**.

BEN: Is that **your** translator, too?

LI: No, it's **Marco's** translator. **Mine** is in **my** backpack. **His** is over there. He always uses **it** in class.

BEN: Where are the workbooks?

LI: I put **them** on the bookshelves over there.

BEN: I always see **you** and Marco together. Are you friends outside of class?

LI: **Marco's** mother and **my** mother are sisters. Marco and I are cousins. We're friends, too.

EXERCISE 2 POSSESSIVE NOUNS

A GRAMMAR NOTES 1–3

Read about the Zhang family. Underline the possessive nouns in the reading.

This is the Zhang family. The older man is Lao Zhang. Lao's wife is Feng. They have two daughters, Hua and Mei. Hua's husband is Gang. They have a son, Bao. Mei's husband is Jinsong. They have a daughter, Ting.

B Complete the sentences. Circle the correct answers.

1. Ting's mothers / mother's mother is Ting's grandmother / grandmother's.

2. Hua's sister / sister's daughter is Hua's / Hua niece.

3. Gang's wife / wife's sister is his / her sister-in-law.

4. Bao's uncle / uncle's apartment is in Shanghai.

5. Bao and Ting are cousins / cousin's. Their mothers / mother's are sisters / sister's.

6. Lao Zhang is the families / family's oldest member.

EXERCISE 3 POSSESSIVE ADJECTIVES

GRAMMAR NOTES 1, 3   Complete the sentences. Use possessive adjectives.

1. My sister studies in Toronto. _____*Her*_____ school is on Victoria Street.

2. She goes to Edgewood University. She likes _____ classes.

3. Her husband's parents work at the United Nations. _____ jobs are interesting.
   _____ mother is a translator, and _____ father is an interpreter.

4. Right now my brother is in Peru. _____ wife is in Belize, and _____
   children are in the United States with their grandparents.

5. The children have a rabbit. _____ fur is soft.

6. Does your brother like _____ job? Does he meet interesting people?

7. Do you like _____ classes? Are they helpful? Are your classmates friendly?

8. Does your grandmother like _____ new apartment? Is she happy there?

EXERCISE 4 POSSESSIVE PRONOUNS

GRAMMAR NOTES 1, 3–4   Replace the underlined words with possessive pronouns.

1. A: Is that your notebook?
                    mine
   B: No, it's not ~~my notebook~~. It's his notebook. My notebook is in my book bag.
                    a.   b.   c.

2. A: Is this their house?

   B: No. Their house is in back of the library.
          a.

   A: Whose house is this?

   B: It's our house.
          b.

3. A: Are those your sunglasses?

　　B: No, they're <u>her sunglasses</u>. <u>My sunglasses</u> are in my bag.
　　　　　　　　　 a.　　　　　　　**b.**

4. A: Is that Jaguar your uncle's car?

　　B: No. <u>My uncle's car</u> is the Ford. That's his wife's car. <u>Her car</u> is the Jaguar.
　　　　　 a.　　　　　　　　　　　　　　　　　　　　　　**b.**

EXERCISE 5 POSSESSIVE ADJECTIVES AND POSSESSIVE PRONOUNS

GRAMMAR NOTES 1, 3–6 **Complete the conversations. Circle the correct answers.**

1. A: I think you have my umbrella.

　　B: No. This is ⃝my / mine umbrella. <u>You / Yours</u> is over there. It's next to <u>her / hers</u>
　　　　　　　　　　 a.　　　　　　　　 **b.**　　　　　　　　　　　　　 **c.**
　　electronic dictionary.

2. A: Whose gloves are these? Yours or Julie's?

　　B: They're <u>her / hers</u>. <u>My / Mine</u> are wool.
　　　　　　　 a.　　　　 **b.**

3. A: Where is <u>their / theirs</u> car?
　　　　　　　　　　 a.

　　B: <u>Their / Theirs</u> car is in the garage.
　　　　 b.

　　A: Is <u>your / yours</u> there, too?
　　　　　 c.

　　B: No. <u>Our / Ours</u> is on the street.
　　　　　 d.

EXERCISE 6 SUBJECT AND OBJECT PRONOUNS, POSSESSIVES

GRAMMAR NOTES 1, 3–6 **Complete the sentences. Circle the correct answers.**

1. It's <u>I / my / me / ⃝mine</u>. Please give it to <u>I / my / me / mine</u>.
　　　　　　　　 a.　　　　　　　　　　　　　　 **b.**
　<u>I / My / Me / Mine</u> need it.
　　　 c.

2. I don't think <u>he / him / his</u> is on the train. I don't see <u>he / him / his</u>.
　　　　　　　　 a.　　　　　　　　　　　　　　 **b.**

3. Our family is from Edmonton. <u>They / Their / Theirs / Them</u> family is from
　　　　　　　　　　　　　　　　　　 a.
　Vancouver, but <u>they / their / theirs / them</u> live in Edmonton now. We live next door
　　　　　　　　　 b.
　to <u>they / their / theirs / them</u>.
　　　 c.

142   Unit 12

EXERCISE 7 PRONOUNS AND POSSESSIVE ADJECTIVES

GRAMMAR NOTES 3–6 Read and complete the article with the correct subject pronoun, object pronoun, possessive pronoun, or possessive adjective.

International Language Institute
NEWSLETTER

GET TO KNOW NEW STUDENTS AT THE ILI

New Student of the Month

Sandra Gomes

My name is Sandra Gomes. ____I____ am from São Paulo,
                                   1.

Brazil. _____ am happy to be a student at the International
              2.

Language Institute. _____ is great to learn English and meet
                           3.

people from all over the world. _____ parents and brother
                                       4.

are in Brazil, but _____ sister is here with _____.
                         5.   6.

_____ share an apartment together. _____ is nice,
       7.   8.

but _____ is far from school. _____ each have a
         9.   10.

bedroom. _____ is bigger than _____. That's fine
                11.   12.

with _____ because _____ like small spaces.
            13.   14.

_____ spend a lot of time together in _____
       15.   16.

apartment. That's because _____ both have a TV, a
                                17.

computer, and a lot of friends who visit _____.
                                                18.

EXERCISE 8 SPELLING OF POSSESSIVE NOUNS

🔘12|02 GRAMMAR NOTES 2, 6 Listen to the sentences. For each sentence, circle the word you hear.

1. Maria   (Maria's)   Marias

2. Maria   Maria's   Marias

3. Maria   Maria's   Marias

4. partner   partner's   partners

5. partner   partner's   partners

6. partner   partner's   partners

EXERCISE 9 EDITING

GRAMMAR NOTES 1–6 Correct the conversations. There are seven mistakes. The first mistake is already corrected. Find and correct six more.

1. A: Is that ~~you~~ *your* dictionary?

   B: No. It's his dictionary.

   A: Who's?

   B: Dans.

   A: That's not his's. It's Juan's.

2. A: Is Maria sister here?

   B: No, she's not.

   A: Is Maria here?

   B: No, but his brother is.

   A: Where is Maria?

   B: I think she's with his sister.

STEP 4   COMMUNICATION PRACTICE

EXERCISE 10 LISTENING

▶12|03 Ⓐ Listen to the conversation. What are Boris and Jasmine talking about? Circle the correct letter.

   a. bikes   **b.** baskets   **c.** sales

▶12|03 Ⓑ Listen again. Work with a partner. Write the name of the owner of each bicycle on the lines next to the bicycles. Use the names from the box. Then explain your answers.

| Amy | Johnny |
| Jasmine | Roger and Ted |

1. _Amy_____

2. _____

3. _____

4. _____

Ⓒ Work with a partner. Take turns. Ask and questions with *whose* about the bikes.

EXAMPLE: A: Whose bike has a basket?
         B: Amy's bike has a basket.

EXERCISE 11 WHOSE BIRTHDAY IS IN DECEMBER?

A Q & A **Prepare to ask and answer questions with your classmates. Complete the questions with *Whose* or *Who's*.**

1. _____Whose_____ birthday is in December?

2. _____Who's_____ good in art?

3. _____ name means something?

4. _____ a good athlete?

5. _____ eyes aren't dark brown?

6. _____ a good cook?

7. _____ first name has more than eight letters?

8. _____ birthday is in the summer?

9. _____ a good dancer?

10. _____ handwriting is beautiful?

B **Walk around the room. Ask your classmates *yes/no* questions about the things in A. Take notes.**

EXAMPLE: A: Juan, is your birthday in December?
B: No, it's not. Is yours?
A: Yes, it is.

C **Ask your classmates the questions in A. Your classmates look at their notes to find the answer.**

EXAMPLE: A: Whose birthday is in December?
B: Maria's birthday is in December.

EXERCISE 12 WHOSE IS IT?

GAME **Work in a large group. Each student in the group puts something that belongs to him or her in a bag. The group then passes the bag to another group. Students in the second group talk about each object. They guess the owner and give a reason why.**

EXAMPLE: A: OK. This is a keychain. Whose keychain is this?
B: I think it's Boris's keychain. There's a tennis racquet on the keychain, and Boris's passion is tennis.
C: Or Sukana's? She likes tennis, too.
D: It's a big keychain and Sukana has a big bag. Let's go with Sukana.
A: Our group thinks it's Sukana's keychain because the keychain has a tennis racket and Sukana likes tennis.

FROM GRAMMAR TO WRITING

A BEFORE YOU WRITE   Read about a student's family. On a separate piece of paper, draw each member of the family. Work with a partner. Compare your drawings. Then draw a picture of your own family. Tell your partner about each member of your family.

This is Jorge. He's on the left. Jorge is my sister's husband. He's twenty-five years old and works for a big company. He's a web architect. He enjoys his job. His passion is computers. That's why he has a computer in his hand.

Dahlia is next to Jorge. Dahlia is my sister and Jorge's wife. She's a jewelry designer. She's twenty-two years old. Her passion is art and jewelry. Her T-shirt and her necklace are her designs.

My mom is next to my sister. She's fifty-three years old. She's a kindergarten teacher. She loves music and has a beautiful voice.

My dad is on the right. He has a band. He's the leader. His passion is music, too. He plays a lot of instruments. He's very talented. He's also a great dad.

B WRITE   Write about the people in your family. Use the paragraphs in A and your drawings to help you. Use pronouns and possessive adjectives.

C CHECK YOUR WORK   Read your description in B. Underline the pronouns and possessive adjectives. Then use the Editing Checklist to check your work.

Editing Checklist

Did you . . . ?

- [ ] use an apostrophe with possessive nouns
- [ ] follow all possessive adjectives with a noun
- [ ] use correct agreement with possessive adjectives
- [ ] check your spelling

D REVISE YOUR WORK   Read your descriptions of your family again. Can you improve your writing? Make changes if necessary.

UNIT 12 REVIEW

Test yourself on the grammar of the unit.

Ⓐ Cross out the underlined words. Replace them with *His, Her, Its,* or *Their*.

1. My parents' car is big.

2. My brother's daughter is a history teacher.

3. That bird is injured. That bird's wing is broken.

4. The students' tests are on the teacher's desk.

5. Our aunt's store is on Main Street.

Ⓑ Complete the conversations. Circle the correct answers.

1. A: You need an umbrella. Take me / mine.

   B: I don't want to use your / yours.

   A: It's OK. I have you / your rain hat.

2. A: Who's / Whose dictionary is on the floor?

   B: It's Ali / Ali's.

Ⓒ Complete the sentences with *Who's* or *Whose*.

1. _____ test is this?

2. _____ compositions are on the floor?

3. _____ in level 3?

4. _____ family lives in the countryside?

5. _____ the director of your school?

Ⓓ Correct the conversation. There are five mistakes.

A: Who's bag is that on the floor?

B: I think it's Maria.

A: No. Her bag is on her arm.

B: Well, it's not mine bag. Maybe it's Rita.

A: Rita, is that yours bag?

Now check your answers on page 447.

Modals: Ability and Permission

PART 5

OUTCOMES

- Express ability in the present and past
- Recognize true and false statements about information in a short article
- Recognize main ideas and details in a conversation about animals
- Discuss abilities of various animals
- Write a paragraph about a pet

OUTCOMES

- Ask, give, and deny permission, using *can* and *may*
- Put items from an article in correct categories
- Recognize important details in a conversation about food allergies
- Talk about rules and regulations
- Ask and answer questions about diets and healthy habits
- Write a note that explains what a person can and cannot eat

Ability: *Can* or *Could*

ANIMALS AND THEIR ABILITIES

OUTCOMES
- Express ability in the present and past
- Recognize true and false statements about information in a short article
- Recognize main ideas and details in a conversation about animals
- Discuss abilities of various animals
- Write a paragraph about a pet

STEP 1   GRAMMAR IN CONTEXT

BEFORE YOU READ

Work with a partner. Answer the questions.

1. Do you have a pet, for example a dog, a cat, or a bird? Do you know someone who has a pet? What kind? What special things can the pet do?

2. Look at the photo. What do you know about parrots?

READ

▶ 13|01 Read this article about an amazing parrot.

A Genius Parrot

Everyone knows parrots can talk. By "talk," we mean they can repeat words. Most parrots can't really express ideas. N'kisi is different. N'kisi is an African grey parrot. He can say almost 1,000 words. He can use basic grammar. He can talk about the present, past, and future. When he doesn't know a form, he can invent one. For example, he used the word "flied," not "flew," for the past tense of the verb "fly."

N'kisi lives in New York City with his owner, Aimee Morgana. He couldn't talk much at first. At first, he could only say a few words. But Aimee was a great teacher, and N'kisi was a good student. Now N'kisi talks to anyone near him.

Donald Broom, a professor of Veterinary Medicine at the University of Cambridge, is not surprised. He says that parrots can think at high levels. In that way, they are like apes and chimpanzees.

Les Rance of the Parrot Society says, "Most African greys are intelligent. They can learn to do easy puzzles. They can say 'good night' when you turn the lights off at night. They can say 'good-bye' when you put a coat on. But N'kisi can do many more things. N'kisi is an amazing bird. He's not just smart. He's a genius."

AFTER YOU READ

A VOCABULARY **Complete the sentences with the words from the box. Use the correct form.**

| genius | intelligent | invent | professor | surprised |

1. Monkeys and dolphins are very _____ animals. They can learn many things.

2. Many people are _____ by the abilities of African grey parrots. They can do all sorts of amazing things.

3. Mozart was a(n) _____. He could write great music at the age of six.

4. He's a very good _____. You can learn a lot in his class.

5. We need to _____ a way you can learn languages while you sleep.

B COMPREHENSION **Read the statements. Check (✓) True, False, or No Information.**

	True	False	No Information
1. N'kisi can say more than 1,100 words.	☐	☐	☐
2. N'kisi can't use basic grammar.	☐	☐	☐
3. N'kisi can talk about the past and the future.	☐	☐	☐
4. N'kisi can understand Italian.	☐	☐	☐
5. Parrots can't think at high levels.	☐	☐	☐
6. N'kisi could only say a few words at first.	☐	☐	☐

C DISCUSSION **Work with a partner. Say two things N'kisi can do. Say two things most African grey parrots can do.**

CAN / CAN'T FOR ABILITY AND POSSIBILITY; *COULD* FOR PAST ABILITY

Affirmative Statements

Subject	Can/Could	Base Form of Verb
I You* He We	can could	talk.

* *You* can be singular or plural.

Negative Statements

Subject	Can't/Couldn't	Base Form of Verb
She It They	can't/cannot couldn't/could not	talk.

Yes/No Questions

Can/Could	Subject	Base Form of Verb
Can	you	understand?
Could		

Short Answers

Affirmative	Negative
Yes, I can.	No, I can't.
Yes, we could.	No, we couldn't.

GRAMMAR NOTES

1 *Can*: Meaning and Form

Can expresses **present ability** or **possibility**. *Can* comes before the verb. The verb is always in the base form.	He **can say** 950 words. *(ability)* We **can teach** your bird to talk. *(possibility)*

2 *Can*: Negative

The **negative** of *can* is *can't*.	I **can't** understand you.
USAGE NOTE *Cannot* is a form of the negative. It is not very common.	I **cannot** understand you.

3 *Can*: Yes/No Questions and Answers

Change the order of the subject and *can* to turn a statement into a *yes/no* question.	**He can** speak about the past. **Can he** speak about the past?
Use **short answers** for a *yes/no* question with *can*.	**Yes, he can.**

4 *Could*: Meaning and Forms

Could expresses **past ability**.	I **could** run fast in high school.
Could not is the full negative form. The more common form is the contraction, *couldn't*.	I **could not** drive five years ago. I **couldn't** drive five years ago.

5 Could: Yes/No Questions and Answers

Change the order of the subject and *could* to turn a statement into a *yes/no* question.	**You could** speak English last year. **Could you** speak English last year?
Use **short answers** for a *yes/no* question with *could*.	**No, I couldn't.**

PRONUNCIATION NOTE

▶13|02 **Stress with *Can* and *Can't***

When *can* comes before a base form of the verb, we usually pronounce it /kən/ and stress the verb.	We can **DANCE**.
When *can't* comes before a base form of the verb, we usually pronounce it /kaent/ and stress both *can't* and the verb.	We **CAN'T DANCE**.

STEP 3   FOCUSED PRACTICE

EXERCISE 1 DISCOVER THE GRAMMAR

GRAMMAR NOTES 1–2, 4 Read the sentences in columns A and B. Underline *can*, *can't*, *could*, and *couldn't*. Circle the base form of the verbs. Then match each sentence in column A with the sentence that follows it in column B.

Column A

_e_ **1.** N'kisi can (invent) new words.

____ **2.** A camel can live up to six months without water.

____ **3.** Cheetahs can go from 0 to 96 km/h in three seconds.

____ **4.** At first, N'kisi couldn't say much.

____ **5.** Dogs can't talk about their love.

____ **6.** The bird couldn't fly south for the winter.

Column B

a. He could only say a few words.

b. They're very fast.

c. It was hurt.

d. They can show their feelings in other ways.

e. He's a smart bird.

g. A human can only go up to five days.

EXERCISE 2 *CAN* AND *CAN'T*

GRAMMAR NOTES 1–2 Complete the sentences with *can* or *can't* and the verbs in parentheses.

1. Many parrots _____*can learn*_____ to speak. My parrot _____,
   (learn)   (say)
   "You're a genius."

2. My dog _____, but he _____ me my shoes. I'm
            (sit)   (bring)
   trying to teach him to bring things to me.

3. My cat _____ mice. He's very good at that. Her cat
            (catch)

   _____ mice. He just sits and watches them.
            (catch)

4. Her dog _____ Spanish and English. She speaks to her dog in
             (understand)
   English, and her husband speaks to the dog in Spanish.

5. Dolphins _____ people in trouble. They are smart and show feelings.
              (help)

EXERCISE 3
YES/NO QUESTIONS
AND ANSWERS

Ⓐ GRAMMAR NOTE 3
Use *can* and the words
in parentheses to write
yes/no questions. Then
guess the answer.

1. (an elephant / swim)   *Can an elephant swim? Yes, it can.* _____

2. (elephants / jump)   _____

3. (a bear / climb a tree)   _____

4. (a chimpanzee / use tools)   _____

5. (chimpanzees / invent games) _____

6. (a penguin / fly)   _____

Ⓑ Check your answers on page 453. Correct any incorrect answers.

EXERCISE 4 PRESENT AND PAST ABILITIES

GRAMMAR NOTES 1, 4–5 Complete the sentences with *can*, *could*, or *couldn't* and the verbs in parentheses.

1. Before N'kisi, there was a world famous African grey called Alex. Alex

    _____could do_____ many amazing things. He _____ up to six
        a. (do)   **b.** (count)

    things in a group. He _____ colors and materials. Before he died, he
                          c. (name)

    _____ the sounds of a few letters.
        d. (read)

        Today you _____ about Alex and his trainer, Dr. Irene
                   e. (read)

    Pepperberg, in a book called *Alex and Me*. You _____ Alex in a DVD
                          f. (see)

    called *Life with Alex*.

2. Some gorillas are smart. Michael was a smart gorilla. He _____ sign
                          a. (use)

    language. He _____ 600 different gestures. You
              b. (make)

    _____ about Michael on the Internet.
        c. (learn)

3. I had two dogs. My dog Charlie was a good watchdog, but he _____
                          a. (do)

    any tricks. My dog Spot was not a good watchdog, but he _____ me
                          b. (bring)

    my slippers.

EXERCISE 5 STRESS WITH *CAN* AND *CAN'T*

▶13|03 PRONUNCIATION NOTE Listen and complete the sentences with *can* or *can't* and the verbs.

1. A zebra _____*can see*_____ the color blue, but it _____ the color orange.

2. You _____ a cow upstairs, but you _____ a cow downstairs.

3. Dolphins _____ with their eyes open, but they _____ on dry land.

4. A pet cat _____ a black bear, but a cat _____ a jaguar.

5. Dogs _____ feelings, but they _____ them.

6. Elephants _____ their trunks to spray water, but they

    _____ .

EXERCISE 6 EDITING

GRAMMAR NOTES 1–6 **Read the conversation. There are seven mistakes. The first mistake is already corrected. Find and correct six more. Add *can* to fix one mistake.**

MARICEL: Can you ~~coming~~ ^{come} to my party? It's next Saturday night. You can to meet my

new dog.

BELLA: Yes, I'd love to. How I get to your home?

MARICEL: You can to take the train or a taxi.

BELLA: Can you meet me at the train station?

MARICEL: I'm sorry. I can't. I no can drive. Maybe Bob can meets you. He has a car, and

he can to drive.

STEP 4   COMMUNICATION PRACTICE

EXERCISE 7 LISTENING

▶13|04 **A Listen to a conversation about dolphins. Check (✓) three things the dolphins in Florida could do.**

☐ catch a ball   ☐ paint pictures   ☐ breathe under water

☑ play basketball   ☐ live on land   ☐ talk

▶13|04 **B Listen again to the conversation. Circle the correct answers.**

1. What can all the dolphins at a marine institute in Mississippi do?
   a. play with a piece of paper   b. get fish for a piece of paper

2. What does Kelly do with her paper?
   a. hides it under a rock   b. eats it

3. Why does Kelly tear her piece of paper?
   a. to play a game with her trainer   b. to get more fish from her trainer

C Work with a partner. Ask *yes/no* questions with *can* and *could* about the dolphins in Florida and about Kelly.

EXAMPLES: A: Could the Florida dolphins play basketball?
           B: Yes, they could play basketball.

           A: Can Kelly plan for the future?
           B: Yes, she can.

EXERCISE 8 FACTS ABOUT ANIMALS

A GAME Work in a group. Discuss which animal matches the facts below. Write the letter of your guess on the line next to the statements about the animal.

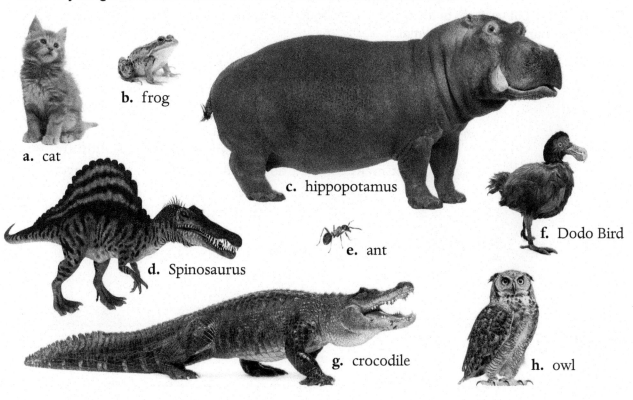

a. cat

b. frog

c. hippopotamus

d. Spinosaurus

e. ant

f. Dodo Bird

g. crocodile

h. owl

_____ **1.** This animal can't turn its head, but it can see almost 360 degrees because its eyes are on the top and sides of its head.

> EXAMPLE: **A:** This animal can't turn its head, but it can see almost 360 degrees around itself. What do you think? Is it the owl?
> **B:** I don't think owls can see all around. I think it's the . . .

_____ **2.** This huge animal spends sixteen hours a day in water. It can make its own sunscreen.

_____ **3.** This animal lived around ninety-five million years ago. Scientists believed this animal could walk on two legs. They also believed it could swim.

_____ **4.** This animal is active at night and can turn its head 270 degrees, but it can't see things close to its eyes.

_____ **5.** This busy little animal can carry many times its weight.

_____ **6.** This animal lived on an island near Madagascar. It was a bird, but it couldn't fly. It was around until about 330 years ago.

_____ **7.** This animal can jump five times its height. It's a very popular pet.

_____ **8.** This animal can swallow stones. It can survive a long time without food. It has very sharp teeth.

B Check your answers on page 453.

A BEFORE YOU WRITE Read about a student's pet. Then complete the chart with information about your pet or a pet you know about. Work with a partner. Use the chart to tell your partner about the animal.

I have a beautiful parakeet. His feathers are bright green. His name is Chichi. He is two years old. He lives in a cage in my living room. Sometimes he flies around the room. Chichi can sing very beautifully. Chichi couldn't do anything when he was younger. But now he can sit on my finger and eat from my hand. He can't speak, but I'm happy about that. I tell him all my secrets, and he doesn't tell anyone. That's a wonderful quality. I love my Chichi.

	Student's Pet	My Pet
Kind of animal	bird/parakeet	
Description	green feathers	
Name	Chichi	
Age	two years old	
Home	cage	
Abilities	sit on finger/eat from hand	

B WRITE Write a paragraph about a pet. Use the paragraph in A and your chart. Use *can, can't, could,* or *couldn't.*

C CHECK YOUR WORK Read your paragraph in B. Underline *can, can't, could,* or *couldn't* and the verb that follows. Use the Editing Checklist to check your work.

Editing Checklist
Did you . . . ?
☐ follow *can, can't, could,* and *couldn't* with the base form of the verb
☐ use *can* for the present and *could* for the past
☐ check your spelling

D REVISE YOUR WORK Read your paragraph again. Can you improve your writing? Make changes if necessary.

UNIT 13 REVIEW

Test yourself on the grammar of the unit.

Ⓐ Complete the sentences with *can, could, can't,* **or** *couldn't* **and the verbs in parentheses.**

1. Last year, I _____ much English. Now I _____
   a. (understand)   b. (understand)
   a lot more.

2. Jill doesn't exercise these days, so she _____ fast. In high school, she
                                              a. (run)
   was fast. She _____ a mile in seven minutes.
                  b. (run)

3. I _____ five years ago. Now I have a driver's license, and I
      a. (drive)

   _____ well.
      b. (drive)

Ⓑ Complete the questions and answers. Use *can, could, can't,* **or** *couldn't.*

1. A: _____ you understand your dreams?

   B: Yes, I _____ .They're easy to understand.

2. A: _____ you write reports last year?

   B: No, I _____ , but now I can.

3. A: _____ Roger speak Korean?

   B: Yes, he _____ . He can speak other languages, too.

Ⓒ Write *yes/no* **questions. Put the words in parentheses in the correct order.**

1. _____ ?
   (your finger / sit / your bird / could / on)

2. _____ ?
   (anything / the parrot / say / can)

3. _____ ?
   (your shoe / bring you / your dog / could)

4. _____ ?
   (the past and the future / talk about / that bird / can)

Ⓓ Correct the conversation. There are four mistakes.

A: Can you to get online?

B: No, I can't. I no could get online last night either.

A: My brother is good with computers. Maybe he can helps. I can to call him after work.

Check your answers on page 447.

UNIT

14

Permission: *Can* or *May*
SPECIAL DIETS

OUTCOMES
- Ask, give, and deny permission, using *can* and *may*
- Put items from an article in correct categories
- Recognize important details in a conversation about food allergies
- Talk about rules and regulations
- Ask and answer questions about diets and healthy habits
- Write a note that explains what a person can and cannot eat

STEP 1 **GRAMMAR IN CONTEXT**

BEFORE YOU READ

Work with a partner. Answer the questions.

1. Are there any foods that you don't eat? What foods?

2. Why don't you eat them?

READ

▶14|01   Read this article about vegetarians and vegans.

Vegetarians and Vegans

What do Confucius, Leonardo da Vinci, Leo Tolstoy, and Mahatma Gandhi have in common? They were all vegetarians. Vegetarians don't eat meat. But they were not vegans. Vegans don't eat meat, fish, eggs, and dairy products.

Are you thinking, "I could never be a vegan"? Well, there are many nutritious meals you can prepare and eat while following a vegan diet. Here is a menu for one day.

For breakfast, you can have oatmeal with fruit. You can't use regular milk in your cereal, but you can substitute soy milk for regular milk. For lunch, you can have a hummus and avocado sandwich and a salad. Cut up lettuce, carrots, and tomatoes. Add nuts and a dairy-free dressing. If you're thirsty, you can make a fruit smoothie. Put water or soy milk in a blender.[1] Then add bananas and strawberries. For dinner, you can prepare spinach lasagna. You may use tofu instead of cheese and soy milk instead of cream. Then follow any spinach lasagna recipe.

Most of us know why vegetarians don't eat meat—for health reasons, or because they don't want to kill an animal in order to eat it. But why can't vegans eat dairy products or eggs? Vegans say when farmers get milk, they hurt the cows. When farmers get eggs, they hurt the hens. Vegans believe that all animals feel pain, pleasure, and love. So they believe it's wrong to eat animals or do anything to hurt them.

---

1 *blender:* a machine that mixes food to make liquid

AFTER YOU READ

Ⓐ VOCABULARY Complete the sentences with the words from the box.

dairy	in common	nutritious	recipe	substitute

1. Schools are trying to give children _____ lunches. They want children to stay healthy and learn good eating habits.

2. He can't eat anything with milk in it. _____ products upset his stomach.

3. Can I have your mother's _____ for lasagna, or is it a secret?

4. We don't have any sugar at home. We can _____ maple syrup for sugar.

5. My best friend and I love the same sports, music, and movies. We have a lot

_____ .

Ⓑ COMPREHENSION In the chart below, check the foods that a vegan and a vegetarian can (✓) and can't (✗) eat.

	apple	cheese	chicken	chocolate	eggs	fish	french fries	hamburger	hummus	ice cream	oatmeal	soy milk
Vegan												
Vegetarian												

Ⓒ DISCUSSION Work with a partner. Compare your answers in B. Explain your answers.

CAN OR *MAY* FOR PERMISSION

Statements

Subject	Can / Can't May / May not	Base Form of Verb	
You	**can** **can't**	**use**	soy.
He	**may** **may not**	**eat**	eggs.

Yes / No Questions

Can / May	Subject	Base Form of Verb	
Can **May**	I	**have**	the recipe?

Answers

Yes, you can.
Yes, you may.
Sure.
Of course.
I'm sorry. It's not possible.

GRAMMAR NOTES

1 *Can* and *May*: Meaning and Form

Use *can* or *may* to **give permission**. ("It's OK to . . .")	
Can and *may* come **before the verb**. The verb is always in the base form.	You **can** *see* the doctor now. You **may** *eat* nuts.
When you don't give permission, use *can't* or *may not*.	She **can't** borrow my cookbook. I need it. You **may not** see the doctor without an appointment.
BE CAREFUL! There is no contraction for *may not*.	You **may not** see the doctor without an appointment. NOT You ~~mayn't~~ see the doctor without an appointment.
USAGE NOTE *Can* is much more common than *may*. We use *may* in formal situations.	You **can** eat your ice cream now. *(mother to child)* You **may** see the doctor now. *(nurse to patient)*

Use *Can I* or *May I* to **ask for permission**. *May* is more formal than *can*.

• *Can I . . .*	**Can I** come in? *(less formal)*
• *May I . . .*	**May I** come in? *(more formal)*

USAGE NOTE We often answer *yes/no* questions with a short affirmative response or a short apology and a reason.	**Yes, you can.** or **Yes, you may.** or **No, I'm sorry. The doctor is not ready for you.**
USAGE NOTE We often use *Can I* or *May I* + *help* to offer help to someone.	**Can I help you?** or **May I help you?**
When we answer, we usually thank someone or say *No thanks* and give a reason.	**Yes, please.** I'm looking for a vegan cookbook. or **No thanks. I don't need anything right now.**

STEP 3   FOCUSED PRACTICE

EXERCISE 1 DISCOVER THE GRAMMAR

GRAMMAR NOTES 1–2 Read the conversation between a patient and a nutritionist. Underline *can*, *can't*, *may*, or *may not* and circle the verbs they go with.

NUTRITIONIST: Can I (help) you?

PATIENT: Thanks. I have a few questions about the diet you gave me. First of all, can I eat meat?

NUTRITIONIST: Yes, you can, but you can only have boiled, grilled, or baked meat.

PATIENT: What about fried chicken? Can I have it? I love fried chicken.

NUTRITIONIST: Sorry. You may not have any fried food on this diet.

PATIENT: Can I eat nuts?

NUTRITIONIST: Yes, you may. But you can't have too many. And remember, there are a lot of things on this diet that you can eat. You may eat as many green vegetables as you want, and you can drink as much green tea as you want.

PATIENT: That sounds good.

NUTRITIONIST: If you have any more questions, you can call me weekdays between 11:00 and 1:00.

EXERCISE 2 STATEMENTS AND QUESTIONS WITH *CAN* AND *MAY*

Ⓐ GRAMMAR NOTES 1–2 Complete the conversations with *can* or *may* and the verbs from the box.

drive	eat	have	help	keep	look	~~return~~	see	take

Conversation 1 (Can)

DOCTOR: You're doing great.

PATIENT: I feel good too, Dr. Lam. When _____*can*_____ I _____*return*_____ to work?
1.

DOCTOR: Next week.

PATIENT: And when _____ I _____?
2.

DOCTOR: Wait another week. Take the train next week.

PATIENT: OK.

DOCTOR: But remember. Watch your diet. Don't eat heavy food and dessert.

PATIENT: _____ I _____ in restaurants?
3.

DOCTOR: Sure. Just watch what you order.

Conversation 2 (May)

RECEPTIONIST: _____ I _____ you?
4.

PATIENT: Thanks. I'd like to make an appointment with Ms. Stein.

RECEPTIONIST: She's free next Tuesday at 10:00. Here are some booklets about nutrition. You

_____ _____ them home and read them.
5.

PATIENT: Thanks. Do you want them back?

RECEPTIONIST: No. You _____ _____ them.
6.

Conversation 3 (Can)

SERVER: Your fish comes with a salad.

BOB: OK. _____ I _____ the dressing on the side?
7.

SERVER: Of course.

BOB: And _____ we _____ the dessert menu?
8.

BOB'S WIFE: Bob, you're on a diet! You can't have dessert.

BOB: But I _____ _____ at the desserts and dream about them.
9.

▶14|02 **Ⓑ LISTEN AND CHECK** Listen to the conversations and check your answers in A.

EXERCISE 3 ASKING PERMISSION WITH *CAN* AND *MAY*

A GRAMMAR NOTES 1–2 Complete the conversation. Write questions with *can* or *may*. Use the information in parentheses.

RECEPTIONIST: (May) _____ *May I help you?* _____

                                           1. (Do you need my help?)

NURAY: Yes, thanks. I'm Nuray Attaturk. I have an appointment with Dr. Lee for 2:00.

RECEPTIONIST: Hi, Ms. Attaturk. (May) _____

                                          2. (I want to see your health insurance card.)

(After Nuray sees Dr. Lee, he gives her a diet to follow.)

DR. LEE: OK, Nuray. Here's your diet. Any questions?

NURAY: (Can) _____

                                      3. (Is it OK to eat snacks?)

DR. LEE: Yes, but you can only have light snacks.

NURAY: (Can) _____

                                      4. (Is it OK to have ice cream?)

DR. LEE: No, you can't, but you can have low-fat yogurt instead.

NURAY: (May) _____

                                      5. (Is it OK to call you with questions?)

DR. LEE: Certainly. But don't worry. Everything is on these papers. Just read the diet and

          follow the directions. You'll feel better in no time.

NURAY: Thanks, Dr. Lee.

○14|03 **B** LISTEN AND CHECK Listen to the conversation and check your answers in A.

EXERCISE 4 EDITING

GRAMMAR NOTES 1–2 Correct the conversations. There are six mistakes. The first mistake is already corrected. Find and correct five more.

1. A: Can we ~~paid~~ *pay* later?

   B: Yes, you can pays half now and half next month.

2. A: May I speaks to the doctor?

   B: I'm sorry. He's with a patient now. Can you calls back later?

3. A: Can I to use salt?

   B: Yes, but not a lot.

4. A: Can I drink coffee or tea?

   B: You may drink tea, but you mayn't drink coffee.

EXERCISE 5 LISTENING

A You are going to listen to a conversation between a doctor and his patient, Sandra. Sandra has a food allergy. Before you listen, work with a partner and answer the questions.

1. Do you have any allergies? What are you allergic to?

2. Do you know people who are allergic to any of the following: cats, dogs, strawberries, soy, nuts, or wheat? Who?

3. What can happen to someone with an allergy?

▶14|04 **B** Listen to the conversation. Then listen again. Check (✓) the foods that Sandra can't eat.

☐ eggs ☑ pad thai ☐ peanuts ☐ wheat

☐ milk ☐ peanut butter ☐ walnuts

C Work with a partner. Talk about foods that Sandra's cousin can't eat.

EXAMPLE: **A:** Well, let's see. It says she can't eat wheat. So I guess she can't eat most kinds of bread.

B: Yes, and she probably can't eat . . .

EXERCISE 6 RULES IN A SCHOOL CAFETERIA

A DISCUSSION Work in groups. Prepare for a discussion in B. Make a list of rules for a school cafeteria for children between the ages of six and twelve. Write your list on the board. Use *can* and *can't*.

EXAMPLE: *You can't run in the cafeteria.*
You can bring a sandwich from home.

B Read your list to your other groups. Explain your rules.

EXAMPLE: **A:** You can't run in the cafeteria.
B: Why not?
A: Children can spill their food and make a mess.

EXERCISE 7 YOU CAN'T EAT PRETZELS AND CHIPS

ROLE PLAY Work with a partner. One of you is a patient. The other is a nutritionist. The patient needs a special diet. The nutritionist tells the patient what he or she can and can't eat.

EXAMPLE: A: Hello. How do you feel?

B: I feel good, but my blood pressure is high and I want to lose some weight. Can you give me a good diet?

A: Yes, of course. You can eat bread, but you can't eat pretzels and chips. They're very salty.

B: Can I have . . . ?

EXERCISE 8 PATIENT INFORMATION

INFORMATION GAP Work with a partner. Student A follows the instructions below. Student B will follow the instructions on page 456.

STUDENT A

- Read the information for Dr. Green's patients.

- Student B will ask you questions about this information. Answer Student B's questions. Use *can*, *may*, *can't*, or *may not* to answer the questions.

Green Clinic

PATIENT INFORMATION

Office Hours: Monday, Wednesday, and Friday between 8:00 and 4:00.

Calls: You can call the doctor weekdays between 11:00 and 12:00 at 344-3500.

Please note: Dr. Green does not answer calls evenings or weekends. In an emergency, call 344-3580.

Learn more:
- Attend free lectures on nutrition on the first Monday of every month.
- Join a support group. For more information, email nutrisupport@greenhealth.com.
- See a list of suggested meals at www.greenhealth.com.

Questions? Email Dr. Green at nutridr@greenhealth.com.

FROM GRAMMAR TO WRITING

A BEFORE YOU WRITE Work with a partner. Read the note from Ana to Maria and Maria's answer. Then discuss: When someone with a special diet visits you, what do you do?

Hi Maria,

My son Jorge would love to go to Rosa's pizza party on Saturday, but he can't eat dairy products. Please don't give him anything with milk or cheese in it. I can give him some food that he can eat at the party.

See you on Saturday,

Ana

Hi Ana,

I'm glad that Jorge can come to the party. I can give him pizza without cheese. My nephew can't eat dairy, either. They can share a cheese-less pizza.

See you Saturday.

Maria

B WRITE You or your son or daughter were invited to a party. You (or your child) would like to go, but can't eat the food. Write a note and then write the answer you would like to get. Use the notes in A and your ideas. Use *can* or *can't*.

C CHECK YOUR WORK Read your paragraph in B. Underline *can* and *can't*. Then use the Editing Checklist to check your work.

Editing Checklist
Did you...?
☐ use *can* for permission
☐ follow *can* or *can't* with the base form of the verb
☐ check your spelling

D REVISE YOUR WORK Read your paragraph again. Can you improve your writing? Make changes if necessary.

UNIT 14 REVIEW

Test yourself on the grammar of the unit.

A Complete the paragraph with the correct forms of the words in parentheses.

It's a great diet. You _____ whatever you like. You just
                              1. (may / eat)

_____ a lot. For example, for breakfast you _____
      2. (not / can / eat)   **3.** (can / have)

a slice of toast, an egg, and an orange. You can put jelly on the toast, but you

_____ butter. You _____ coffee, tea, or milk.
      4. (not / may / use)   **5.** (may / drink)

B Write these questions to a doctor. Use *can* and the words in parentheses.

1. (When / I / return to work) _____

2. (When / I / take a shower) _____

3. (I / go / to the gym) _____

4. (I / ride / my bike) _____

C Ask questions about what students can and cannot do during a test. Put the words in parentheses in the correct order.

1. (can / eat / during the test / we)   **4.** (can / drink water / we)

_____   _____

2. (a pencil / may / use / I)   **5.** (use / a black pen / I / may)

_____   _____

3. (I / can / during the test / make calls)   **6.** (can / a dictionary / we / use)

_____   _____

D Correct the conversation. There are five mistakes.

A: May I sees a menu?   B: Sure. Here you go.

A: And can we to have some water?   B: I'll be right back with the water. . . . Ready?

A: May I has the chicken?   B: Of course. A very good choice.

A: And can you brings me a small salad?   B: Certainly. And may I gets you anything else?

Now check your answers on page 447.

Present Progressive

PART 6

OUTCOMES

- Use the present progressive for events happening now and in the extended present
- Identify details in an online article
- Recognize where people are based on a conversation
- Describe what people are wearing and doing
- Write a paragraph about what is happening now

OUTCOMES

- Ask and answer questions about situations that are happening now
- Answer questions about details in a conversation
- Recognize where people are and what they are doing based on a conversation
- Ask and answer questions about a movie
- Write a conversation that describes what is happening now

OUTCOMES

- Use the simple present and the present progressive
- Describe emotions, experiences, and preferences with non-action verbs
- Recognize details in a short article about technology
- Recognize details of short phone messages
- Discuss reasons for people's actions
- Discuss the ways your prefer to communicate
- Write a description of a picture

Present Progressive: Affirmative and Negative Statements

PEOPLE WATCHING

OUTCOMES
- Use the present progressive for events happening now and in the extended present
- Identify details in an online article
- Recognize where people are based on a conversation
- Describe what people are wearing and doing
- Write a paragraph about what is happening now

STEP 1   **GRAMMAR IN CONTEXT**

BEFORE YOU READ

Work with a partner. Answer the questions.

1. Do you like to watch people? Why or why not?

2. When you watch people, what questions do you ask yourself about them?

3. Where is a good place to go to observe people? Why?

READ

▶15|01   Read this article about people watching.

People Watching

You're waiting for a train or a plane, and you're bored. What can you do? You can look at the people around you. I'm at Los Angeles International Airport, and I'm doing that now.

Across from me, I can see two businessmen. They're wearing suits and ties. One man is working on his laptop. The other man is reading a report. Both men are not looking around. They're working hard. They're not traveling for fun. They're traveling for business.

I can also see a mother and her little girl. The little girl is about three years old, and she's sitting on her mother's lap. I'm not certain they're mother and daughter, but I think so. They look alike. They're both wearing jeans. They're having fun. The mother is taking a selfie,[1] and they're both making funny faces.

---

1 *selfie:* a picture you take of yourself

A woman in her thirties is standing in front of the departure and arrival signs. She's wearing a business suit, but she isn't working now. She's talking to someone on the phone. She's smiling. She isn't speaking English. I think she's speaking Korean. Maybe she's talking to her mother. Maybe she's talking to a friend.

It's fun to look at other people. For some people, it's a way to relax. For others, such as writers and artists, it's a way to get ideas.

Writers, artists, photographers, psychologists, and detectives are people watchers. What about you?

AFTER YOU READ

A VOCABULARY **Complete the sentences with the words from the box.**

| bored | departure | detective | psychologist | suit |

1. The _____ is trying to find the murderer. He's questioning the family and neighbors.

2. Most lawyers and bankers wear a _____ to work.

3. My son is always angry and is having problems at school. A _____ is helping him.

4. We need to check in at the airport two hours before our _____.

5. Children are rarely _____ on planes. They always have a lot to do and to look at.

B COMPREHENSION **Complete the sentences. Circle the correct answers.**

1. The author of the article <u>is</u> / <u>isn't</u> looking at people at a train station.

2. The businessmen <u>are</u> / <u>aren't</u> resting before their flight.

3. The little girl <u>is</u> / <u>isn't</u> smiling.

4. The woman in her thirties <u>is</u> / <u>isn't</u> enjoying her phone conversation.

5. The woman in her thirties <u>is</u> / <u>isn't</u> speaking English.

C DISCUSSION **Work with a partner. Look at the reading again. Take turns. Tell your partner three things about the people in the reading.**

PRESENT PROGRESSIVE

Affirmative Statements

Subject	Be	Base Form of Verb + -ing
I	am	
He		
She	is	
It		relaxing.
We		
You	are	
They		

Negative Statements

Subject	Be	Not	Base Form of Verb + -ing
I	am		
He			
She	is		
It		not	sleeping.
We			
You	are		
They			

GRAMMAR NOTES

1 **Present Progressive: For This Moment in Time**

Use the present progressive (sometimes called the present continuous) for actions that are or are not happening **at the moment of speaking or writing**.

They**'re eating**.
They**'re not drinking**.

With this use of the present progressive, we often use these time expressions:

• *now*
• *right now*
• *at the moment*

The machine **isn't working** *now*.

Right now, she**'s resting**.

At the moment, he**'s talking** on the phone.

BE CAREFUL! We don't usually use non-action verbs in the present progressive even for something that is happening now.

I **want** some coffee.
NOT I ~~am wanting~~ some coffee.

2 Present Progressive: For Extended Periods of Time

Use the present progressive for actions that are happening **at this time**, but may not be happening at this moment.

| Past | **Now** | Future |
| | This year | |

This year, **he is studying English**.
(At this moment, he is not studying English.)

With this use of the present progressive, we often use these time expressions:

- *nowadays*
- *these days*
- *this year*

Nowadays, people **are traveling** a lot.

These days, the weather **is changing**.

This year, we're **studying** English.

3 Present Progressive: Forms

The present progressive always has a form of *be* + **the verb in the -*ing* form**.

Use *am*, *is*, or *are* and the **verb + -*ing*** to form the present progressive.

I **am watching** people.
He **is reading**.
They **are looking** at their phones.

Put *not* after *am*, *is*, or *are* to form the negative.

I **am not watching** people.
He **is not reading**.
They **are not looking** at their phones.

BE CAREFUL! Do not repeat the verb *be* when the same subject is doing two actions.

They **are singing** and **dancing**.
NOT They are singing and ~~are~~ dancing.

USAGE NOTE Use **contractions** in speaking and informal writing.

She's holding his hand.
I'm texting.
We **aren't** listening.

IN WRITING If a verb ends in a silent -*e*, drop the final -*e* and add -*ing*.

- *close*
- *smile*
- *make*

She's **closing** the window.
He's **smiling** at me.
They're **making** dinner.

REFERENCE NOTES

For more information on **non-action verbs**, see Unit 17 on page 196.

For a list of **non-action verbs**, see Appendix 15 on page 437.

For a list of **spelling rules for the present progressive**, see Appendix 16 on page 437.

EXERCISE 1
DISCOVER THE GRAMMAR

A GRAMMAR NOTES 1, 3

A student is people watching in her psychology class. Underline all the uses of the present progressive.

I'm in my psychology class. This semester we're studying child psychology. Today's class is almost over. Julia and Maria are closing their books. Our teacher is returning a test. Bob has a smile on his face. He always gets a good grade. Ryan isn't smiling. Maybe his grade is low. Shoko is texting under the table. Jon isn't listening to the teacher. He's thinking about lunch. I can hear his stomach. It's making noises.

B Write the base form of the underlined words in A.

1. _____study_____   4. _____   7. _____

2. _____   5. _____   8. _____

3. _____   6. _____

EXERCISE 2   AFFIRMATIVE AND NEGATIVE STATEMENTS

GRAMMAR NOTES 1–3 Complete the sentences with the present progressive forms of the verbs in parentheses.

1. I'm tired of studying. I _'m taking_ (take) a break and _____ (look) around.

2. Julie and Maria _____ (play) games, and Bob _____ (text) someone.

3. Shoko and Ryan _____ (do) homework, and Jon _____ (read) the paper.

4. It _____ (rain) outside now. People _____ (use) umbrellas.

5. Some people _____ (stand) at the door. They _____ (wait) for the rain to stop.

6. I _____ (not / do) homework. I'm looking at the people in the library.

7. It _____ (not / snow) now. It _____ (rain).

8. They _____ (not / study) at this moment. They _____ (relax).

9. This semester, Hugo _____ (take) five courses. He _____ (work) hard.

10. This week in psychology class, we _____ (learn) about the behavior of three-year-old children.

EXERCISE 3 AFFIRMATIVE STATEMENTS

GRAMMAR NOTES 1–3 Circle the correct words to complete the email message.

Hi Antonio,

Remember me? I'm Hye Won Paik from Korea. We were together at the English Language
Institute. I 'm work / ('m working) for a Korean cosmetics company now. I'm in Madrid this week
— **1.**
on business, and I stay / 'm staying at the Hotel Ritz. I meeting / 'm meeting with clients from
— **2.** — **3.**
all over Spain. Right now, I sit / 'm sitting in the hotel lobby and watch / watching people.
— **4.** — **5.**
I 'm think / 'm thinking about you, too. Do you remember the fun we had in English class six
— **6.**
years ago? If you're free and in Madrid this week, please write or call.

Your friend from long ago,
Hye Won

EXERCISE 4 AFFIRMATIVE AND NEGATIVE STATEMENTS

GRAMMAR NOTES 1–3 Complete the paragraphs with the present progressive forms of
the verbs in parentheses.

Hye Won is a director of a cosmetics company. This week she _'s traveling_ on
1. (travel)
business. She _____ with clients in Spain.
2. (meet)

It's 8:00 in the evening. Hye Won _____ dinner with a client.
3. (have)
They _____ at Casa Paco, a top restaurant in Madrid. Hye Won and the
4. (eat)
client _____ about business right now. They _____ customs in
5. (not / talk) **6.** (compare)
Spain and Korea.

On this business trip, Hye Won _____ a week in Madrid and two days
7. (spend)
in London.

Hye Won loves her job and her lifestyle. She says, "I'm glad I'm not married.
I _____ my freedom. I _____ for a husband at the moment.
8. (enjoy) **9.** (not / look)
Maybe later." Hye Won's parents _____ to worry, but Hye Won is very happy.
10. (begin)

EXERCISE 5
EDITING

GRAMMAR NOTES 1, 3

Correct a student's journal. There are seven mistakes. The first mistake is already corrected. Find and correct six more.

I'm ~~sit~~ *sitting* in the park. It's a beautiful day. The leaves changing

color. Today there are a lot of children in the park. They laughing

and are playing. They no are studying. They're lucky. It's hard to

study on a beautiful day.

I trying to study for a test. I'm wait for my classmate, Grace.

We like to work together.

STEP 4   COMMUNICATION PRACTICE

EXERCISE 6   LISTENING

15|02   **A** Listen to two telephone conversations. Then find George and Sara in the picture. Write their names next to them.

B Listen again to the telephone conversations. Complete the sentences. Then check your answers with a partner's.

1. George is _____ in front of Joey's _____.

2. George is _____ a red _____ and _____.

3. George is _____ a bag of _____.

4. Sara is _____ in front of _____ Bank.

5. Ali is _____ in front of _____ _____.

6. Sara is _____ a black _____ and a gray _____.

C Work with a partner. Take turns. Describe other people in the picture. Use the present progressive. Your partner points to the person.

EXAMPLE: This man is wearing a navy sports jacket. He's standing next to a woman. They're . . .

EXERCISE 7 WHO'S WEARING WHAT?

A GAME Work in a group. Prepare for the game in B. Look around your class. Who's wearing the following?

a belt	a necklace	a sweater	earrings
a blouse	a ring	a T-shirt	jeans
a button-down shirt	a scarf	a watch	running shoes
a dress	a skirt	boots	sandals

EXAMPLE: A: Soraya is wearing a green sweater.
　　　　　　B: Mohammed is wearing a button-down shirt.

B The class sits in two rows back-to-back. Take turns with the person behind you. Say your name. Can you remember your partner's clothes? Don't look. Tell your partner what he or she is wearing. After you finish, students in one row move to the next seat.

EXAMPLE: A: I'm Mustafa.
　　　　　　B: Hi, Mustafa. I'm Shoko.
　　　　　　A: OK, Shoko, I think you're wearing jeans and a white sweater. Am I correct?
　　　　　　B: That's right. And you're wearing black pants and a black shirt.
　　　　　　A: Actually, my shirt is dark green, not black.

EXERCISE 8 COMPARING PHOTOS

CONVERSATION Work in a group. Ask a classmate from another group to take two photos of your group. In each photo, look or do something different. Look at the two photos and talk about the differences.

EXAMPLE: A: In the first photo, Juan is holding a notebook, but he isn't holding a notebook in the second photo.
B: And in the first photo, Eleni is wearing a watch. She isn't wearing a watch in the second photo. And look, I'm smiling in this photo, but I'm not smiling in that one.

EXERCISE 9 FIND THE DIFFERENCES

GAME Work with a partner. Find ten differences between picture A and picture B. The first pair to find the ten differences wins.

EXAMPLE: In picture A, the two girls are talking and laughing. In picture B, they aren't talking or laughing. They're eating.

FROM GRAMMAR TO WRITING

A BEFORE YOU WRITE
A student is looking at people in a school cafeteria. Read her observations. Then look around your classroom, hallway, or school cafeteria. Take notes about two people. Work with a partner. Tell your partner about the people.

I'm in our school cafeteria. It's 12:30 p.m. Two girls are waiting to pay for their food. One girl is tall. The other is not. The tall girl is wearing black pants and a black T-shirt. The other girl is wearing jeans and a red sweater. The tall girl is carrying a tray with yogurt and a salad. The shorter girl is carrying a tray with a sandwich, a salad, an apple, and cookies. She's talking a lot. The other girl is listening. She isn't saying a word. She isn't smiling. I think they're classmates. I don't think they're friends.

	What's the person doing?	What's the person wearing?	What else is happening?
Person #1			
Person #2			

B WRITE Write a paragraph about the people around you. Use the paragraph in A and your chart. Use the present progressive.

C CHECK YOUR WORK Read your paragraph in B. Underline the present progressive verbs. Use the Editing Checklist to check your work.

Editing Checklist

Did you ... ?
- [ ] use the present progressive for things that are happening now or nowadays
- [ ] include a form of *be* + the base form of the verb + *-ing* for the present progressive
- [ ] check your spelling

D REVISE YOUR WORK Read your paragraph again. Can you improve your writing? Make changes if necessary.

UNIT 15 REVIEW

Test yourself on the grammar of the unit.

Ⓐ **Complete the sentences. Circle the correct answers.**

1. I'm not / I no am sleeping.

2. We are prepare / We're preparing for a test.

3. She isn't playing / She no is playing tennis now.

4. They doing / They're doing homework.

5. He is read / He's reading a mystery.

Ⓑ **Complete the sentences with the present progressive forms of the verbs from the box.**

| carry | drive | listen to | run | stand and talk |

1. A man _____ music on his iPod.

2. Two women _____ on a street corner.

3. Some children _____ to catch their school bus.

4. A young man _____ a red sports car.

5. An older man _____ a bag.

Ⓒ **Complete the sentences with the present progressive forms of the verbs in parentheses. Use affirmative or negative forms.**

1. John _____ his friend. He _____ him. John says texting is faster.

a. (text)   b. (call)

2. Lulu is laughing. She _____ . She _____ a very funny show.

a. (cry)   b. (watch)

3. Julie _____ fast. She _____ to win a race.

a. (swim)   b. (try)

Ⓓ **Correct the paragraph. There are four mistakes.**

My classmates and I am sitting in a computer lab. One student writing a composition. Two students are check their email. A teacher is helps a student. The other students are reading.

Now check your answers on page 448.

Present Progressive: *Yes/No* and *Wh-* Questions

MOVIES

OUTCOMES
• Ask and answer questions about situations that are happening now
• Answer questions about details in a conversation
• Recognize where people are and what they are doing based on a conversation
• Ask and answer questions about a movie
• Write a conversation that describes what is happening now

STEP 1   GRAMMAR IN CONTEXT

BEFORE YOU READ

Work with a partner. Answer the questions.

1. What kinds of movies do you like?
   a. action
   b. animation
   c. comedy
   d. drama
   e. horror
   f. science fiction
   g. other

2. Look at the picture on the laptop computer. What kind of movie is this? What do you know about this movie?

READ

▶ 16|01   Ann has a cold. Her co-worker Don is calling her on the phone to see how she is. Read their conversation.

A Very Funny Movie

ANN: Hello.

DON: Hi, Ann. How are you feeling today? Any better?

ANN: Uh-huh. I'm coughing less.

DON: Good. Is the fever going down?

ANN: Yes, it is. I'm just resting and watching movies.

DON: Oh? What are you watching?

ANN: *My Big Fat Greek Wedding.*

DON: I remember that movie. It was really funny. What's happening now?

ANN: In this scene, Toula's parents and Ian's parents are meeting for the first time.

DON: Where are you watching it? On your computer?

ANN: Yes.

DON: It's amazing. It's still funny after so many years.

ANN: I know. But, tell me, what's going on at work?

DON: We're working on ten things at the same time.

ANN: Is Mr. Brooks going crazy?[1] Who's doing my work?

DON: Mr. Brooks is impossible, and *I'm* doing your work. But not tomorrow.

ANN: Why? Are you taking the day off?

DON: Yes, I am. I'm catching *your* cold. I guess I need some good movies.

---

1 *going crazy:* feeling upset because there are too many things to do

AFTER YOU READ

Ⓐ VOCABULARY **Complete the sentences with the words from the box.**

catching a cold	coughing	fever	scene	still

1. A: Why are you watching that _____ again?

    B: It's my favorite part of the movie.

2. A: Why are you staying home?

    B: I feel terrible. I think I'm _____ .

3. A: Why is he so hot? Does he have a _____ ?

    B: Yes, he does.

4. A: Do you _____ like to go to the movies?

    B: Yes, I do. Now the movie theater in my area has big, comfortable chairs.

5. A: He's _____ and sneezing because he's allergic to those flowers. He isn't sick.

    B: Oh. Let's put the flowers in another room.

Ⓑ COMPREHENSION **Match each question with its answer.**

_____ **1.** Why is Ann staying home?   **a.** Yes, she is.

_____ **2.** Is she feeling better today?   **b.** No, Don is.

_____ **3.** What kind of movie is Ann watching?   **c.** He's getting sick.

_____ **4.** What's happening in the movie?   **d.** A comedy.

_____ **5.** Is Mr. Brooks doing Ann's work?   **e.** She has a cold.

_____ **6.** What's happening to Don?   **f.** Toula's and Ian's parents are meeting.

Ⓒ DISCUSSION **Work with a partner. Compare your answers. Then look at the reading. What does Don ask Ann? What does Ann ask Don?**

PRESENT PROGRESSIVE: *YES/NO* QUESTIONS AND *WH-* QUESTIONS

Yes/No Questions

Be	Subject	Base Form of Verb + *-ing*	
Am	I		
Are	you		
Is	he she it	resting?	
Are	we you they		

Short Answers

Affirmative				Negative			
Yes,	you	are.		No,	you're	not.	
	I	am.			I'm		
	he she it	is.			he's she's it's		
	you we they	are.			you're we're they're		

Wh- Questions

Wh- Word	*Be*	Subject	Base Form of Verb + *-ing*	
Why	is	she	**staying**	home?
What	are	you	**watching**?	
Where		they	**showing**	the movie?

Answers

She's sick.
My Big Fat Greek Wedding.
At the Cineplex.

Wh- Questions About the Subject

Wh- Word	*Be*	Base Form of Verb + *-ing*	
Who	is	**staying**	home?
What		**happening**?	

Answers

Ann is.
They're singing.

GRAMMAR NOTES

1 Present Progressive: *Yes/No* Questions

Yes/no **questions** in the present progressive **ask if something is happening now** or nowadays.

| To form a *yes/no* question, reverse the subject and the verb *be*. | **He is singing.**
↙↘
Is he singing? |

Wh- **questions** in the present progressive **ask for information about something happening now** or nowadays.	
Wh- questions in the present progressive begin with a *wh-* word and use *yes/no* question **word order**.	**Where is** he **working**? **What are** they **doing**? **Who are** you **meeting**?
IN WRITING Use *whom* only for very formal written English.	**Whom** is the president meeting?

3 Present Progressive: Questions About the Subject

Questions about the **subject** use **statement word order**—noun + verb. They often begin with *Who* or *What*.	A: **Who is resting?** B: Ann is resting. *(Both the question and the answer have the same word order.)*
When you are forming a question, it is important to know if you are asking about the subject or the object.	
Questions about the **subject** follow this form: *Wh-* **word** + *is* + *-ing* **form of the verb** (+ **object**).	**Who is pushing Maria?** *(The question is about the subject.)*
Questions about the **object** follow this form: *Wh-* **word** + **form of** *be* + **subject** + *-ing* **form of the verb**.	A: **Who are Billy and Pete pushing?** B: Maria. *(The question is about the object—Maria.)*

STEP 3   FOCUSED PRACTICE

EXERCISE 1   DISCOVER THE GRAMMAR

GRAMMAR NOTES 1–3   Read the questions in the chart. Then answer the questions.

Column A	Column B	Column C
What's happening now?	How are you feeling today?	Is the fever going down?
What's going on at work?	What are you watching?	Is Mr. Brooks going crazy?
Who's doing my work?	Where are you watching it?	Are you getting sick?

1. Which column has *yes/no* questions? _____

2. Which column has questions about the subject? _____

3. Which column has other *wh-* questions? _____

EXERCISE 2
YES/NO QUESTIONS

Ⓐ GRAMMAR NOTE 1 Change each statement to a yes/no question. Write the question on the line for Speaker A.

1. She is buying the tickets online.

   A: *Is she buying the tickets online?*

   B: _____

2. They are sitting in the first row.

   A: _____

   B: _____

3. They are watching a horror movie.

   A: _____

   B: _____

4. My hat is blocking your view.

   A: _____

   B: _____

5. You are enjoying the movie.

   A: _____

   B: _____

Ⓑ Write the answer to each question in A. Choose the correct answer from the box below and write the answer on the line for Speaker B.

Yes, I am. Are you?	No, it isn't. I can see the screen.	Yes. It's very scary.
No. They're in the fifth row.	Yes, she is. She always gets tickets online.	

EXERCISE 3 WH- QUESTIONS

GRAMMAR NOTE 2 Write questions with the correct forms of the words in parentheses. Use the present progressive.

1. A: (What / you / do?) *What are you doing?*

   B: I'm getting something to eat.

2. A: (What / he / buy?) _____

   B: Popcorn. He always eats popcorn at the movies.

3. A: (Where / they / sit?) _____

    B: In the fifth row in the center.

4. A: (Why / she / put her coat on that seat?) _____

    B: She's saving the seat for her friend.

5. A: (Who / he / wait for?) _____

    B: His roommate. They're meeting in front of the movie theater.

EXERCISE 4
WH- QUESTIONS ABOUT THE SUBJECT

GRAMMAR NOTE 3

The following sentences describe scenes from famous movies. Write questions about the underlined words.

1. <u>Jack and Rose</u> are standing on the top deck of the *Titanic*.

                                                                            (Titanic, 1997, Drama / Romance)

   Who's standing on the top deck of the Titanic? _____

2. <u>Jon and Sara</u> are drinking frozen hot chocolate at Serendipity.

                                                         (Serendipity, 2001, Fantasy / Romance)

_____

3. <u>E.T.</u> is phoning home.

                            (E.T. the Extra-Terrestrial, 1982, Fantasy / Science Fiction)

_____

4. <u>Elsa</u> is dancing on the ice and singing, "Let It Go."

                                              (Frozen, 2013, Fantasy / Animation)

_____

5. <u>Michael Corleone</u> is saying, "Keep your friends close, but your enemies closer."

                                        (The Godfather: Part II, 1974, Crime / Drama)

_____

6. Gru and people in the park are exercising to the song, "Happy."

(*Despicable Me 2*, 2013, Animation/Comedy)

_____

7. Dr. Serizawa is saying, "Let them fight."

(*Godzilla*, 2014, Thriller/Action)

_____

EXERCISE 5 *YES/NO* AND *WH-* QUESTIONS

Ⓐ GRAMMAR NOTES 1–2 Complete Ann and Don's conversation with the correct forms of the words in parentheses. Use the present progressive.

ANN: Hi, Don. *How are you feeling* ? _____ ?
          1. (how / you / feel)   **2.** (you / feel / any better)

DON: No, I'm not.

ANN: _____ ?
           3. (you / take / the medicine)

DON: Yes, I am. _____ ?
               4. (where / you / call from)

ANN: I'm at an Italian restaurant. Don. Listen to this. Meryl Streep is eating here, too.

DON: No kidding! _____ ?
               5. (who / she / eat / with)

ANN: I think she's with her daughter. I'm not sure.

DON: _____ ?
               6. (people / ask for her autograph)

ANN: No. Nobody's bothering her, but everyone knows she's here.

DON: Well, when you pass her table, say, "Bon appétit!" Say it the same way she said it in

     the movie *Julie and Julia*.

▶16|02 Ⓑ LISTEN AND CHECK Listen to the conversation and check your answers in A.

EXERCISE 6 EDITING

GRAMMAR NOTES 1–3 There are six mistakes. The first mistake is already corrected. Find and correct five more.

           who's
1. A: Excuse me, ~~who~~ collecting tickets?

   B: He isn't here now. Wait a minute. He'll be right back.

2. A: What you doing?

   B: I'm turning off my cell phone.

3. A: Is Dad buy popcorn?

   B: Yes, he is.

4. A: What taking him so long?

   B: He's waiting in a long line.

5. A: Excuse me, is someone sits here?

   B: No, no one sitting here. Have a seat.

STEP 4   COMMUNICATION PRACTICE

EXERCISE 7 LISTENING

16|03 **A** Listen to the telephone conversation. Answer the questions.

1. Where is Joy?
   a. in Chicago   **b.** in Miami

2. Where is it raining?
   a. in Chicago   **b.** in Miami

3. What are Joy and her family doing today?
   a. They're watching movies.   **b.** They're watching TV.

16|03 **B** Listen again to the telephone conversation. Complete the chart.

Who	Kind of movie	Where / How
Joy's mother	*a comedy*	on her iPad on the balcony at home
	a documentary	
Brian (Joy's son)		at the Cineplex movie theater
	an animated film	
Joy		

C Work with a partner. Look at the chart in B. Take turns. Ask questions about the people, the kinds of movies, and the places they're watching them.

EXAMPLE: **A:** So, where is Joy's mom watching the movie?

B: On the balcony. What about Joy's husband? Is he watching the documentary on his iPad?

EXERCISE 8 HOME ALONE

ROLE PLAY Student B is watching a movie when Student A calls. Student A asks Student B questions about the movie. Work with a partner. Complete the telephone conversation with your partner. Then switch roles.

A: Hi, _____(name)_____. This is _____(name)_____. Are you busy?

B: Oh, hi, _____(name)_____. I'm watching a movie. Let me turn it off.

A: No. Don't turn it off. What are you watching?

B: _____(name of movie)_____.

A: What's happening?

B: Well, at the moment . . .

EXERCISE 9 CHARADES

GAME Choose an action from the list below. Act it out in front of the class. Classmates raise their hands as soon as they guess the activity. Students get one point for each correct guess.

EXAMPLE: *(Student A performs an action.)*

B: Are you watching a horror movie?

A: No, I'm not.

C: Are you watching a comedy?

A: Yes, I am. *(Student C gets a point.)*

- watch a comedy / a horror movie / an action film

- play soccer / tennis / volleyball

- eat an apple / popcorn / an ice cream / a sandwich / a steak

- ride or drive a car / a bike / a motorcycle / a horse

- play the guitar / the piano / the drums / the saxophone

- Other: _____

FROM GRAMMAR TO WRITING

A BEFORE YOU WRITE Work with a partner and have a conversation. Begin the conversation with the dialogue below. Your partner is looking at a movie star. Ask more questions about the star. Take notes on your partner's answers. Then switch roles.

A: Hi, _____(B's name)_____ . It's _____(A's name)_____ .

B: Hi, _____(A's name)_____ . How are you? Why are you calling?

A: Guess who I am looking at right now?

B: Who?

A: _____(name of famous movie star)_____ .

B: You're kidding! What's _____(he or she)_____ doing?

A: Well, _____(he or she)_____ is . . .

B WRITE Write a telephone conversation between you and your partner about a movie star. Use your notes from your conversation in A. Use the present progressive.

C CHECK YOUR WORK Read your telephone conversation. Underline the present progressive verbs. Use the Editing Checklist to check your work.

Editing Checklist
Did you . . . ?
☐ include the verb *be* in all present progressive statements and questions
☐ use correct word order for questions
☐ include a subject in all questions except questions about a subject
☐ check your spelling

D REVISE YOUR WORK Read your questions again. Can you improve your writing? Make changes if necessary.

UNIT 16 REVIEW

Test yourself on the grammar of the unit.

A Write present progressive *yes/no* questions with the correct forms of the words in parentheses.

1. (you / work) _____

2. (he / buy tickets online) _____

3. (they / watch a mystery) _____

4. (your cousin / enjoy the movie) _____

B Write present progressive *wh-* questions with the correct forms of the words in parentheses.

1. (Where / they / go) _____

2. (What movie / she / watch) _____

3. (Why / Bob / stay home) _____

4. (Who / watch / the children) _____

C Complete the conversations with the correct forms of the words in parentheses. Use the present progressive. Use contractions.

1. A: Why _____? _____ a funny movie?
      a. (laugh / the kids)   b. (watch / they)

   B: No, they _____ a game.
                      c. (play)

2. A: What _____?
              a. (do / you)

   B: I _____ a movie. I _____ to
            b. (make)   c. (plan)
   study film in college.

3. A: What _____ outside?
              a. (happen)

   B: They _____ a movie about our neighborhood.
                  b. (make)

D Correct the conversation. There are four mistakes.

A: What you watching?   B: We're watching a detective show.

A: What happening?   B: A boy is missing from his home.

A: The police are looking for him?   B: Yes, they are.

A: Where they looking?   B: Everywhere.

Now check your answers on page 448.

OUTCOMES
- Use the simple present and the present progressive
- Describe emotions, experiences, and preferences with non-action verbs
- Recognize details in a short article about technology
- Recognize details of short phone messages
- Discuss reasons for people's actions
- Discuss the ways your prefer to communicate
- Write a description of a picture

STEP 1 GRAMMAR IN CONTEXT

BEFORE YOU READ

Work with a partner. Answer the questions.

1. How do you use your phone? Circle your answers.

   a. to email
   b. to get directions
   c. to listen to music

   d. to make phone calls
   e. to network with friends
   f. to search the Internet

   g. to take photos
   h. to text

2. What three ways do you use your phone the most?

READ

▶17|01 Read this article about smartphones.

SMARTPHONE MANIA

Smartphones are everywhere. People under twenty[1] don't know a world without them. They come with many features. They come in different colors and sizes. Some smartphones are waterproof and shockproof.[2]

People use their smartphones for a lot more than talking. Xavier uses his phone all the time, but rarely makes phone calls.

He texts and plays games. Right now, he's running late,[3] so he's texting his friend.

It's easy to understand the popularity of these phones. People want to connect with others, and at the same time, they want to be mobile.[4] Smartphones make it possible to do both. Smartphones are big business, and the technology is constantly improving.

---

1 *under twenty:* less than twenty years old
2 *waterproof and shockproof:* don't break when they fall in water and fall on the ground

3 *running late:* not on time
4 *mobile:* able to move around

What about in the future? Nobody knows, but here are the wishes of two people:

Robert says, "I want my phone to teach me a foreign language while I sleep."

Emily says, "I often forget to charge my phone. I want a phone with endless power."

Well, Emily may get her wish a lot sooner than Robert. But, of course, with the speed at which things are changing these days, you never know what the future will bring.

AFTER YOU READ

A VOCABULARY Match the words in **bold** with their meanings.

1. I **connect** with Hiro once or twice a week.
   a. dance
   b. make contact

2. That watch is **waterproof**. You can swim with it on.
   a. not hurt by water
   b. dry

3. That new computer comes with a lot of **features**.
   a. parts that do many things
   b. memory

4. He calls her **constantly**. Is he in love?
   a. from time to time
   b. all the time

5. Your work is **improving**.
   a. getting better
   b. getting worse

B COMPREHENSION Complete the sentences. Circle the correct answers.

1. Fifteen years ago, almost no one had a _____.
   a. personal computer
   b. cell phone
   c. smartphone

2. Xavier is texting a friend because he is _____.
   a. late
   b. playing a game
   c. tweeting

3. People want to get phone calls, but they don't want to _____.
   a. stay home to get calls
   b. be mobile
   c. make phone calls

4. Emily wants her phone to have _____.
   a. a beeper
   b. power all the time
   c. an alarm

5. Robert wants to learn a language when he is _____.
   a. at school
   b. at work
   c. asleep

C DISCUSSION Work with a partner. Compare your answers in B. Then discuss the following question: What is the main reason smartphones are popular?

SIMPLE PRESENT AND PRESENT PROGRESSIVE

The Simple Present
I **work**.
He **works** on Mondays.
She **doesn't work** with me.
They **don't work** with us.
Does he **work** with you?
Do you **work** for a phone company?

The Present Progressive
I'm working now.
He's working now.
She **isn't working** with him.
They **aren't working** with us.
Is he **working** with us?
Are you **working** now?

NON-ACTION (STATIVE) VERBS

State of Being	Emotion	Sense/ Appearance	Need/ Preference	Mental Action	Possession	Measurement
be	love hate like dislike	hear see feel taste smell sound look	want need prefer	agree disagree guess understand know remember believe think mean worry	have own belong	cost weigh owe

GRAMMAR NOTES

1 **Simple Present**

Remember to use the **simple present** to tell or ask about **habits**, **customs**, **routines**, and **facts**. (See Unit 8.)

Past — Now — Future
She shops every Saturday.

I **charge** my phone every evening.
Do you **charge** your phone in the morning?

2 Present Progressive

Remember to use the **present progressive** to tell or ask about an action happening **right now** or **these days**. (See Unit 15.)

He**'s checking** email now.

Is Enrique **checking** email?

Jon **is teaching** computer science this year.

3 Non-action Verbs

Some verbs do not describe actions. These verbs are called **non-action** or **stative verbs**.

Non-action verbs do the following:

• express emotion	We **like** that computer.
• describe sense or appearance	The music **sounds** relaxing.
• express a need or preference	I **prefer** email.
• describe a thought	Jennifer **knows** you.
• show possession	It **belongs** to me.
• give a measurement	It **costs** two hundred dollars.
• express a state	I **am** tired now.

BE CAREFUL! We usually do not use non-action verbs in the present progressive (-*ing*) form.

I **own** a smartphone. It **costs** a lot.

NOT I'm owning a smartphone. It's costing a lot.

USAGE NOTE Some non-action verbs can also have an active meaning. When they have an active meaning, they can use the present progressive.

I **have** a new phone. I**'m having** trouble with it.

I**'m thinking** about my phone. I **think** I need to return it.

I'm **tasting** the soup. It **tastes** delicious.

REFERENCE NOTES

For a list of **non-action verbs**, see Appendix 15 on page 437.

For more information about the **simple present**, see Unit 8 on page 88, Unit 9 on page 100, and Unit 10 on page 111.

For more information about the **present progressive**, see Unit 15 on page 174 and Unit 16 on page 185.

EXERCISE 1
DISCOVER THE GRAMMAR

A GRAMMAR NOTES 1–3

Read the paragraph. Circle the simple present verbs. Underline the present progressive verbs.

B There are five non-action verbs in A. Find them and write the base form of each verb on the lines below.

_____ *have* _____

_____

_____

_____

EXERCISE 2
SIMPLE PRESENT; NON-ACTION VERBS; PRESENT PROGRESSIVE

A GRAMMAR NOTES 1–3

Complete the conversation. Use the simple present or present progressive forms of the verbs in parentheses. Use contractions when possible.

Raisa (has) a new phone with a lot of great features. She likes her phone a lot. Her phone keeps her in touch with[1] her friends. Right now, Raisa is texting friends. They are making plans for the evening. She and her friends often text. They don't talk much on the phone. They also connect through social media. Raisa often adds new friends to her social media sites. Sometimes she doesn't know them very well. Raisa's grandmother, Olga, worries about that. Olga doesn't use social media. She prefers to talk on the phone or connect through email.

_____

1 *in touch with:* connected to

ELI: What _____ *are* _____ you _____ *doing* _____?
　　　　　　　　1. (do)

MONA: I _____ Instagram. Look! That's Joy Lin from high school. She
　　　　　2. (check)

　　_____ three kids now. The twins _____ pirate costumes,
　　　　3. (have)　　　　　　　　　　　　　**4.** (wear)

　　and the older girl _____ a princess dress. The boy _____
　　　　　　　　　　5. (wear)　　　　　　　　　　　　**6.** (look)

　　like Joy, doesn't he?

ELIA: Yes, I _____ they all look like Joy.
　　　　　　　7. (think)

MONA: _____ you _____ social media a lot?
　　　　8. (use)

ELI: No, not really. I _____ to text or email friends. I _____
     9. (prefer)   **10.** (believe)

     it's more personal. Also, I _____ about my privacy.
                                11. (worry)

     _____ you _____ about your privacy?
     12. (worry)

MONA: Sometimes, but I _____ to connect with my friends on social media.
                       13. (love)

17|02 **B** LISTEN AND CHECK Listen to the conversation and check your answers in A.

EXERCISE 3 SIMPLE PRESENT; NON-ACTION VERBS; PRESENT PROGRESSIVE

A GRAMMAR NOTES 1–3 Complete the conversation. Use the simple present or present progressive forms of the verbs in parentheses. Use contractions when possible.

JEN: I'm worried about Tim. He _____*isn't doing*_____ well in school. He was always a good
                               1. (not / do)

     student, but this term he _____ games or _____ friends all
                              2. (play)   **3.** (text)

     the time. I _____ he _____ Spanish. Bob and I
               4. (think)   **5.** (fail)

     _____ about getting him a Spanish tutor.
     6. (talk)

RAY: What _____ Tim _____?
          7. (want)

JEN: I _____. Right now, he _____ some new game. He
        8. (not / know)   **9.** (play)

     _____ those computer games. I _____ he
     10. (love)   **11.** (think)

     _____ addicted to them.
     12. (become)

RAY: My friend's daughter was like that. Now she _____ her own company.
                                               13. (own)

17|03 **B** LISTEN AND CHECK Listen to the conversation and check your answers in A.

EXERCISE 4 SIMPLE PRESENT; NON-ACTION VERBS; PRESENT PROGRESSIVE

GRAMMAR NOTES 1–3 Complete the paragraphs with the correct forms of the verbs from the box. Use contractions when possible.

| answer | ask | know | look | ~~need~~ | swim | take | talk | want |

Phuong _____*needs*_____ a new phone. He _____ a waterproof phone
           1.   2.

because he _____ every day. He _____ for a phone with a good
               3.   4.

camera because he often _____ photos.
                             5.

Right now, Phuong _____ to a saleswoman. He _____ her a
                        6.   7.

lot of questions. The saleswoman _____ all his questions. She
                                       8.

_____ a lot about phones. She's good at her job.
    9.

EXERCISE 5 EDITING

GRAMMAR NOTES 1–3 Correct the paragraph. There are six mistakes. The first mistake is already corrected. Find and correct five more.

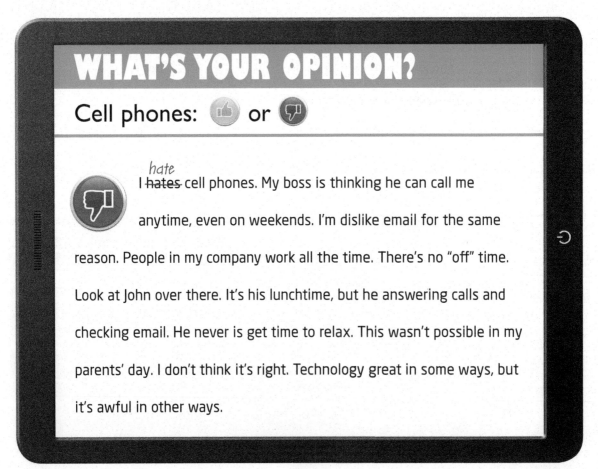

WHAT'S YOUR OPINION?

Cell phones: 👍 or 👎

        hate
I ~~hates~~ cell phones. My boss is thinking he can call me

anytime, even on weekends. I'm dislike email for the same

reason. People in my company work all the time. There's no "off" time.

Look at John over there. It's his lunchtime, but he answering calls and

checking email. He never is get time to relax. This wasn't possible in my

parents' day. I don't think it's right. Technology great in some ways, but

it's awful in other ways.

EXERCISE 6 LISTENING

▶17|04 **A** Listen to Karina's phone messages. Put a check in the box if the call if is a business call or a call from a family member.

	Business	Family
Message 1	☑	☐
Message 2	☐	☐
Message 3	☐	☐
Message 4	☐	☐

▶17|04 **B** Listen to the messages again. Draw lines from the caller to his or her relationship to Karina to the reason for the call.

Name of caller	Relationship to Karina	Reason for the call
Bob	aunt	wants advice on smartphones
Lydia	boss	wants a business report
Natalya	daughter	wants Karina's travel plans
Gina	assistant	wants a ride from the station

C Work with a partner. Make guesses about Karina's life.

EXAMPLE: **A:** I think Karina is a businesswoman. I think she works hard and travels a lot.

   B: I agree. I think she is a saleswoman. She has a daughter. I think her daughter is in her teens because she can take the train alone.

EXERCISE 7 CONSIDER THE POSSIBILITIES

PROBLEM SOLVING Work with a partner. Read about things people are doing. Guess why they are doing them.

1. Paul and Ana usually shop at Electronics Plus for their electronics. Today they're shopping at Goodbuys.

   EXAMPLE: A: Paul and Ana are shopping at Goodbuys today because there is a big sale there.

   B: That's one possibility. Maybe they're shopping at Goodbuys because Electronics Plus is closed.

2. Maria usually texts friends. Today she's calling and speaking to them.

3. Shoshana is speaking to someone on the phone. She sounds angry. She has a bill in her hand.

4. Ali usually brings his lunch to work. Today he's eating out.

5. Olivia is smiling. She's reading a text.

6. Joaquin usually wears jeans and a T-shirt in class. Today he's wearing a suit.

7. Rosa and Said are waiting in a very long line. It's raining, but they're laughing. Everyone in the line is between thirteen and twenty-two years old.

8. Uri is talking to someone on the phone. His face is turning red.

EXERCISE 8 PROS AND CONS OF SMARTPHONES

Ⓐ DEBATE Form two groups. Prepare for a debate in B. One group talks about why smartphones are good, and the other group talks about why they are not good. Look at the chart below or use your own ideas.

Why Smartphones Are Good	Why Smartphones Are Not Good
many features	expensive
immediate information	noises
connect anywhere / anytime	you are always available
entertainment / fun	battery dies
	no privacy

Ⓑ Work with the other group. Have a debate about why smartphones are or are not good.

EXAMPLE: A: I think smartphones are great. Everyone in my family has a smartphone, and we do all sorts of things with our phones. My mother emails her friends. My father . . .

B: But those phones are expensive, and the cost is always going up.

EXERCISE 9 TEXTS, CALLS, OR EMAILS?

A DISCUSSION Prepare for a discussion in B. Complete the chart. Make notes about the ways you prefer to communicate or get information and why. Give reasons why.

Which do you prefer?	I prefer . . .
ebooks or print books	
phone calls or texts or email messages	
smartphones or laptop computers	
electronic planners or paper planners	
news on your computer or news on TV	

B Work in a group. Discuss which forms of communication or media you prefer and why.

EXAMPLE: A: Do you like ebooks or print books?

B: It depends. I read ebooks for fun because they're easy to carry, but I prefer print textbooks. I remember more when I read a print book.

C: I prefer ebooks to printed books. I don't have space for books.

A BEFORE YOU WRITE Read about the man in the picture. Then look at the picture of the woman. Make up a story about her. Explain why she's doing the things in the picture. Work with a partner. Tell your partner your story about the woman.

John is on the train. He's going to work. He's reading his mail. He's also having breakfast and listening to music. John is a busy man. He's a vice president of a company. He enjoys his job, but he's busy all the time. He has a wife and three children under four. His family is great, but at home he rarely has time alone. That's why John loves his long train ride to work.

B WRITE Write your story about the woman in A. Use the paragraph in A and your ideas. Use the simple present and the present progressive.

C CHECK YOUR WORK Read your paragraph. Underline the verbs in the simple present and circle the verbs in the present progressive. Then use the Editing Checklist to check your work.

Editing Checklist
Did you . . . ?
☐ add -s or -es to the simple present third-person singular (*he, she, it*)
☐ use *is, am, are* + the base form of the verb and *-ing* for the present progressive
☐ use the simple present for habits, customs, facts, and with non-action verbs
☐ use the present progressive for actions happening now or nowadays

D REVISE YOUR WORK Read your paragraph again. Can you improve your writing? Make changes if necessary.

UNIT 17 **REVIEW**

Test yourself on the grammar of the unit.

A Complete the sentences with the simple present forms of the verbs in parentheses. Use the affirmative or negative form.

1. They _____ a car.
   (not / own)

2. He _____ to drive.
   (not / like)

3. She _____ a new bike.
   (have)

4. She _____ a lock for it.
   (need)

5. They _____ to buy bikes, too.
   (want)

B Complete the paragraph with the simple present or present progressive forms of the verbs in parentheses.

John _____ his new computer now. He _____ the
1. (use)   2. (surf)
Internet. He _____ about his computer. His computer _____
3. (read)   4. (have)
a lot of great features. John _____ to learn how to use all of them.
5. (want)

C Complete the conversation with the simple present or present progressive forms of the verbs in parentheses.

A: What _____ Tom _____ right now?
        1. (do)

B: He _____ to fix his printer again.
        2. (try)

A: What _____ the problem now?
        3. (be)

B: I _____.
        4. (not / know)

A: I think he _____ a new printer. His printer is very old.
        5. (need)

D Correct the conversations. There are five mistakes.

1. A: Where you calling from?   B: Downtown. I walk along Second Street.

2. A: Is she play tennis at West Park?   B: No, she's not. She no like West Park.

3. A: Does he understands Greek?   B: Yes, he does. He was in Greece for a year.

Now check your answers on page 448.

Appendices

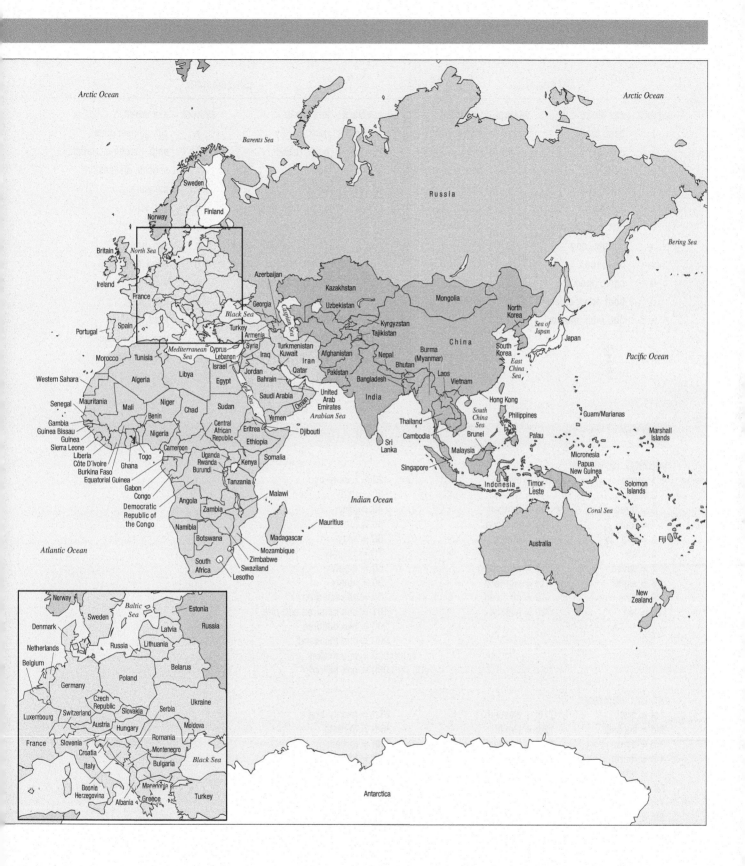

3 Pronunciation Table

A|01 These are the pronunciation symbols used in this text. Listen to the pronunciation of the key words.

VOWELS				CONSONANTS			
SYMBOL	KEY WORD	SYMBOL	KEY WORD	SYMBOL	KEY WORD	SYMBOL	KEY WORD
i	beat, feed	ə	banana, among	p	pack, happy	z	zip, please, goes
ɪ	bit, did	ɚ	shirt, murder	b	back, rubber	ʃ	ship, machine, station, special, discussion
eɪ	date, paid	aɪ	bite, cry, buy, eye	t	tie		
ɛ	bet, bed	aʊ	about, how	d	die	ʒ	measure
æ	bat, bad	ɔɪ	voice, boy	k	came, key, quick	h	hot, who
ɑ	box, odd, father	ɪr	ear, beer	g	game, guest	m	men
ɔ	bought, dog	ɛr	bare	tʃ	church, nature, watch	n	sun, know
oʊ	boat, road	ɑr	bar	ʤ	judge, general, major	ŋ	sung, ringing
ʊ	book, good	ɔr	door	f	fan, photograph	w	wet, white
u	boot, food, student	ʊr	tour	v	van	l	light, long
ʌ	but, mud, mother			θ	thing, breath	r	right, wrong
				ð	then, breathe	y	yes, use, music
				s	sip, city, psychology	t̬	butter, bottle

4 Numbers

CARDINAL NUMBERS

1 = one	11 = eleven	21 = twenty-one
2 = two	12 = twelve	30 = thirty
3 = three	13 = thirteen	40 = forty
4 = four	14 = fourteen	50 = fifty
5 = five	15 = fifteen	60 = sixty
6 = six	16 = sixteen	70 = seventy
7 = seven	17 = seventeen	80 = eighty
8 = eight	18 = eighteen	90 = ninety
9 = nine	19 = nineteen	100 = one hundred
10 = ten	20 = twenty	101 = one hundred and one

200 = two hundred
1,000 = one thousand
1,000,000 = one million
1,000,000,000 = one billion

ORDINAL NUMBERS

1st = first	11th = eleventh	21st = twenty-first
2nd = second	12th = twelfth	30th = thirtieth
3rd = third	13th = thirteenth	40th = fortieth
4th = fourth	14th = fourteenth	50th = fiftieth
5th = fifth	15th = fifteenth	60th = sixtieth
6th = sixth	16th = sixteenth	70th = seventieth
7th = seventh	17th = seventeenth	80th = eightieth
8th = eighth	18th = eighteenth	90th = ninetieth
9th = ninth	19th = nineteenth	100th = one hundredth
10th = tenth	20th = twentieth	101st = one hundred and first

200th = two hundredth
1,000th = one thousandth
1,000,000th = one millionth
1,000,000,000th = one billionth

5 Days, Months, and Seasons

DAYS OF THE WEEK

Weekdays	Weekend
Monday	Saturday
Tuesday	Sunday
Wednesday	
Thursday	
Friday	

MONTHS OF THE YEAR

Month	Abbreviation	Month	Abbreviation
January	Jan.	July	Jul.
February	Feb.	August	Aug.
March	Mar.	September	Sept.
April	Apr.	October	Oct.
May	May	November	Nov.
June	Jun.	December	Dec.

SEASONS

Spring
Summer
Autumn or Fall
Winter

6 Titles

Mr. (Mister) /mɪstər/   unmarried or married man
Ms. /mɪz/   unmarried or married woman
Miss /mɪs/   unmarried woman
Mrs. /mɪsɪz/   married woman
Dr. (Doctor) /dɑktər/   doctor (medical doctor or Ph.D.)

7 Time

It's one o'clock.
(It's 1:00.)

It's five after one.
(It's 1:05.)

It's one-ten.
It's ten after one.
(It's 1:10.)

It's one-fifteen.
It's a quarter after one.
(It's 1:15.)

It's one twenty-five.
It's twenty-five after one.
(It's 1:25.)

It's one-thirty.
It's half past one.
(It's 1:30.)

It's one forty-five.
It's a quarter to two.
(It's 1:45.)

It's one-fifty.
It's ten to two.
(It's 1:50.)

1 You can ask and give the time in this way:

A: **What time is it?**
B: It's one **o'clock**.

2 We often write time with numbers.

It's one o'clock. = It's **1:00**.
It's two-twenty. = It's **2:20**.

3 We use the abbreviation **a.m.** for times from midnight to noon.
It's 10:00 **a.m.**

We use the abbreviation **p.m.** for times from noon to midnight.
It's 10:00 **p.m.**

4 When people say 12:00 a.m., they mean midnight. When people say 12:00 p.m., they mean noon.

8 Regular Plural Nouns: Spelling Rules

1 Add **-s** to most nouns.

book	book**s**
table	table**s**
cup	cup**s**

2 Add **-es** to nouns that end in **-ch**, **-s**, **-sh**, or **-x**.

watch	watch**es**
bus	bus**es**
dish	dish**es**
box	box**es**

3 Add **-s** to nouns that end in **vowel + y**.

day	day**s**
key	key**s**

4 Change the **y** to **i** and add **-es** to nouns that end in **consonant + y**.

baby	bab**ies**
city	cit**ies**
strawberry	strawberr**ies**

5 Add **-s** to nouns that end in **vowel + o**.

radio	radio**s**
video	video**s**
zoo	zoo**s**

6 Add **-es** to nouns that end in **consonant + o**.

potato	potato**es**
tomato	tomato**es**

EXCEPTIONS:

kilo	kilo**s**
photo	photo**s**
piano	piano**s**

9 Irregular Plural Nouns

SINGULAR	PLURAL
half	halves
knife	knives
leaf	leaves
life	lives
shelf	shelves
wife	wives

SINGULAR	PLURAL
child	children
foot	feet
man	men
mouse	mice
person	people
tooth	teeth
woman	women

SINGULAR	PLURAL
clothes	clothes
deer	deer
fish	fish
pants	pants
scissors	scissors
sheep	sheep

10 Plural Nouns: Pronunciation Rules

1 The **final sounds** for regular plural nouns are /s/, /z/, and /ɪz/.

boots	boys	horses

2 The plural is pronounced /s/ after the **voiceless sounds** /p/, /t/, /k/, /f/, and /θ/.

cups	cuffs
hats	myths
works	

3 The plural is pronounced /z/ after the **voiced sounds** /b/, /d/, /g/, /v/, /m/, /n/, /ŋ/, /l/, /r/, and /ð/.

crabs	doves	rings
cards	drums	girls
rugs	fans	stores

4 The plural **s** is pronounced /z/ **after all vowel sounds**.

day	days
toe	toes

5 The plural **s** is pronounced /ɪz/ **after the sounds** /s/, /z/, /ʃ/, /tʃ/, and /ʤ/. (This adds another syllable to the word.)

races	churches
causes	judges
dishes	

11 Non-Count Nouns

Non-count nouns are singular.

ACTIVITIES
baseball
biking
football
golf
hiking
running
soccer
swimming
tennis

CITY PROBLEMS
crime
pollution

FOOD AND DRINKS
bread
broccoli
butter
cake
cheese
chicken
chocolate
coffee
corn
fat
fish
flour
fruit
ice cream

juice
lettuce
meat
milk
pasta
pizza
salad
soda
soup
spaghetti
spinach
tea
water
yogurt

IDEAS AND FEELINGS
friendship
happiness
love

GASES
air
oxygen
smoke

MATERIALS
clay
cotton
glass
gold
leather
paper
silk
silver
wood
wool

SCHOOL SUBJECTS
art
English
geography
history
mathematics
music
photography
psychology
science

VERY SMALL THINGS
cereal
corn
dust
pepper
rice
salt
sand
sugar

WEATHER
fog
ice
rain
snow
wind

NAMES OF CATEGORIES

clothing	(BUT: coats, hats, shoes …)
equipment	(BUT: computers, phones …)
food	(BUT: bananas, eggs …)
furniture	(BUT: beds, chairs, lamps …)
homework	(BUT: assignments, problems …)
jewelry	(BUT: earrings, necklaces …)
mail	(BUT: letters, packages …)
money	(BUT: dollars, euros, pounds …)
time	(BUT: minutes, months …)
work	(BUT: jobs, projects …)

OTHER
Some non-count nouns don't fit into any list. You must memorize these non-count nouns.

advice
garbage/trash
help
information
news

12 Quantifying Non-Count Nouns

a bottle of (milk, soda, ketchup)
a bowl of (cereal, soup, rice)
a can of (soda, beans, tuna fish)
a cup of (hot chocolate, coffee, tea)
a foot of (snow, water)
a gallon of (juice, gas, paint)

a head of (lettuce)
a loaf of (bread)
an inch of (snow, rain)
a pair of (pants, gloves)
a piece of (paper, cake, pie)
a pint of (ice cream, cream)

a quart of (milk)
a roll of (toilet paper, paper towels)
a slice of (toast, cheese, meat)
a tablespoon of (flour, sugar, baking soda)
a teaspoon of (sugar, salt, pepper)
a tube of (toothpaste, glue)

13 The Simple Present: Spelling Rules

1 Add **-s** for most verbs.

work	work**s**
buy	buy**s**
ride	ride**s**
return	return**s**

2 Add **-es** for verbs that end in **-ch**, **-s**, **-sh**, **-x**, or **-z**.

watch	watch**es**
pass	pass**es**
rush	rush**es**
relax	relax**es**
buzz	buzz**es**

3 Change the **y** to **i** and add **-es** when the base form ends in **consonant + y**.

study	stud**ies**
hurry	hurr**ies**
dry	dr**ies**

4 Do not change the **y** when the base form ends in **vowel + y**. Add **-s**.

play	play**s**
enjoy	enjoy**s**

5 A few verbs have **irregular forms**.

be	**is**
do	**does**
go	**goes**
have	**has**

14 The Simple Present: Pronunciation Rules

1 The third-person singular in the simple present always ends in the letter **-s**. There are three different pronunciations for the final sound of the third-person singular.

/s/	/z/	/ɪz/
talk**s**	love**s**	danc**es**

2 The final sound is pronounced /s/ after the voiceless sounds /p/, /t/, /k/, and /f/.

top	to**ps**
get	ge**ts**
take	ta**kes**
laugh	lau**ghs**

3 The final sound is pronounced /z/ after the voiced sounds /b/, /d/, /g/, /v/, /m/, /n/, /ŋ/, /l/, /r/, and /ð/.

describe	descri**bes**
spend	spen**ds**
hug	hu**gs**
live	li**ves**
seem	see**ms**
remain	remai**ns**
sing	si**ngs**
tell	te**lls**
lower	lowe**rs**
bathe	bat**hes**

4 The final sound is pronounced /z/ after all **vowel sounds**.

agree	agre**es**
try	tr**ies**
stay	stay**s**
know	kn**ows**

5 The final sound is pronounced /ɪz/ after the sounds /s/, /z/, /ʃ/, /ʒ/, /tʃ/, and /dʒ/. /ɪz/ adds a syllable to the verb.

miss	mi**sses**
freeze	free**zes**
rush	ru**shes**
massage	massa**ges**
watch	wat**ches**
judge	ju**dges**

6 **Do** and **say** have a change in vowel sound.

do /du/	does /dʌz/
say /sɛɪ/	says /sɛz/

15 Non-Action Verbs

STATE OF BEING	EMOTIONS	MENTAL STATES	POSSESSION AND RELATIONSHIP	SENSES	WANTS AND PREFERENCES
be	dislike	agree	belong	feel	need
	hate	believe	cost	hear	prefer
	like	disagree	have	look	want
	love	guess	owe	see	
	miss	know	own	smell	
		remember		sound	
		think		taste	
		understand			

16 The Present Progressive: Spelling Rules

1 Add *-ing* to the base form of the verb.

read	read**ing**
stand	stand**ing**

2 If the verb ends in a **silent -e**, drop the final *-e* and add *-ing*.

leave	leav**ing**
take	tak**ing**

3 In **one-syllable** verbs, if the last three letters are consonant-vowel-consonant (CVC), double the last consonant and add *-ing*.

C V C
↓ ↓ ↓
s i t   sit**ting**

C V C
↓ ↓ ↓
p l a n   plan**ning**

EXCEPTION: Do not double the last consonant in verbs that end in *-w*, *-x*, or *-y*.

sew	sew**ing**
fix	fix**ing**
play	play**ing**

4 In verbs of **two or more syllables** that end in consonant-vowel-consonant, double the last consonant only if the last syllable is stressed.

admít	admit**ting**	*(The last syllable is stressed.)*
whísper	whisper**ing**	*(The last syllable is not stressed, so don't double the -r.)*

5 If the verb ends in *-ie*, change the *ie* to *y* before adding *-ing*.

die	d**ying**
lie	l**ying**

Stress
´ shows main stress.

17 The Simple Past: Spelling Rules

1 If the verb ends in a **consonant**, add **-ed**.

return returned
help helped

2 If the verb ends in **-e**, add **-d**.

live lived
create created
die died

3 In **one-syllable** verbs, if the last three letters are consonant-vowel-consonant (CVC), double the last consonant and add **-ed**.

C V C
↓ ↓ ↓
h o p   hopped

C V C
↓ ↓ ↓
g r a b   grabbed

EXCEPTION: Do not double the last consonant in **one-syllable** verbs that end in **-w**, **-x**, or **-y**.

bow bowed
mix mixed
play played

4 In verbs of **two or more syllables** that end in consonant-vowel-consonant, double the last consonant only if the last syllable is stressed.

prefér   preferred   *(The last syllable is stressed.)*

vísit   visited   *(The last syllable is not stressed, so don't double the* **-t***.)*

5 If the verb ends in **consonant + y**, change the **y** to **i** and add **-ed**.

worry worried
carry carried

6 If the verb ends in **vowel + y**, add **-ed**. (Do not change the **y** to **i**.)

play played
annoy annoyed

EXCEPTIONS:
lay laid
pay paid
say said

18 The Simple Past: Pronunciation Rules

1 The regular simple past always ends in the letter **-d**. There are three different pronunciations for the final sound of the regular simple past.

/t/   /d/   /ɪd/
raced   lived   attended

2 The final sound is pronounced /t/ after the voiceless sounds /p/, /k/, /f/, /s/, /ʃ/, and /tʃ/.

hop hopped
work worked
laugh laughed
address addressed
publish published
watch watched

3 The final sound is pronounced /d/ after the voiced sounds /b/, /g/, /v/, /z/, /ʒ/, /dʒ/, /m/, /n/, /ŋ/, /l/, /r/, and /ð/.

rub rubbed   rhyme rhymed
hug hugged   return returned
live lived   bang banged
surprise surprised   enroll enrolled
massage massaged   appear appeared
change changed   bathe bathed

4 The final sound is pronounced /d/ after all **vowel sounds**.

agree agreed
die died
play played
enjoy enjoyed
snow snowed

5 The final sound is pronounced /ɪd/ after /t/ and /d/. /ɪd/ adds a syllable to the verb.

start started
decide decided

19 Irregular Past Tense Verbs

BASE FORM	PAST FORM	BASE FORM	PAST FORM	BASE FORM	PAST FORM	BASE FORM	PAST FORM
become	became	feel	felt	leave	left	sit	sat
begin	began	fight	fought	lend	lent	sleep	slept
bite	bit	find	found	lose	lost	speak	spoke
blow	blew	fly	flew	make	made	spend	spent
break	broke	forget	forgot	meet	met	stand	stood
bring	brought	get	got	pay	paid	steal	stole
build	built	give	gave	put	put	swim	swam
buy	bought	go	went	quit	quit	take	took
catch	caught	grow	grew	read*	read*	teach	taught
choose	chose	hang	hung	ride	rode	tear	tore
come	came	have	had	ring	rang	tell	told
cost	cost	hear	heard	run	ran	think	thought
do	did	hide	hid	say	said	throw	threw
draw	drew	hit	hit	see	saw	understand	understood
drink	drank	hold	held	send	sent	wake	woke
drive	drove	hurt	hurt	shake	shook	wear	wore
eat	ate	keep	kept	shoot	shot	win	won
fall	fell	know	knew	shut	shut	write	wrote
feed	fed	lead	led	sing	sang		

*Pronounce the base form /rid/. Pronounce the past form /rɛd/.

20 Capitalization and Punctuation Rules

	USE FOR . . .	EXAMPLES
capital letter	• the pronoun *I*	My friend and **I** are on vacation.
	• proper nouns	**Ali** is from Turkey.
	• the first word of a sentence	**They** live in Spain.
apostrophe (')	• possessive nouns	Is that **Marta's** coat?
	• contractions	**That's** not hers. **It's** mine.
comma (,)	• after items in a list	He bought apples**,** pears**,** oranges**,** and bananas.
	• to connect two sentences with *and* or *but*	They watched TV**,** and she played video games.
	• after the name of a person you are writing to	Dear John**,**
exclamation point (!)	• at the end of a sentence to show surprise or a strong feeling	You're here**!** That's great**!** Stop**!** A car is coming**!**
period (.)	• at the end of a statement	Today is Wednesday**.**
	• after abbreviations	The party is on Nov**.** 3.
question mark (?)	• at the end of a question	What day is today**?**

Glossary of Grammar Terms

action verb A verb that describes an action. It can be used in the progressive.

> Sachiko **is planning** a big party.

adjective A word that describes (or modifies) a noun or pronoun.

> That's a **great** idea.

adverb A word that describes (or modifies) an action verb, an adverb, an adjective, or a sentence.

> She drives **slowly**.

adverb of frequency A word that tells the frequency of something.

> We **usually** eat lunch at noon.

adverb of manner A word that describes a verb. It usually answers the question *how*.

> She speaks **clearly**.

affirmative statement A sentence that does not use a negative verb form (*not*).

> **I have a car.**

apostrophe A punctuation mark used to show possession and to write a short form (contraction).

> He**'s** in my father**'s** car.

base form The form of the verb without any ending such as *-ing*, *-ed*, or *-s*. It is the same as the infinitive without *to*.

> Arnold will **come** at 8:00. We should **eat** then.

be going to future A verb form used to make predictions, express general facts in the future, or talk about definite plans that were made before now.

> Mei-Ling says it**'s going to be** cold, so she**'s going to take** a coat.

capital letter The big form of a letter of the alphabet. Sentences start with a capital letter.

> **A, B, C**, etc.

comma Punctuation used to separate single things in a list or parts of a sentence.

> We went to a restaurant**,** and we ate chicken**,** potatoes**,** and broccoli.

common noun A noun for a person, an animal, a place, or a thing. It is not capitalized.

> The **man** got a **book** at the **library**.

comparative form An adjective or adverb ending in *-er* or following *more*. It is used in comparing two things.

> My sister is **older** and **more intelligent** than my brother.
> But he studies **harder** and **more carefully**.

consonant The letters $b, c, d, f, g, h, j, k, l, m, n, p, q, r, s, t, v, w, x, y, z$.

contraction A short form of two words. An apostrophe (') replaces the missing letter.

> **It is** late and **I am** tired. **I should not** stay up so late.
> **It's** late and **I'm** tired. **I shouldn't** stay up so late.

count noun A noun you can count. It usually has a singular and a plural form.

> In the **park**, there was a **man** with two **children** and a **dog**.

definite article *The*; makes a noun specific.

> We saw a movie. **The** movie starred Sean Penn.

demonstrative adjective An adjective used to identify the noun that follows.

> **This** man is resting, but **those** men are busy.

demonstrative pronoun A pronoun used in place of a demonstrative adjective and the noun that follows.

> **This** is our classroom, and **these** are my students.

direct object A noun or pronoun used to receive the action of a verb.

> She sold a **car**. He bought **it**.

exclamation point A punctuation mark (!) used at the end of a statement. It shows strong emotion.

> Help**!** Call the police**!**

formal language Language we usually use in business settings, academic settings, and with people we don't know.

> **Good morning, ladies and gentlemen. May** we begin?

gerund The *-ing* form of a verb. It is used as a noun.

> **Skiing** is fun, but we also enjoy **swimming**.

imperative A sentence used to give an instruction, a direction, a command, or a suggestion. It uses the base form of the verb. The subject (*you*) is not a part of the sentence.

> **Turn** right at the corner. **Drive** to the end of the street. **Stop!**

indefinite article *A* and *an*; used before singular, nonspecific non-count nouns.

> Jaime brought **a** sandwich and **an** apple for lunch.

infinitive *To* + the base form of a verb.

> **To travel** is my dream. I want **to see** the world.

informal language The language we usually use with family and friends, in email messages, and in other informal settings.

> **Hey, Doug, what's up?**

inseparable phrasal verb A phrasal verb that cannot have an object between the verb and the particle.

> She **ran into** John.

irregular verb A verb that does not form the simple past by adding *-d* or *-ed*.

> They **ate** a fancy meal last night. The boss **came** to dinner.

modal A word that comes before the main verb. Modals can express ability, possibility, obligation, and necessity.

> You **can** come early, but you **mustn't** be late, and you **should** wear a tie.

negative statement A statement with a negative verb form.

> He **didn't study**. He **wasn't** ready for the test.

non-action verb A verb that does not describe an action. It can describe an emotion, a state, a sense, or a mental thought. We usually don't use non-action verbs in the progressive.

> I **like** that actor. He **is** very famous, and I **believe** he won an Oscar.

non-count noun A noun we usually do not count. We don't put *a*, *an*, or a number before a non-count noun.

> All you'll need is **rice, water, salt,** and **butter**.

noun A word that refers to a person, animal, place, thing, or idea.

> **Paula** has a **friend** at the **library**. She gave me a **book** about **birds**.

noun modifier A noun that describes another noun.

> Samantha is a **chemistry** professor. She loves **spy** movies.

noun phrase A phrase formed by a noun and words that describe (modify) it.

> It was **a dark brown leather jacket**.

object A noun or pronoun following an action verb. It receives the action of the verb.

> I sent **a letter**. He read **it**.

object pronoun A pronoun following a verb or a preposition.

> We asked **him** to show the photos to **them**.

period A punctuation mark (.) used at the end of a statement.

> I'd like you to call on Saturday**.** We need to talk**.**

phrasal verb A two-part (or three-part) verb that combines a verb and a preposition or particle (for example, *on* or *up*). The meaning of the parts together is often different from the meaning of the verb alone.

> We **put on** our gloves and **picked up** our umbrellas.

phrase A group of words that can form a grammatical unit.

> She lost **a red hat**. He found it **under the table**.

plural The form that means more than one.

> **We** sat in **our chairs** reading **our books**.

possessive An adjective, noun, or pronoun that shows possession.

> **Her** book is in **John's** car. **Mine** is at the office.

preposition A small word that goes before a noun or pronoun object. A preposition often shows time or place.

> Maria saw it **on** the table **at** two o'clock.

prepositional phrase A phrase that consists of a preposition followed by a noun or a noun phrase.

> Chong-Dae saw it **under the black wooden table**.

present progressive A verb form that shows an action happening now or planned for the future.

> **I'm working** hard now, but **I'm taking** a vacation soon.

pronoun A word that replaces a noun or a noun phrase. There are subject pronouns, object pronouns, possessive pronouns, and demonstrative pronouns.

> **He** is a friend—I know **him** well. **This** is his coat; **mine** is black.

proper noun The actual name of a person, place, or thing. A proper noun begins with a capital letter.

> **Tom** is living in **New York**. He is studying **Russian** at **Columbia University**.

quantifier A word or phrase that comes before a noun and expresses an amount of that noun.

> Jeannette used **a little** sugar, **some** flour, **four** eggs, and **a liter of** milk.

question mark A punctuation mark (?) used at the end of a question.

> Where are you going**?** When will you be back**?**

quotation marks Punctuation marks (" . . . ") used before and after the actual words a person says.

> I said, **"Where are you going?"** and **"When will you be back?"**

regular verb A verb that forms the simple past by adding *-d* or *-ed*.

> We **lived** in France. My mother **visited** us there.

sentence A group of words with a subject and a verb.

> **We opened the window.**
> **Did they paint the house?**

separable phrasal verb A phrasal verb that can have an object between the verb and the particle.

> She **put on** her coat. She **put** it **on** before he **put** his coat **on**.

simple past A verb form used to show a completed action or idea in the past.

> The plane **landed** at 9:00. We **caught** a bus to the hotel.

simple present A verb form used to show habitual actions or states, general facts, or conditions that are true now.

> Kemal **loves** to ski, and it **snows** a lot in his area, so he**'s** very happy.

singular The form that means only one.

> I put on my **hat** and **coat** and closed the **door**.

small letter The small form of a letter of the alphabet. We use small letters for most words except for proper nouns and the word that starts a sentence.

> **a**, **b**, **c**, etc.

subject The person, place, or thing that a sentence is about.

> **The children** ate at the mall.

subject pronoun A pronoun used to replace a subject noun.

> Irene works hard. **She** loves her work.

superlative form An adjective or adverb ending in *-est* or following *most*. It is used in comparing three or more things.

> We climbed the **highest** mountain by the **most dangerous** route.
> She drives the **fastest** and the **most carelessly** of all the drivers.

syllable A group of letters with one vowel sound. Words are made up of one or more syllables.

> One syllable—**win**
> Two syllables—**ta ble**
> Three syllables—**im por tant**

verb A word used to describe an action, a fact, or a state.

> He **drives** to work now. He **has** a new car, and he **is** a careful driver.

vowel The letters *a*, *e*, *i*, *o*, or *u*, and sometimes *y*.

wh- question A question that asks for information. It begins with *what, when, where, why, which, who, whose,* or *how*.

> **What**'s your name?
> **Where** are you from?
> **How** do you feel?

will future A verb form used to make predictions, to talk about facts in the future, to make promises, to offer something, or to state a decision to do something at the time of speaking.

> It **will** probably rain, so I'**ll take** an umbrella. I'**ll give** you my extra one.

yes/no question A question that has a *yes* or a *no* answer.

> **Did you arrive on time?** Yes, I did.
> **Are you from Uruguay?** No, I'm not.
> **Can you swim well?** Yes, I can.

Unit Review Answer Key

UNIT 1

A 1. are 3. am 5. are
2. is 4. is

B 1. 'm 3. 're 5. 're
2. 's 4. 's

C 1. He's not **or** He isn't 3. We're not **or** We aren't
2. They're 4. She's

D My father and mother are from India, but they're in Canada now. My parents are doctors. My father ^is^ a sports doctor, and my mother ~~she~~ is a family doctor. My parents and I love sports. My father ~~are~~ ^is^ a soccer fan, and my mother ^is^ a baseball fan. I'm a soccer fan. My father and I ~~am~~ ^are^ fans of Lionel Messi and Nuno Gomes. My sister ~~no is~~ ^isn't **or** is not^ good at sports. She's not a sports fan. She loves movies.

UNIT 2

A 1. Where's 4. Are
2. How's 5. Is
3. What's

B 1. I am
2. it isn't **or** it is not
3. they aren't **or** they are not
4. we are
5. you're not **or** you aren't **or** you are not

C 1. What's today's date? **or** What is today's date?
2. Where's the men's room? **or** Where is the men's room?
3. Why's he absent? **or** Why is he absent?
4. When's your first class? **or** When is your first class?
5. Who's your teacher? **or** Who is your teacher?

D 1. ~~She~~ ^Is^ she your teacher?
2. What ^'s **or** is^ your name?
3. Where ^'s **or** is^ your class?
4. ~~Is~~ ^Are^ Bob and Molly good friends?
5. Why ^are^ you late?

UNIT 3

A 1. was 3. Were 5. Was
2. was 4. were

B 1. c 2. b 3. d 4. a

C 1. was 3. Were 5. were 7. was
2. was 4. was 6. wasn't

D John ~~is~~ ^was^ at a job interview yesterday. It ~~were~~ ^was^ for a job at a bank. The questions ~~no were~~ ^weren't **or** were not^ easy, but John's answers were good. He was happy. It ^was^ a good day for John.

UNIT 4

A 1. a 3. Ø 5. Ø
2. an 4. Ø

B 1. cities 4. fish
2. watches 5. people
3. clothes

C A: Hi, are you the photographer?
B: Yes, I'm Amy Lin.
A: Nice to meet you. I'm Ali Mohammed.
B: Are you from London?
A: Yes, I am. I'm here for your Thanksgiving Day holiday.

D Melanie Einzig is ^an^ artist and ~~an~~ ^a^ photographer. She was born in Minnesota, but lives in New ~~york~~ ^York^. Einzig captures moments in time. Her ~~photograph~~ ^photographs^ are striking. They are in ~~museum~~ ^museums^ in San ~~francisco~~ ^Francisco^, Chicago, and Princeton.

UNIT 5

A 1. a 3. Ø 5. Ø
2. Ø 4. an

B 1. a small hotel 4. kind and helpful
2. an interesting garden 5. a great choice
3. big and comfortable

C 1. I'm at the new museum
2. It has interesting things
3. It has unusual bowls
4. It has beautiful carpets
5. The museum is a great place

D The Grand Canyon National Park in Arizona is ~~a~~ *an* awesome place to visit. Almost five million people visit the park every year. It is a ~~park beautiful~~ *beautiful park*. The weather is good in the late spring and summer, but the park ~~crowded is~~ *is crowded* during those months. There are seven ~~differents~~ *different* places to stay in the park. I like El Tovar. It is ~~a~~ *an* old hotel with a great view.

UNIT 6

A 1. on
2. under
3. behind
4. next to
5. in front of

B 1. at / across
2. at / on

C 1. on the / in the / on the
2. inside / above / under

D A: Is Jon ~~on~~ *at* school?
B: No. He's ~~in~~ *at* home.
A: Where does he live?
B: He lives ~~at~~ *on* Oak Street ~~at~~ *in* New City.
A: Does he live in an apartment?
B: Yes. He lives ~~in~~ *on* the third floor.

UNIT 7

A 1. Let's get
2. Why don't we
3. Don't buy
4. Let's meet
5. Don't touch

B 1. Wear
2. Don't wear
3. Bring
4. Don't bring
5. pay

C 1. Let's
2. don't we
3. don't you
4. Let's

D 1. Why ~~you~~ don't *you* ask Andrij for help?
2. You look really tired. ~~You take~~ *Take* a short nap.
3. Let's ~~to~~ walk to work. Let's not drive.
4. Don't ask Boris to fix the car. ~~Asks~~ *Ask* Mickey.
5. I'm on a diet, so buy ~~please~~ *please* yogurt. Don't ~~to~~ get sour cream.

UNIT 8

A 1. loves
2. doesn't have
3. invites
4. don't give
5. have

B 1. always celebrate
2. sometimes wears
3. often sits
4. usually dance
5. are usually

C 1. thinks
2. don't work
3. comes
4. is

D Some people don't ~~enjoys~~ *enjoy* holidays and family gatherings. Bill Jones ~~visits usually~~ *usually visits* his wife's sister on holidays. He likes his wife's sister, but he ~~don't~~ *doesn't* like her husband. Mary Brown doesn't like holidays because she lives far from her family. She ~~have~~ *has* a very important job, but she doesn't have close friends. She usually watches movies and ~~wait~~ *waits* for the holiday to be over. ~~Always she is~~ *She is always* happy to return to work.

UNIT 9

A 1. Do
2. Is
3. Does
4. Are
5. Am

B 1. Do you have
2. Does his roommate speak
3. Does your roommate watch
4. Is your roommate
5. Are your roommate's parents

C 1. Are the neighbors noisy?
2. Does the building have an elevator?
3. Is the apartment near buses?
4. Does the bedroom have two closets?
5. Is the bedroom big?

D 1. A: Does he have a big TV in his room?
B: Yes, he ~~has~~ *does*.
2. A: Does she ~~needs~~ *need* help?
B: No, she ~~don't~~ *doesn't*.
3. A: ~~Do you are~~ *Are* you friends?
B: Yes, we ~~aren't~~ *are*. **or** ~~Yes~~ *No*, we aren't.

UNIT 10

A 1. Why
2. When
3. Who
4. How
5. Where

B 1. What do you dream about?
2. What time does your mother get up?
3. What time do you go to bed?
4. Where does your brother sleep?
5. Who snores in your family?

C 1. Who meets his uncle at the diner on Saturdays?
2. Who does John meet at the diner on Saturdays?
3. Where does John meet his uncle on Saturdays?
4. When does John meet his uncle at the diner?

D 1. Where ~~do~~ you live?
2. Why ~~he daydreams~~ *does he daydream* in class?
3. When does she ~~gets~~ *get* up?
4. How ~~do~~ they feel about sleeping pills?
5. Who ~~does~~ *do* you dream about?
6. What time ~~he~~ *does* he wake up?

UNIT 11

A 1. There aren't   4. There isn't
2. There's   5. There's
3. There are   6. There are

B 1. A: Are there   3. A: Are they
   B: there are   B: they aren't
2. A: Is she   4. A: Is there
   B: she is   B: there isn't

C 1. There's / It's   3. There's / She's
2. There are / They're

D Visit the new Shopper's Mall on Route 290. There~~'s~~ *are* over 100 stores. There *is* a movie theater, and ~~they~~ *there* are ten great places to eat. Come early. Every morning at 10:30, there ~~are~~ *is* a free show for children. The mall is three miles from the Tappan Bridge on Route 290.

UNIT 12

A 1. ~~My parents'~~ *Their*   4. ~~The students'~~ *Their*
2. ~~My brother's~~ *His*   5. ~~Our aunt's~~ *Her*
3. ~~That bird's~~ *Its*

B 1. A: mine   2. A: Whose
   B: yours   B: Ali's
   A: your

C 1. Whose   3. Who's   5. Who's
2. Whose   4. Whose

D A: ~~Who's~~ *Whose* bag is that on the floor?
   B: I think it's ~~Maria~~ *Maria's*.
   A: No. Her bag is on her arm.
   B: Well, it's not ~~mine~~ *my* bag. Maybe it's ~~Rita~~ *Rita's*.
   A: Rita, is that ~~yours~~ *your* bag?

UNIT 13

A 1. a. couldn't understand
      b. can understand
2. a. can't run
      b. could run
3. a. couldn't drive
      b. can drive

B 1. A: Can   3. A: Can
   B: can   B: can
2. A: Could
   B: couldn't

C 1. Could your bird sit on your finger?
2. Can the parrot say anything?
3. Could your dog bring you your shoe?
4. Can that bird talk about the past and the future?

D A: Can you ~~to~~ get online?
   B: No, I can't. I ~~no could~~ *couldn't* get online last night either.
   A: My brother is good with computers. Maybe he can ~~helps~~ *help*. I can ~~to~~ call him after work.

UNIT 14

A 1. may eat   4. may not use
2. can't eat   5. may drink
3. can have

B 1. When can I return to work?
2. When can I take a shower?
3. When can I go to the gym?
4. When can I ride my bike?

C 1. Can we eat during the test?
2. May I use a pencil?
3. Can I make calls during the test?
4. Can we drink water?
5. May I use a black pen?
6. Can we use a dictionary?

D A: May I ~~sees~~ *see* a menu?
   B: Sure. Here you go.
   A: And can we ~~to~~ have some water?
   B: I'll be right back with the water....Ready?
   A: Yes. May I ~~has~~ *have* the chicken?
   B: Of course. A very good choice.
   A: And can you ~~brings~~ *bring* me a small salad?
   B: Certainly. And may I ~~gets~~ *get* you anything else?

UNIT 15

A
1. I'm not
2. We're preparing
3. She isn't playing
4. They're doing
5. He's reading

B
1. is listening to
2. are standing and talking
3. are running
4. is driving
5. is carrying

C
1. a. is texting
   b. isn't calling **or** 's not calling
2. a. isn't crying ('s not crying)
   b. 's watching **or** is watching
3. a. 's swimming **or** is swimming
   b. 's trying

D
My classmates and I ~~am~~ *are* sitting in a computer lab.
One student *is* writing a composition. Two students are
~~check~~ *checking* their email. A teacher is ~~helps~~ *helping* a student. The
other students are reading.

UNIT 16

A
1. Are you working?
2. Is he buying tickets online?
3. Are they watching a mystery?
4. Is your cousin enjoying the movie?

B
1. Where are they going?
2. What movie is she watching?
3. Why is Bob staying home?
4. Who's watching the children?

C
1. a. are the kids laughing
   b. Are they watching
   c. 're playing
2. a. are you doing
   b. 'm making
   c. 'm planning
3. a. 's happening
   b. 're making

D
A: What *are* you watching?

B: We're watching a detective show.

A: What *'s* happening?

B: A boy is missing from home.

A: ~~The police are~~ *Are the police* looking for him?

B: Yes, they are.

A: Where *are* they looking?

B: Everywhere.

UNIT 17

A
1. don't own
2. doesn't like
3. has
4. needs
5. want

B
1. is using
2. is surfing **or** 's surfing
3. is reading **or** 's reading
4. has
5. wants

C
1. is, doing
2. is trying **or** 's trying
3. is
4. don't know
5. needs

D
1. A: Where *are* you calling from?

   B: Downtown. I ~~walk~~ *'m walking* along Second Street.

2. A: Is she ~~play~~ *playing* tennis at West Park?

   B: No, she's not. She ~~no like~~ *doesn't like* West Park.

3. A: Does he ~~understands~~ *understand* Greek?

   B: Yes, he does. He was in Greece for a year.

UNIT 18

A
1. watched
2. visited
3. an hour ago
4. Last night
5. didn't land

B
1. helped
2. stayed
3. didn't snow
4. didn't ask
5. didn't want

C
1. canceled
2. didn't stay
3. didn't rain
4. played
5. didn't enjoy

D
Hello from London. Our friends ~~did invited~~ *invited* us
here for a week. Yesterday we ~~visit~~ *visited* Big Ben, and we
~~tour~~ *toured* Buckingham Palace. This morning, we ~~watch~~ *watched*
a cricket match. Later, we walked around Piccadilly
Circus and ~~are~~ enjoyed coffee and sandwiches at a
small nearby café.

UNIT 19

A
1. saw
2. were
3. was
4. began
5. said
6. wanted

B
1. grew up
2. drew
3. didn't make
4. began
5. was

C 1. left
2. lost
3. ran

4. didn't see
5. didn't take

D The writer William Sidney Porter *was* born in North Carolina in 1862. He wrote under different names, but he ~~did~~ became best known as O. Henry. His stories ~~were~~ had surprise endings. O. Henry was a very successful writer, but he ~~spended~~ *spent* time in prison.

UNIT 20

A 1. Did they go to the theater?
2. Did we miss the beginning?
3. Did you have good seats?
4. Did it have a good ending?

B 1. When did Olivia do her homework?
2. Where did John go last summer?
3. Who helped Claudia with her report?
4. How long did Mia and Lily work?

C 1. What play did you see last night?
2. Where did you see it?
3. How long was the show?
4. Did you enjoy the performance?
5. Who was the star of the show?
6. Did you go out after the show?

D 1. Where ~~he did~~ *did he go* last night?
2. What ~~saw he~~ *did he see*?
3. Did he ~~enjoyed~~ *enjoy* it?
4. Who ~~he met~~ *did he meet* **or** *met him*?
5. When ~~they left~~ *did they leave*?
6. Who ~~did pay~~ *paid* for dinner?

UNIT 21

A 1. was born
2. grew up
3. attended
4. went
5. started
6. became
7. expanded

B 1. When did she go to college?
2. Who did they meet?
3. Where did he study?
4. How long did they live in Canada?

C 1. Were
2. Did
3. Was
4. Did
5. Did

D Steve Paul Jobs ~~did start~~ *started* college in 1970, but he ~~no did~~ *didn't* **or** *did not* finish it. In In 1976, Jobs and his friend ~~begin~~ *began* to make their own computers. They worked in Jobs' garage. That was the beginning of Apple® Computers. Their company ~~become~~ *became* a big success. Apple® changed the field of computers, and by the age of thirty, Jobs was a multimillionaire.

UNIT 22

A 1. is going to build
2. 's going to cost
3. 's going to have
4. are going to be
5. is not going to begin

B 1. are not going to increase
2. 're not going to play **or** aren't going to play
3. 're going to visit him
4. 's going to retire
5. 'm not going to do

C 1. Q: When is she going to the dentist?
    A: On Monday at 5:30.
2. Q: Where is she meeting Yu Chen?
    A: At Pappa Pizza.
3. Q: Is she meeting Yu Chen on Monday?
    A: No, she isn't.

D This city *is* going to change under our new mayor. People~~'s~~ *are* going to ride bikes, and they're going *to* use public transportation. ~~They're no~~ *They're not* **or** *They aren't* going to drive big cars. There are probably going to be higher tolls on bridges and more bike paths on the roads.

UNIT 23

A 1. won't
2. won't
3. will
4. will
5. won't

B 1. Will many people travel to the moon in twenty years?
2. Will the climate change in the future?
3. What will people eat in 2050?
4. Will people look different in 2100?
5. How will people get around in the year 2035?

C 1. Will...be
2. Will...have
3. Will...be
4. Will...rain
5. Will...work

D I usually bring my lunch to work, but tomorrow
won't
I ~~no will~~ bring it because it's my birthday. My
take
co-workers will ~~takes~~ me out to a restaurant. We'll

~~to~~ order a few different dishes, and we'll share them.
sing
They'll ~~singing~~ "Happy Birthday," and they'll give me
be
a small gift. I'm sure it will ~~is~~ a lot of fun.

UNIT 24

A 1. go   4. may
    2. buy   5. Will
    3. might not

B 1. may snow **or** might snow
    2. may not get **or** might not get
    3. may need **or** might need
    4. may not see **or** might not see
    5. may stay **or** might stay

C 1. Will   4. will
    2. may   5. will
    3. might **or** may

D 1. He might ~~goes~~ on vacation next week.
go
              work
    2. He may ~~works~~ late tomorrow.
    3. They might ~~to~~ visit him tomorrow. Are you free?
    4. I might not help him. I might ~~to~~ help her instead.
may **or** *might*
    5. She ~~maybe~~ take a yoga class.

UNIT 25

A 1. to start   4. to become
    2. to sell   5. flying / seeing
    3. to return

B 1. to work   3. quitting / going
    2. to change   4. improving

C 1. She enjoys helping people.
    2. We expect to graduate in June.
    3. They are trying to study.
    4. He avoids eating candy and ice cream. **or** He avoids
       eating ice cream and candy.

D Carol volunteers at a hospital. She enjoys taking
to
care of patients. Some patients refuse ⌃ do exercise,
pushing ⌃ *to*
but Carol keeps ~~to push~~ them. Carol intends study
to take ⌃
physical therapy in college. She needs ~~taking~~ a lot of
go
science courses. She expects to ~~goes~~ to college next
to
fall. She hopes ⌃ get a degree in physical therapy in

five years.

UNIT 26

A 1. some   2. the   3. an   4. any

B 1. We don't need any glasses.
    2. I don't want any help.
    3. There aren't any menus on the table.
    4. He doesn't have any free time.

C 1. a   3. the   5. a
    2. a   4. the   6. a

D 1. A: What are you looking for?
some   *some*
      B: I need ~~a~~ stamps. I wrote ~~any~~ letters, and I want

        to mail them.
The   *any*
    2. A: ~~A~~ refrigerator looks empty. There isn't ~~some~~

        yogurt.
any
      B: There aren't ~~an~~ eggs either. We need to go
                          time **or** *any time*
        shopping, but I don't have ~~a time~~ today. Let's go

        shopping tomorrow.

UNIT 27

A 1. How many   4. How many
    2. How many   5. How much
    3. How much

B 1. How much chocolate do you eat in a week?
    2. How many teaspoons of sugar do you take?
    3. How much time do you spend online?
    4. How many sisters do you have?
    5. How much coffee do you drink every day?

C 1. much   4. a lot of
    2. a lot of   5. a little
    3. a can of

D 1. There were only a ~~little~~ people at the meeting.
few
               peaches
    2. There are a few ~~peach~~ in the refrigerator.
much
    3. How ~~many~~ milk do you need?
many
    4. How ~~much~~ bottles of juice did they buy?
many
    5. There are not ~~much~~ books in their home.

UNIT 28

A
1. The child ate *too many* cookies.
2. We have *too much* homework.
3. I bought *too much* milk.
4. There are *too many* trucks on that road.
5. It takes *too much* time to get there by bus.

B
1. too much
2. too few
3. too much
4. too many
5. too little

C
1. not enough
2. not enough
3. enough
4. enough
5. not enough

D   I want to move. I don't like the climate here. There's too ~~many~~ *much* snow in winter. There are too ~~little~~ *few* nice, sunny days. There's too ~~many~~ *much* air pollution from all the traffic on the streets, and there aren't ~~jobs enough~~ *enough jobs*. There also aren't enough ~~park~~ *parks* and places for children to play.

UNIT 29

A
1. should
2. had better
3. shouldn't
4. ought to
5. I'd better not

B
1. had better not forget
2. had better buy
3. had better not wait
4. had better go

C
1. should take
2. shouldn't work
3. should call
4. shouldn't forget

D
1. Where should we ~~meets~~ *meet* after work? ~~Ought~~ *Should* we go to the Rainbow Diner?
2. We *'d or had* better take an umbrella tonight. It's going to rain.
3. Should I ~~to~~ make a reservation for my flight now? I think I ~~outta~~ *ought to* make it soon.
4. What ~~I should~~ *should I* see during my business trip to Uruguay?
5. Should we ~~leaves~~ *leave* Brazil tonight or tomorrow?

UNIT 30

A
1. don't have to
2. has to
3. must not
4. doesn't have to
5. have to

B
1. can't
2. has
3. have to
4. don't have to
5. have to

C
1. had to work
2. have to read
3. have to answer
4. had to give
5. didn't have to bring

D   Drew's test starts at 8:10. He must ~~to~~ be in the room at 8:00. He must not ~~came~~ *come* late. He ~~have to has~~ *has to have* two pencils. He must ~~brings~~ *bring* a photo ID. Cell phones are not allowed in the room. He ~~doesn't have to~~ *must not or can't* bring his cell phone with him.

UNIT 31

A
1. much, taller
2. more popular
3. worse
4. better
5. brother's

B
1. younger than
2. shorter than
3. more expensive than
4. hotter than

C
1. less expensive
2. more expensive
3. higher
4. lower

D   The train is much ~~fast~~ *faster* than the bus and the seats are ~~comfortabler~~ *more comfortable*. The bus is much ~~more~~ *slower* than the train, but the views from the bus are more interesting. Which ~~are~~ *is* cheaper, the train or the bus? The bus is much less ~~expensiver~~ *expensive*, but for me the train is ~~more good~~ *better* because I'm a busy student with very little free time.

UNIT 32

A
1. quickly
2. fluently
3. well
4. slowly
5. clearly

B
1. good
2. seriously
3. hard
4. badly
5. quickly

C
1. good
2. briefly
3. clearly
4. fast
5. honestly

D A: Did your speech go ~~good~~ *well*? Did they appreciate

your jokes?

B: Well…they laughed ~~polite~~ *politely*, but I'm not sure they

laughed ~~sincere~~ *sincerely*.

A: It's hard to be funny.

B: I ~~hard~~ *hard* worked, and I prepared carefully, but I

was ~~nervously~~ *nervous*.

UNIT 33

A 1. big enough   4. as
   2. as   5. very
   3. too

B 1. warm enough   4. fast enough
   2. too late   5. very good
   3. too short

C 1. not as thin as my father **or** not as thin as he is
   2. not as cheap as my new one **or** not as cheap as my new coat
   3. as tall as my brother **or** as tall as he is
   4. as old as I am **or** as old as me

D   This year, the party wasn't *as* good as last year. The

music was very ~~much~~ loud. It was hard to dance

because the room was ~~too way~~ *way too* hot. I like to dance,

so I felt ~~too~~ *very* bad about that. Also, the drinks weren't

~~enough cold~~ *cold enough*, and the food wasn't *as* tasty as last year.

UNIT 34

A 1. the funniest
   2. the biggest
   3. the best
   4. The largest / the most dangerous

B 1. the hottest   4. the most interesting
   2. the oldest   5. the most popular
   3. the busiest

C 1. the most intelligent animals
   2. the most colorful birds
   3. the worst seats
   4. the longest days

D A: What's *the* hardest part of your job here at the zoo?

B: The ~~difficultest~~ *most difficult* part for me is telling people not to

bother or feed the animals.

A: And which animal is the ~~most smart~~ *smartest*?

B: Bill the gorilla. He's one of *the* funniest and smartest

~~animal~~ *animals*. He's also one of the *most* interesting. And I

think he's one of the cutest, too!

Key to Exercises with Guessed Answers

UNIT 13

EXERCISE 3

2. Can elephants jump?   No, they can't.
3. Can a bear climb a tree?   Yes, it can.
4. Can a chimpanzee use tools?   Yes, it can.
5. Can chimpanzees invent games?   Yes, they can.
6. Can a penguin fly?   No, it can't.

EXERCISE 8

1. b	3. d	5. e	7. a
2. c	4. h	6. f	8. g

UNIT 18

BEFORE YOU READ

1. The Eiffel Tower, Paris, France
   The Great Wall of China, Beijing, China
   Machu Picchu, Peru

UNIT 27

EXERCISE 9

1. a	4. b	7. a	10. c
2. a	5. c	8. b	
3. c	6. b	9. c	

UNIT 31

EXERCISE 5

2. A: Which river is longer, the Amazon or the Nile?
   B: The Nile is longer than the Amazon.
3. A: Which mountain has a higher elevation, Mount Everest or Mount Denali?
   B: Mount Everest has a higher elevation than Mount Denali. **or** Mount Everest is higher than Mount Denali.
4. A: Which ocean is bigger, the Atlantic or the Pacific?
   B: The Pacific Ocean is bigger than the Atlantic Ocean.
5. A: Which city has a higher elevation, La Paz, Bolivia or Sydney, Australia?
   B: La Paz, Bolivia has a higher elevation than Sydney, Australia. **or** La Paz, Bolivia is higher than Sydney, Australia.
6. A: Which country has a bigger population, Japan or South Korea?
   B: Japan has a bigger population than South Korea. **or** Japan's population is bigger than South Korea's. **or** Japan's population is bigger than South Korea's is.
7. A: Which city is more expensive, New York or Venice?
   B: New York is more expensive than Venice.

UNIT 34

EXERCISE 2

2. the elephant	5. the sailfish
3. the giraffe	6. the Macaroni Penguin
4. the hummingbird	

UNIT 10

EXERCISE 9 DREAMS

INFORMATION GAP Work with a partner. Student B, follow the instructions below.
Student A, follow the instructions on page 117.

STUDENT B

- You have a dream again and again. Read about your dream below. Student A will ask you questions about this dream. Answer Student A's questions.

  You are at school. You are in the third grade. You see your third-grade teacher. Your teacher is very big. You are small. Your teacher says, "Your schoolwork is great. You are my favorite student." You smile. Then you laugh. Then you wake up.

- Student A has a dream again and again. Find out about the dream. Ask Student A the questions below. Write down his or her answers.

  1. Where are you in your dream? _____
  2. Who comes to you? _____
  3. What does he say? _____
  4. What do you do? _____
  5. How do you feel? _____
  6. What happens next? _____

- Talk about your dreams. What do they mean?

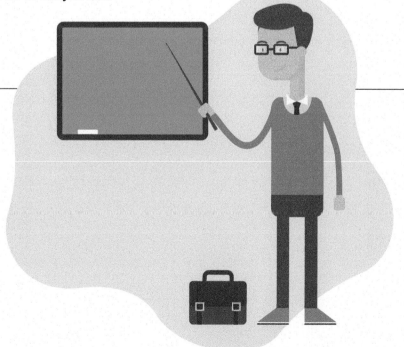

EXERCISE 8 PATIENT INFORMATION

INFORMATION GAP Work with a partner. Student B follows the instructions below. Student A will follow the instructions on page 167.

STUDENT B

- Student A has information about Dr. Green's Clinic. Ask Student A the questions below to get the information.

- Listen carefully to Student A's answers. Write down the answers.

1. When can I see the doctor?

   _____

2. When can I call her?

   _____

3. Can I contact her by email?

   _____

4. What can I do in an emergency?

   _____

5. Are there any free lectures on nutrition?

   _____

6. Can I join a support group?

   _____

7. How can I get good meal suggestions?

   _____

EXERCISE 8 WHO INVENTED THE ATM?

INFORMATION GAP Work with a partner. Student B follows the instructions below. Student A follows the instructions on page 252.

STUDENT B

- Your partner has a chart that is missing some information. Your chart contains the missing information. Answer your partner's questions, so that he or she can write the missing information into his or her chart.

EXAMPLE: A: Who invented the ATM?
B: Don Wetzel invented the ATM.
A: When did he invent it?

Invention	Inventor	Year	Country
ATM	Don Wetzel	1968	United States
credit card	Frank McNamara, Ralph Schneider	1950	United States
dishwasher	Josephine Cochrane	1886	United States
eyeglasses	Salvino D'Armate, Alessandro della Spina	1280	Italy
subway	Sir John Fowler	1863	United Kingdom
YouTube	Steven Chen, Chad Hurley, Jawed Karim	2005	United States

- The chart below is missing some information. Your partner has a chart that contains your missing information. Ask your partner questions to find the missing information. Write your partner's answers into your chart.

EXAMPLE: B: Who invented the bicycle?
A: Baron de Sauerbrun.
B: When did he invent it?

Invention	Inventor	Year	Country
bicycle	*Baron de Sauerbrun*		
	Marion Donovan		
paper			
	Conrad Gessner		
thermometer			
World Wide Web			

EXERCISE 10 COOKIES AND PIE

INFORMATION GAP Work with a partner. Student B will follow the instructions below. Student A will follow the instructions on page 332.

STUDENT B

- Look at the list of ingredients for chocolate chip cookies. Answer Student A's questions about them.

  EXAMPLE: A: How much flour do you need for the chocolate chip cookies?
  B: Two and a half cups.

Chocolate Chip Cookies

7 ounces of chocolate chips

2½ cups flour
(= two and a half cups)

3 teaspoons baking powder

1 cup chopped walnuts

1 cup butter

¾ cup sugar
(= three-quarters of a cup)

¾ cup brown sugar

2 eggs

1 teaspoon vanilla extract

- Now look at the recipe for apple pie. Ask your partner questions to find out how much you need of each ingredient to make apple pie. Write the amounts to complete the recipe.

  EXAMPLE: B: How much flour do you need for the apple pie crust?
  A: Two cups of flour.

Apple Pie

THE CRUST

_____ flour

1 teaspoon salt

⅔ cup shortening
(= two-thirds of a cup)

_____ cold water

THE FILLING

_____ sugar

_____ flour

½ teaspoon ground cinnamon

½ teaspoon ground nutmeg

a pinch of salt

_____ medium-size apples

_____ butter

Index

This index is for the full and split editions. All entries are in the full book. Entries for Volume A of the split edition are in black. Entries for Volume B are in blue.

Credits *Continued from page xxix*

(bottom right) Alona_s/Fotolia; **369:** (top left) Arcady/Fotolia, (top right) Ambassador806/Fotolia; **370:** nezezon/Fotolia; **371:** Fredy Sujono/Fotolia; **372:** (background) picsfive/Fotolia; **374–375:** doethion/Fotolia; **376:** Joseph Sohm/Fotolia; **377:** Rigucci/Shutterstock; **381:** (left) merrvas/Fotolia, (right) Dan Breckwoldt/Shutterstock; **385:** (left) Bart Everett/Shutterstock, (right) trekandphoto/Fotolia; **386:** andreykr/Fotolia; **387:** (left) dglavinova/Fotolia, (right) Dmitry Sitin/Fotolia; **388:** TTstudio/Fotolia; **389:** (center) holbox/Shutterstock, (right) Sergii Figurnyi/Fotolia; **391:** R. Gino Santa Maria/Shutterstock; **395:** kasto/Fotolia; **397:** Photographee.eu/Fotolia; **398:** (top) Africa Studio/Fotolia, (bottom) Comaniciu Dan/Shutterstock; **399:** (background) paladin1212/Fotolia; **401:** pathdoc/Fotolia; **405:** Elnur/Shutterstock; **406:** Elnur/Fotolia; **409:** sebra/Fotolia; **411:** txakel/Fotolia; **412:** (top to bottom) prapann/Fotolia, Adeus Buhai/Fotolia, Piotr Pawinski/Fotolia, Murat BAYSAN/Fotolia, bright/Fotolia; **413:** (background) Scisetti Alfio/Fotolia; **415:** mzphoto11/Fotolia; **416:** (center left) Olga Khoroshunova/Fotolia, (center) DK Images, (center right) Elena Shchipkova/123RF, (bottom) Mega Pixel/Shutterstock; **420:** (top left) Eric Isselée/Fotolia, (bottom right) Leysan/Fotolia; **421:** Eric Isselee /123RF; **423:** tristan tan/Shutterstock; **425:** J. Bicking/Shutterstock; **426:** Eric Isselee/Shutterstock; **455:** Mayrum/Fotolia; **458:** (background) B.Melo/Fotolia, (center left) LeNi/Shutterstock, (bottom left) Denise Kappa/Shutterstock

ILLUSTRATION CREDITS

Steve Attoe – pages 180, 204

ElectraGraphics, Inc. – pages (top) 73, 112

Suzanne Mogensen – page 65

Dusan Petricic – page 131

Dave Sullivan – page 101

Gary Torrisi – pages 19, 68, 71, (bottom) 73, 81, 109, 136, 144, 178, 203